HOME TO BILOELA

'The story behind the headlines. The sheer brutality of bureaucracy and the fierce love of a mother. What an incredible woman Priya is.'
Justine Clarke, actor

'An amazing story that shows how powerful we can all be when we authentically join together. If all Australians could be familiar with this story we could ensure that something as unthinkable as this never happens again.'
Claudia Karvan, actor

'This book tore my heart out and had me crying tears of anger and devastation but also hope and love. This isn't just an important story for the growth of this country and necessary change in our world, but an essential read.'
Susie Youssef, writer and actor

'Priya's deeply moving account of seeking asylum is a powerful story of survival, humanity and hope and how the persistence of a small town finally brought home a family to a place of healing.'
Leah Vandenberg, actor and *Play School* presenter

HOME TO BILOELA

The story of the Tamil family
that captured our hearts

PRIYA NADESALINGAM
WITH **REBEKAH HOLT**
AND NIROMI DE SOYZA

ALLEN&UNWIN
SYDNEY・MELBOURNE・AUCKLAND・LONDON

First published in 2023

Copyright © Priya Nadesalingam, Rebekah Holt, Niromi de Soyza 2023

All rights reserved. No part of this book may be reproduced or transmitted in any form or by any means, electronic or mechanical, including photocopying, recording or by any information storage and retrieval system, without prior permission in writing from the publisher. The Australian *Copyright Act 1968* (the Act) allows a maximum of one chapter or 10 per cent of this book, whichever is the greater, to be photocopied by any educational institution for its educational purposes provided that the educational institution (or body that administers it) has given a remuneration notice to the Copyright Agency (Australia) under the Act.

Allen & Unwin
Cammeraygal Country
83 Alexander Street
Crows Nest NSW 2065
Australia
Phone: (61 2) 8425 0100
Email: info@allenandunwin.com
Web: www.allenandunwin.com

Allen & Unwin acknowledges the Traditional Owners of the Country on which we live and work. We pay our respects to all Aboriginal and Torres Strait Islander Elders, past and present.

A catalogue record for this book is available from the National Library of Australia

ISBN 978 1 76106 968 0

Photo on p. 295 by Stephanie Coombes
Set in 11.75/18 pt Bembo Std by Midland Typesetters, Australia
Printed and bound in Australia by the Opus Group

10 9 8 7 6 5 4 3 2 1

MIX
Paper | Supporting responsible forestry
FSC® C001695
www.fsc.org

The paper in this book is FSC® certified. FSC® promotes environmentally responsible, socially beneficial and economically viable management of the world's forests.

For those who got us back to Bilo

Contents

My Story		xi
1	Biloela	1
2	Dawn Raid	5
3	No Answer	11
4	Sri Lanka	15
5	Little Star	21
6	Not on My Watch	28
7	MITA	33
8	These are My Friends and This is What Happened	37
9	English Teacher	41
10	There and Back Again	45
11	Vigil	52
12	Into Detention	58
13	The Children	62
14	Under Guard	70
15	War	74
16	India	83
17	The Boat	89
18	Australia	96
19	Meeting Nades	103
20	First Winter	114
21	Angela's Speech	120
22	At the Minister's Discretion	128
23	Disturbing Behaviour	136
24	Tharnicaa	146

25	This is Not a Place for Children to Be	154
26	The Plane	156
27	I Began to Scream	161
28	Tullamarine	165
29	'You Can't Take Us Overseas'	170
30	We Will Fight for You	175
31	Back to Christmas Island	182
32	They Did It	188
33	Not Quite Out of Sight	192
34	The Front Door to Australia	195
35	Hello, I'm Your Friend	200
36	Three Guards	206
37	I Want to Go Home	210
38	That's Always Going to Be a Problem	216
39	Medevac	220
40	We are Better Than This	223
41	A Rising Fever	230
42	They've Gone, All Gone	239
43	Reunion	243
44	Now Everyone Knows About This Family	246
45	I Want to Go Back to Our Bilo House	253
46	Election	257
47	Back in Biloela	268
48	We Did It	273
49	Afterwards	279

Postscript: Priya	288
Acknowledgements	297
About the authors	301

A note on Tamil naming protocols

Sri Lankan Tamils, both men and women, take on their father's first name as their surname. Upon marriage, a woman takes her husband's first name as her surname. Any children will also take their father's first name as their surname. For example, if Priya's father's first name had been Kumar she would have been known as Kokilapathampriya (Priya) Kumar. When Priya married Nadesalingam (Nades) Murugappan (Nadesalingam being his first name and Murugappan being his father's first name), she became known as Priya Nadesalingam. In accordance with local custom, she did not take Nades' father's first name (Murugappan) because that would mean she was married to Nades' father.

Nades' full name is therefore Nadesalingam Murugappan, and Priya and the girls are known as Priya, Kopika and Tharnicaa Nadesalingam. This means we can't call the family either 'the Nadesalingams' or 'the Murugappans'. For this reason, it became easier for their supporters to call them the Biloela family.

MY STORY

Since I was seven years old, I haven't had a permanent home. My entire life, I have moved from city to city, country to country, so many times that I've lost count. I'm not a wanderer by nature. If it were up to me, I would've stayed in one place and called it home. But the decisions were always made for me, either by things outside my control or by those more powerful than me.

Now, after ten years in Australia, I have received permanent residency. I know now that this country will be my forever home. But even that wasn't easy, I had to live through what I can only describe as a tsunami to get back to this town. I'm telling you my story so you will understand why some people become refugees and seek asylum elsewhere. Also, how those in power will do everything they can to control those who don't have the means to defend themselves and how a small town in rural Queensland called Biloela earned its place in Australian history by fighting for those without a voice.

Priya Nadesalingam

HOME TO BILOELA

Chapter 1

BILOELA

In the latter half of 2017, in the small Queensland town of Biloela, Mayor Neville Ferrier was called by reception staff. There was a woman who wanted to talk to him, but she wouldn't give her name.

Ferrier believes part of his role is to talk to anyone if they are a constituent, even if he's yelled at. He believes he should take the brunt of public office, rather than his reception staff.

Nev is a quiet and solid figure, not given to flowery language. His rural background shows up in many mannerisms, not least that he appears as ready to fix a fence as he is to discuss the local power plant. Unusually for a politician, he leaves a lot of space for other people to speak and remains a technically difficult interview for a journalist because his sentences gently trail away.

When the mayor brought the woman through to his office, he realised he didn't recognise her, which was unusual in a town with a population of only 5500.

HOME TO BILOELA

While the stranger continued to insist she couldn't tell Ferrier her name, what she did tell him, and with some urgency, was that she held grave fears for the safety of one particular family in Biloela. They were Tamil asylum seekers, and she believed their lives were at risk because the entire family were being assessed for deportation back to Sri Lanka.

The family she described were Priya and Nades and their two Biloela-born daughters Kopika, then aged two, and Tharnicaa, only a few months old. This would be the first time the mayor would hear the names of a family who were soon to become the most famous residents of his town.

———

By 2017, even in the conservative heartland of rural Biloela, the strident anti-refugee policies of the then Australian government were crystal clear to anyone who could switch on a TV. While Ferrier didn't know Priya and Nades personally, he did know that Teys, the local meatworks where Nades worked, was reliant on workers like Nades. People willing to do deeply unpleasant jobs, jobs that Ferrier says many Australians aren't keen to do. Jobs that remain filled by people from approximately twenty-four nations other than Australia.

And besides, a simpler chord of disbelief struck Ferrier. This couple had two baby daughters, both born in Biloela. Surely the government wouldn't take a local family with baby girls away from the town?

After the woman left, a concerned Ferrier discreetly contacted his local federal MP, Ken O'Dowd, a member of the Liberal National Party of Queensland and consequently a member of the Coalition government then in power in Canberra. The very government the stranger had said was narrowing its sights on Priya and her family in Biloela.

Pragmatically, Ferrier felt any chance the family had of staying would probably be through him using his existing relationships. Ferrier knew O'Dowd and had friends in his office. He hoped that his quiet and reasonable concerns would be met with mutual respect and that his back-channel lobbying would quietly secure an outcome that kept the family safely in Biloela.

Of course, like many local politicians in rural Australia who are constantly dealing with the realities of workforce shortages, Ferrier also knew that the Minister for Immigration held huge discretionary powers. Meaning he could, and frequently did, change the outcomes of people's lives, just by taking a few minutes to grant a visa.

An Australian Immigration minister's signature was the manifestation of what many had come to call 'God Powers'. But while the volume of anti-refugee rhetoric was almost always dialled up to ten, it was undeniable that the minister was regularly and quietly dishing out visas for refugees who, for whatever reason, they decided deserved ministerial discretion.

While trying to reach O'Dowd, Ferrier ruminated that perhaps his mysterious visitor worked for the government herself and that her work prevented her from doing anything other than taking the risk of coming to him. By this time, medical staff, including doctors, had faced the threat of serious legal action by the Australian government for speaking out on behalf of seriously ill refugees in detention centres.

While the mayor was trying to contact the local MP, Priya was at home with her daughters, minutes from the council offices. Waiting for her husband to return from the meatworks to their home on Rainbow Street, she was oblivious to what was going on just up the road.

With her visa valid until March 2018—a date all the way in the next year—Priya was actively engaged and fully cooperative with departmental requirements and was hoping her family would be one that benefited from the 'God Powers' of the Immigration minister. It was not an unreasonable expectation either, given that her friends, local health workers and nuns, as well as Nades' employers, were all drafting letters to ask for just that—the minister's discretion. Discretion that was granted every day to other asylum seekers.

But by the time the stranger spoke to the mayor, a race had already started. Looking back, it's hard to see just when it started, because no one has ever said.

While Ferrier waited to get through to someone, anyone, at Ken O'Dowd's office, he had no idea of the race Biloela would have to run to save Priya and Nades and their daughters. A race that would play out across multiple Australian detention centres, thousands of kilometres from their home. A race that would propel the name and fate of his small town into international headlines and the mouths of parliamentarians from all sides of politics.

No one in Biloela, the town named after the local Indigenous word for cockatoo, was aware of what lay ahead over the next five years. But the name of the tiny inland town would soon have better brand recognition than most of the politicians involved in the extraordinary events that lay ahead.

Nev never saw the stranger again.

Chapter 2
DAWN RAID

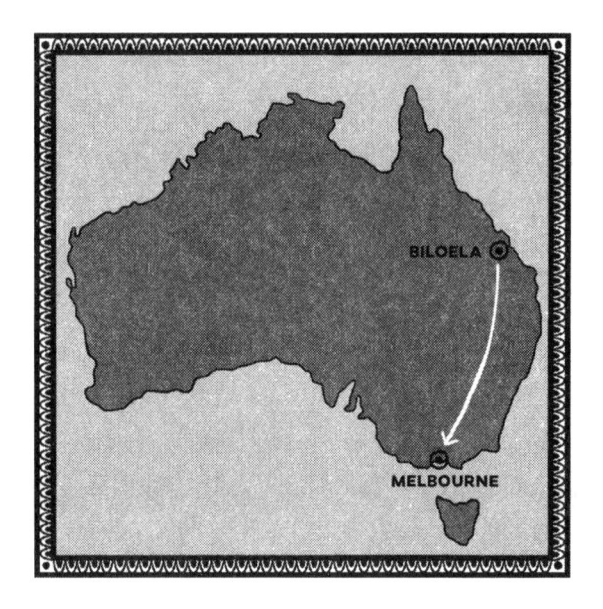

Biloela   **5 March 2018**

I was woken up by someone banging on our front door. It sounded hurried and urgent. 'Who is it at this time of the morning?' Nades muttered as he rolled out of bed.

The banging continued. It was a little light outside; you could hear the birds chirping. Kopika was asleep nestled next to me, and Tharnicaa was back in her cot after having been breastfed an hour ago.

HOME TO BILOELA

Then I heard a male voice say, 'Police.'

My first thought was that they must be looking for someone who'd run through our neighbourhood. As I got up to investigate, I heard several heavy footsteps inside the house. Suddenly there were police officers in front of me. I was startled!

'Put your hands up and go sit in the lounge!' one of the officers commanded.

At this, Kopika woke up and began to cry. As if he read my mind, the officer told me not to pick her up and to keep my hands up. 'Go to the front room!' he said firmly.

I was still in my cotton nightdress, so I didn't feel comfortable standing in front of strangers in that state or raising my hands up. I tried to ask them what they wanted from us and if I could change my clothes. But all I got was, 'Just do as you're told!' I felt humiliated.

The living room was a sea of blue uniforms and I couldn't tell you how many police officers were inside our house. Nades was sitting on the sofa with his hands up. It was a pathetic sight. It broke my heart to see my honest, hardworking husband being treated like a common criminal.

Kopika clung to me, but I couldn't hold her because I was told to keep my hands up. I sat down next to Nades, trying hard not to scream with anger. I felt that I was a child again back in Sri Lanka, when I had watched helplessly as soldiers turned up at our house at dawn and took my mother and grandfather away. I had not imagined that a similar scene would play out here in Biloela, Australia.

As some officers stood watching us, others were going through our things. They confiscated our mobile phones and the children's

Dawn Raid

birth certificates. Some were packing our belongings into boxes and suitcases.

Just then Tharnicaa started crying in her cot in the bedroom. I stood up to go and get her, but one of the officers yelled at me to sit back down.

A woman in street clothes came over to me. She was a nurse and needed to examine me as I was a diabetic. While she was checking me, Nades asked the officers in his calm voice what was going on.

'Your visas have expired,' came the reply. The officer added that we were now illegally living in Australia and they had come to deport us.

Nades and I looked at each other in disbelief. This was definitely a mistake. My visa was due to arrive today. My caseworker had said so two days ago, on Friday. Nades tried to explain this to them, but no one would listen.

I asked if we could call my caseworker.

'No,' said the police officer. 'You'll be taken to Melbourne detention centre for deportation and, if you don't cooperate, we'll put you in handcuffs.'

Melbourne was the only Australian city with a direct flight to Sri Lanka. It made sense that they'd fly us there. Our worst nightmare was coming true: we were about to be deported back to Sri Lanka.

I began to feel ill. Nades whispered to me that we should do what they asked, that this surely was a misunderstanding, and our caseworker would explain the situation to the police later.

Nades told them politely that we'd cooperate, and asked if we could please feed the kids, go to the bathroom and change into our day clothes. The police officers looked at each other and one of them said that he'd give us five minutes at the most, but we weren't allowed to shut any doors. We protested, but they took no notice.

So, watched by the police officers, we went to the toilet, quickly washed and changed clothes. This really upset both Nades and me as we had been brought up in a conservative culture, where privacy is respected even inside the family.

But we were now refugees, a status less than human. They kept hurrying us the whole time. In the end, we were forced out of the house without feeding the children, leaving Tharnicaa's bottle of milk in the microwave. Most of our belongings were also left behind. Even now, five years later, I don't understand why they came at dawn or why they were in such a rush to get us to Melbourne.

Outside the house, there were other people in uniform. Because of my previous time in detention centres, I recognised them as officers from Australian Border Force (ABF) and guards from Serco, the private company that staffs some prisons and all of the immigration detention centres in Australia.

The Serco guards took Nades ahead of us to a car, but the children and I were forced into a separate van. I didn't know what was going on. Nades pleaded with them not to separate us. We were cooperating after all. But they told him to get moving.

That moment, something snapped inside me, and I began to scream. I demanded that my husband be kept with us. I didn't want my children to experience what I went through as a child, watching my parents being dragged away and not knowing if I'd ever see them again. I was not going to have it.

As they began to strap the girls into children's car seats in the front of the van, I tried to get to them, but I was forced into the back of the vehicle, two rows behind the children, and held down on both sides by two guards. I screamed and struggled to free myself, but I couldn't.

In the 90 minutes it took to reach Gladstone Airport, my children hardly stopped crying. I couldn't bear to listen to them. I begged the guards several times to let me hold my children and, if I could, to breastfeed Tharnicaa. But no one seemed to care. One of the guards told me that they'd fall asleep if I stopped talking.

I screamed at him, asking if he was a father, because no parent would think this was okay. It broke my heart that, as their mother, I couldn't touch my own children or comfort them. What had we done to deserve this lowly treatment? It was as if the Australian government was punishing us for being refugees, as if they were making us see that we were nobodies, and our suffering mattered to no one.

At Gladstone Airport, we were hauled onto a charter flight to Melbourne, along with the boxes of our belongings the officers had packed. The police left us at this stage, and ABF officers and Serco guards got on the flight with us.

At least, once we were inside the plane, Nades and I were allowed to sit together and hold our children. But I couldn't stop crying. I was terrified of us returning to Sri Lanka.

Nades touched me on my shoulder and whispered, 'Don't worry, Priya, it'll all work out in the end. We've done nothing wrong.'

I desperately hoped he was right. It was only after we returned to Biloela years later that he told me that, deep down, he wasn't feeling so confident. He was worried sick that returning to Sri Lanka would be the death of him, leaving me widowed and the children fatherless. He said that at this time he'd regretted getting married and bringing two innocent children into this world and subjecting them to so much trauma.

HOME TO BILOELA

The flight from Gladstone to Melbourne lasted over four hours but felt longer without food or water. The children were asleep from exhaustion. Looking at their faces I decided that I was going to do everything in my power to stop us being deported. I'd rather be dead than go back to Sri Lanka.

Chapter 3

NO ANSWER

Vashini Jayakumar, a young Brisbane-based Tamil refugee and mother, was in the habit of calling her dear friend Priya every morning at around 9 am. The pair had become like sisters when Vashini had lived in Biloela and worked at Teys meatworks alongside Nades, but Vashini had not long ago moved to Brisbane, seven hours south, where her parents and sister were living.

The daily telephone call was something they both relied on for different reasons. Because Vashini had been recognised by Australia as a refugee and granted a five-year visa, it meant she had slightly more certainty than Priya.

But Vashini had recently been through a difficult marriage separation. The ordeal left her isolated, and the morning call had become a steadying way for both women to start their days.

When Priya didn't answer the phone on 5 March 2018, it was so alarming that Vashini didn't hesitate to immediately call friends in the Biloela community, asking them to go and check the house on Rainbow Street.

'I was so panicked. I was worried . . . we began to hear stories that the government had been deporting people and taking the men, mostly the single men. I rang people in Biloela and then I checked with them—what's happened?'

When her friends got there the house was empty, washing left hanging on the line and food on the table. Vashini was told that neighbours in the street had heard and seen the forceful raid and was alarmed to hear that, 'Many men in uniforms had been at the house; even police were there.'

In an act of singular determination that most people, let alone a young refugee, wouldn't dare attempt, Vashini immediately started calling any government department she could think of who might know where Priya and the family had been taken. Vashini wasn't listed as a next of kin or a contact person for the family so it would take considerable resolve and a credible phone manner for her to do what she did next.

First she called the Department of Immigration.

'I was on the phone all day, trying to find them. They were saying, "Oh, we don't know what happened. We don't have any details about the family." And then I rang the Australian Federal Police and they transferred me to Home Affairs.' Vashini started calling on Monday and kept calling through to Tuesday. Finally she got an answer.

'I got the answer from the Australian Federal Police. They said, "They are in a detention centre."'

But Vashini wasn't told which detention centre or where, so she called three centres trying to find out. She knew that if they were going to be deported, then every minute they didn't have legal representation was a minute wasted.

―――

A day after the dawn raid, she found them. They were in MITA, the Melbourne Immigration Transit Accommodation in Broadmeadows, a detention centre. But the staff manning the phones in reception wouldn't put her call through, telling her, 'They don't have access to the phone. We have to get your name and details and give it to them, and then they can call you back.' It was now almost midday on the second day.

Later that night, after nearly two whole days, Vashini's phone finally rang.

'I remember it was evening and Priya rang me back, she was so panicked. She was stressed and she told me, "We've been taken into custody and they're threatening us: *You need to sign the paper. We're gonna deport you.*"'

Vashini immediately knew what she needed to do. She contacted friends in the Australian Tamil community to alert them that the family needed urgent legal help. They hadn't yet been deported, but Vashini feared it could happen at any moment.

―――

What was complicating everything was that Priya and Nades had had their phones taken away. In the many immigration detention centres spread across the vast country of Australia, any asylum seeker who had arrived by sea was not allowed their own mobile phone until the law was changed in late June 2018.

HOME TO BILOELA

While government officials would point out there were landlines and a small number of computers that those in detention could access, the reality was that detainees with no phone had no way of interacting immediately with the outside world.

The implications of this were many, and included the inability to contact lawyers, quickly sign vital paperwork those lawyers needed, or even to take family photos, until a federal court ruling returned phones. But that would be nearly four months after the dawn raid had ripped the Biloela family from their home. This meant Vashini's marathon effort on the phone had been exactly what was required—and the only way to find the family, who had effectively had all means of communication cut off.

What Priya didn't know was that while Vashini had been calling the Melbourne immigration detention centre, another family friend in Biloela was just about to join the race to find her and her family and, like Vashini, she wasn't going to helplessly stand by.

Chapter 4
SRI LANKA

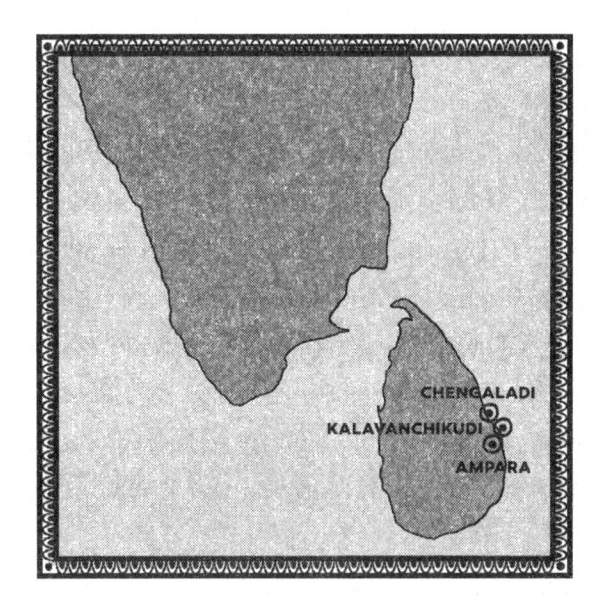

Ampara   1976–1983

I was born in a village called Irakkamam in the Ampara District in the south-east of Sri Lanka in 1976. I was named Kokilapathampriya, meaning lover of music. Everyone called me 'Priya' for short. My older brother—my *anna*, as we say—was treated like a little prince because he was the firstborn son. I would eventually also get a younger brother, and my little sister was born when I was fourteen years old.

HOME TO BILOELA

Irakkamam village was known for its two lakes, rice fields and a sugar factory. Most of its people were Sinhalese Buddhists; the Tamil Hindus were in the minority and there were also some Muslims. But I didn't know of these differences because I grew up in a Tamil neighbourhood.

Everyone I knew was a Tamil Hindu. Our family lived in the large house of my Amma's parents together with her ten brothers and sisters and their families. It was set in the middle of 400 acres, full of coconut, guava and mango trees. I was never short of attention or food.

My Appa was a very handsome man. He was the only son of Indian-origin Tamils and owned a restaurant business in town. His marriage to Amma nearly didn't happen. A marriage broker had arranged *penn paakirathu*, where Appa and his family would meet Amma's family. When Appa saw his future bride, he thought her too skinny. So, through his family, he asked if he could marry one of her younger sisters. My Thaatha (grandfather) refused this, of course, saying he couldn't let his younger daughter get married before the older one.

So Appa decided to look for a bride elsewhere. Six months and many failed attempts later, he came back to ask for Amma's hand in marriage and Thaatha agreed. It was never up to Amma to make that decision.

Although Appa's family were now Sri Lankans with no ties in India, if one of my brothers got into a fight with some boy at school, he would be accused of being the 'Indian's son' who started the fight. The Sri Lankan Tamils labelled the Indian Tamils as *Thoattakkaattaan*, an insulting term referring to the Indian labourers brought down by the British to work in the tea plantations. It is interesting how easily people stick labels on others so they can ignore the individual behind them.

Kalavanchikudi   1983–1987

Not long after my younger brother—my *thambi*—was born, things began to change. A Tamil militant group, the Tamil Tigers, attacked an Army patrol in the northern city of Jaffna. They wanted a separate homeland for the Tamils in the north and east of the country. After this, the Sinhalese began to attack Tamils in my neighbourhood; my father's restaurant was targeted, my grandparents' fields were burned down and my friends' houses were torched. Many Tamils in the area lost their properties and some their lives. Everyone we knew was fleeing Ampara to somewhere safe for the Tamils, as the Sinhalese took over the lands where Tamils had lived for generations. My family fled to the east coast, a Tamil stronghold. We became refugees in our own country.

My immediate family and some of my aunties moved north-east to the beachside village of Kalavanchikudi in the Batticaloa District, and my grandparents moved further north to my grandmother's home town, Trincomalee. This way, my extended family were split all down the east coast of Sri Lanka.

My early memories of growing up in Kalavanchikudi are wonderful. Those were carefree years; we'd swim in the waterhole with our dogs, then dry out in the sun and drink fresh coconut milk or eat mangoes and guava straight from the trees. We'd walk our pet cow Valli to the fields through palm-lined sandy lanes as if she was our pet dog. I missed living in our old home in Ampara with all my family, but I was happy in this new village. Amma started working as a seamstress and Appa found work in another town called Chengaladi, 50 kilometres north.

HOME TO BILOELA

Two of my aunties lived with us, taking care of the house and us kids. I loved listening to their chatter, especially in the evenings, when they talked into the night about everything from movies to general town gossip, sipping black tea with *hakkuru* (palm sugar). They were fond of me and treated me as their own child, often cooking my favourite food for dinner: *kurakkan* (finger millet) flour *puttu* and fish curry. We'd all sit together and eat with our fingers.

In 1984 when I was eight years old, I started at Kalavanchikudi school and I finished there in 1992. But in between, I had to be moved to another school, which I'll tell you about later. My first year of schooling was very basic. We didn't have formal classrooms, books or pencils. We sang songs and learned to write the alphabet on sand. It was only in Grade 2 that we sat in a classroom with tables and chairs. I loved to chat, so I made friends easily. The teachers were kind and caring.

There was never any pressure for me to perform well, so school gave me the opportunity to enjoy every day and play with friends. Although I wanted to be a doctor when I grew up, I was not academic. I wasn't particularly interested in singing or dancing like some girls, but I liked athletics. I'd usually win several prizes at our athletics carnivals.

As a daughter, I was totally under the control of Amma, especially because Appa worked long hours in his new job. She wouldn't let me go anywhere on my own, ride a bicycle or shop for myself. She'd make all my clothes in the fashion that she preferred. She allowed only four friends to visit me at home, but never let me visit them. Having so little choice in life didn't bother me because I understood that being a girl brought some restrictions with it; my behaviour could make or break my family's reputation. It could

Sri Lanka

affect the future chances of marriage not only for me but also for my female relatives. So I obeyed the rules set out by my parents, elders, religion and culture. I did what they expected me to do.

Our lives in Kalavanchikudi wouldn't stay peaceful for long. We began to hear distant sounds of explosions and machine guns firing. One morning, when my grandparents had come to visit us, we were woken up by a sudden heavy knock on our door and shouting in Sinhala. I jumped out of bed and ran behind Thaatha. When he opened the door, there were soldiers everywhere in the front yard. They ordered all of us out. Some soldiers stood pointing their guns at us and some went inside and turned the house upside down. Then the boss of the soldiers shouted something in Sinhala and Amma shouted back at him in Tamil.

Next thing you know, they were taking Amma and Thaatha away. I remember feeling terrified. I held on to Amma's legs as the soldiers dragged her away by the shoulders. My aunts pulled me away. I was so scared that I'd never see them again. My aunties consoled me by saying that we'd get them back and all would be okay. All I had to do was to pray to Goddess Durgai Amman.

My prayers were answered when Thaatha and Amma were released fourteen days later. They had been interrogated the whole time about helping the Tigers because a neighbour had informed the Army that we had weapons in the house. It was true that Amma's two brothers were senior Tiger figures and my *anna* was a Tiger sympathiser, but we never had any guns in the house.

What the Sinhalese soldiers didn't understand was that every Tamil had some connection to the militants, not just my family. After the 1983 Tamil massacres, many Tamil youths had joined militant groups, and fighting had been going on in the north and east of the country since then. From that day onwards, fear of dawn raids pervaded our existence.

In 1987, the Indian Army came to Sri Lanka to keep the peace, but it started fighting alongside the Sri Lankan Army against the Tamil Tigers. Soon, artillery shells and bombs began falling in our neighbourhood and the distant machine gun sounds were getting closer and closer. As a young girl, all I knew was that my family and I were in danger because we were Tamils.

As the fighting increased over time, I started to hear about and sometimes see the bad things that the Sinhalese were doing to the Tamils. Around the end of that year, the Army set up a camp next to our school. This scared Amma and she immediately decided that all of us would move some 40 kilometres north to Chengaladi, near Batticaloa. With that, my childhood came to an end, and an uncertain future took over.

Chapter 5

LITTLE STAR

For the Biloela locals, there was nothing unusual about the morning of 5 March 2018, until a steady stream of unmarked and unexpected vehicles drove into the tiny town. The vehicles had come from the port town of Gladstone, 90 minutes away, where the nearest ABF office was located. Once in Biloela, they were joined by local police staff, some in marked cars, others not, some in uniform, some in plain clothes.

By 6.30 am it was 26 degrees. Life in the country starts early, and people were up and about. Miners were heading home after the night shift, crossing paths with the new shift travelling the same roads the other way. The cleaners at the school just down the road from Priya's house were just finishing up. The locals who liked a daily walk were greeting each other out on the path that runs alongside the highway, past the large 'Welcome to Biloela' sign.

The sign, which bears a large stylised profile of a cockatoo, is set into a roundabout that greets all incoming traffic. The bird is the namesake of the small town and was soon to become the emblem of the two toddlers who were asleep in their home on Rainbow Street.

The council worker who empties the rubbish bins at Lions Park and gets a coffee every morning at exactly 6.30 am would have seen the unusual line-up of official, unmarked vehicles about the time he took his first sip. Walking past Rainbow Street at 8 am, a high school student noticed what looked like a crime scene. Passing one end and pausing, he could see three or four police cars and a white van parked outside one of the homes. A cluster of plain-clothes police gathered around the front steps looked to be debriefing after whatever had just happened.

At Biloela Hospital, staff were changing shifts and wouldn't have had the time to look up and see the ABF cars and vans making their way back past the Welcome to Biloela sign for the second time that morning, returning to Gladstone with four extra passengers. The physiotherapy team were expecting to see Priya for an appointment later in the day, as was her social worker, Bronwyn.

But none of them would see her again for over four years.

———

Less than a week before the dawn raid, Biloela Hospital social worker Bronwyn Dendle had sat on the floor of Priya's Rainbow Street home during one of her regular visits. While her colleague spoke to Priya, Bronwyn sat with 22-month-old Kopika as the little girl carefully traced around her hand to draw a star. While Kopika's small hands pressed one of Bronwyn's down and drew its outline, she enthusiastically led Bronwyn through a verse of 'Twinkle, Twinkle Little Star'—a song she had recently learned at a church playgroup.

Little Star

As a mother of five, this wasn't Bronwyn's first nursery rhyme. Priya had been regularly seeing Bronwyn since Kopika was nine months old. She had been referred to her through outpatient services, and in a small town the size of Biloela, that means seeing your clients everywhere. With Bron's youngest child only eighteen months older than Kopika, it was inevitable the two families would often see each other at the playground, park or supermarket.

Amplifying the smallness of Biloela was Bronwyn's natural tendency to get involved in her community. Bronwyn is a capable and highly approachable woman who has trouble recalling the exact number of committees or groups she was a part of in 2018. 'Maybe ten, probably a lot bloody more!'

The social worker hadn't had any significant experience with other refugees prior to meeting Priya and says she had no knowledge about the Sri Lankan civil war when they first met. 'I knew nothing about it at all. And so just in general, rapport building, getting someone's story—normal social worker stuff—I started to get a bit of an understanding of Priya's story and was just like, Oh my God, this really happens to people. At first when she was talking about the stuff in Sri Lanka, I had to do a google to see, what happened, search Civil War, Sri Lanka and do a bit of a read.'

Bronwyn then started asking a local medical staffer who was also Sri Lankan Tamil about the civil war. 'I went and said to him, what's the go? Like, what happened? And that's when he was telling me about the oppression that he had experienced even with his studies and why he had to leave to further them. Just the blatant discrimination that happened. So I think that really poked at the social justice part of me. I was saying, what the hell? This is not right.'

HOME TO BILOELA

By 2018 Bronwyn was meeting Priya regularly to talk about some of the trauma she'd survived, and her ongoing concerns around what would happen if the family's refugee status wasn't resolved. While Bronwyn didn't understand the complex and increasingly impenetrable Australian immigration system that anyone who arrives by sea must navigate, she could see it was dragging on for years, and causing Priya much concern and confusion.

'As I got to know her, then I would see her at Woolies when I was doing my shopping with the kids and Kopika would be in the trolley and the family would say, "Oh, I've got another extension on my visa." And we'd be chatting about that, "Oh, that's such a relief, I'm so pleased, this is great." So we'd have those conversations regularly. The more I learned about the rubbish that they'd been subjected to with all of the visa stuff the more it made me furious because it didn't make sense to me that they were here, they were settled, they were working. It just didn't make sense to me that they couldn't stay.'

By this stage Bronwyn had been observing what the family had to deal with for nearly two years, including when Nades had his work rights taken away and then returned to him, despite having full-time employment, an Australian-born toddler and a pregnant wife.

Bronwyn was watching at close hand the family wrestling with the deeply flawed, confusing and internationally criticised Australian immigration system that saw tens of thousands of asylum seekers spend years treading water as they were given visas, got work and paid taxes but still didn't have clear pathways to a permanent life in Australia.

Little Star

When Priya became pregnant again with Tharnicaa, in 2016, she was given a new referral to see Bronwyn, as there were concerns she was at a higher risk than usual.

Adding to Priya's stress were her worries about her ongoing application for a visa, as the whole process had been confusing. Priya, like many refugees, struggled to understand why they were still going through this, years after having been given visas and security clearances to leave detention. She had a valid bridging visa but was applying for a different kind of visa—a Safe Haven visa—something refugees who were living and working rurally could apply for. They were intended to be issued for periods of five years.

Priya made her application in a phone call with an immigration official. Her migration agent and an interpreter were also on the line. She was then eight months pregnant, and the process didn't go well. She felt sick on the day of the interview; she struggled to understand her interpreter, and the migration agent kept dropping in and out of the call.

The application was denied, as was Kopika's. The Immigration Assessment Authority upheld that decision. Priya was no longer at risk if she returned to Sri Lanka, the authority found. Nor would her husband's involvement in the Tamil Tigers affect her safety.

Such was the murkiness of the entire process that Priya, the woman at the centre of it, had no idea her entire family were about to be targeted in a dawn raid by ABF staff. While—as Vashini knew—individual Tamil men had been deported back to Sri Lanka, detaining and attempting to deport an entire family would be highly unusual and aggressive, even for the Liberal National government. This was for several reasons, not least that in 2018 the Liberal Party was fond of proclaiming that they, unlike the opposition Labor Party, had 'got the children out of detention'.

This statement was definitely fudging the facts. While there were far fewer children in the onshore immigration detention centres than there had been under the opposition, there were still babies, young children and minors in the centres, which by March 2018 had become increasingly harsh.

Bronwyn recalls asking about Priya's visa as she sat on the floor with Kopika tracing stars that March morning in the Rainbow Street house. 'I asked her, "Have you heard any more about your visa?" 'Cause we knew the time was coming again where it was reaching its expiry date . . . I can't remember the lady's name that she was in regular contact with from the Immigration department. And she said, there's something in the post or they're sending something out to do with the visa. I just remember thinking, Oh good, it'll be another extension and we'll see how we go. And then that was the last time I saw them.'

Less than a week after Bronwyn had been sitting with Kopika and singing 'Twinkle, Twinkle Little Star', she was walking out of a 3 pm training session at the hospital when a colleague said someone was trying to find her.

'The health assistant said, "Bronwyn, the community nurses are looking for you. They've got some terrible news." And I was like, "Oh gosh, what's happened?" I'm thinking, Do I have to go to the Emergency Department or something? Has there been a big accident?'

There hadn't been an accident. As happens in a small town, Bronwyn would hear about the dawn raid because the hospital receptionist went to an aqua aerobics class with Priya's neighbour. The receptionist told a nurse who explained to Bronwyn that the neighbour was in shock, and had told the class at the Biloela pool about the scene that greeted her when she ran out of her house at 6.30 am after hearing screams.

'She was telling all her friends in the aqua aerobics class. Priya had been crying out and there was yelling and she looked out and the local police had blocked off the street. She was really panicked, thinking something terrible had happened. Then she ran into the yard and was saying, "Is everything all right? Can I talk to Priya?" And they wouldn't let her near her. There were these big men and they were in suits and there were guns and the kids were screaming. Then they went in these vans and they wouldn't put them in together, they separated them.

'I remember getting teary straightaway and kind of saying, "What? Taking them where?" All they said was, "I don't know, we don't know."'

Chapter 6

NOT ON MY WATCH

At Biloela Hospital, a shocked Bronwyn sought out the other nurses who knew Priya and the family. 'I walked into the community nurses and just burst into tears. And they were hugging me, and they were feeling very sad as well. It was just that sense of wrongness. I knew they were in danger but it wasn't what was panicking me at that point—it was the injustice of it. So I sat there for a bit while I calmed down and I thought, Okay, now what?'

Bronwyn rang one of the community organisations that had dealt with the family to see if they had heard the news, and had a conversation that would shock and galvanise her for thousands of hours to come.

The worker Bronwyn talked to said they had heard about Priya and the family being taken. Bronwyn recalls being told, 'A lot of people in that situation, they have these little cyanide tablets, and they take them rather than be sent back. So who knows, they're probably dead by now, or they're back there.'

'That was when the injustice and angry tears turned into panic—holy shit . . . And she was just saying, "Bron, the advice I'll give you is you've just gotta shake this off. You did the best you could. You've gotta shake this off and take your next client, that's the only way you can cope in the industry that we're in."

'That was when I went, "Not on my watch, sweetheart. Hell no, we're doing something." I distinctly remember putting the phone down, then standing up and saying out loud to the other community nurses, "This whole situation is fucked. This is not happening."

'Apparently this has happened before. This is not uncommon. And it was probably one of the nurses who said, "Oh Bronwyn, be careful." That's probably the beginning of where I saw that there were people that really, genuinely cared and loved them and knew that it was wrong, but were kind of, "Oh, be careful because you don't wanna get into trouble or you don't wanna upset the apple cart."'

By then it was close to the end of the day, so Bronwyn left the hospital and headed home, but she couldn't shake it off.

'I go home and have this big rant to my mum and my husband, just firing up about it all, and this big rant on Facebook. Then other people were contacting me going, "Oh, what's happened at work today?" And I said, "Well, I had this client family disappear."'

———

Come Wednesday and Thursday, Bronwyn combined family and work responsibilities with buttonholing absolutely anyone she could in Biloela to tell them about what had happened to Priya and the family. 'Life did go on to a certain extent—I've got five kids, I'm getting them to school, I'm doing after-school activities, I'm doing lunches, I'm shopping. So there's a couple of days where there wasn't a lot I could do other than tell every man and his dog, ad nauseam. I'm sure people were ducking and weaving away from me so they didn't have to hear about what had happened again.'

On Friday evening Bronwyn went to a pub in Biloela for dinner with her husband, but just after she sat down, her phone rang. 'It came up as an unknown number. I never answer those because of telemarketing. But my phone rang and I don't know why, but I decided to answer.'

The call was from Melbourne. It was Aran Mylvaganam and Ben Hillier from the Tamil Refugee Council, a voluntary organisation that worked with Tamil asylum seekers. They knew where Priya and Nades were. Bronwyn went outside to take the call more privately.

'I remember standing on the footpath outside the restaurant, saying, "Where are they? What's happened?" They explained, "Well, they're in the Melbourne immigration detention centre."'

Aran wasn't just calling Bronwyn to pass on information, though. He wanted to know if Bronwyn could be a local contact for a press release he was writing about Priya and her family.

After the last three days, Bronwyn knew she shouldn't go any more public than she already had because of her role at the hospital. She'd begun to notice tensions as the week had played out. But she told him to put her phone number on it anyway.

While her husband and dinner waited inside, Bronwyn made it clear to Aran that while she knew nothing about the legal issues, what she absolutely did know was that the family being ripped out of the Biloela community had been devastating. That detail caught Aran's and Ben's attention. They asked Bronwyn more about the impact on the community. Bronwyn explained how devastated Priya's neighbour had been after witnessing the raid and that even she, an experienced social worker, had to leave work early because she had been so distraught. She was beginning to hit her stride in explaining why people from Biloela were so upset: 'Because we knew them, we worked with them, we loved them, we saw them everywhere.'

Bronwyn's insistence that night, on the footpath talking to two people she didn't know, would establish the essential and inarguable truth that the family were loved and valued community members of Biloela. She didn't know that what she was doing, by clearly and fairly affirming that this family were cherished, was the start of a process of unravelling years and years of nuanced and relentless negative messaging about refugees.

———

The press release Aran and Ben wrote would highlight the fact that taking the family had been devastating for the small town. But, more crucially, it would humanise and give Priya a proxy voice during a time in which she wasn't even allowed to have a mobile phone. But they still needed someone to talk to the media. Was Bronwyn sure she couldn't speak?

Priya's family wasn't Bronwyn's only pressing concern. There was also the matter of keeping a roof over her own large family. By 2018 the farming family were on the end of a bad run of seven years of annual floods that had ripped through their corner of Queensland, wiping out fences, crops and stock.

'We'd lost everything. Tens of thousands of dollars every flood; financially we were in a really precarious situation. I had this full-time job at the hospital that was good pay. There weren't a lot of other jobs going around at the time. And particularly not for that amount of money. We've got five kids. We needed my income.

'While the social justice part of me is like, to hell with it all. I'll quit my job, I'll live on air, it actually wasn't quite that easy in practice. Because how am I gonna make those repayments? We'd go bankrupt if I didn't have this income.'

Standing on the main street of Biloela, Bronwyn knew she had to find someone to front the media, and she had a good idea who that might be.

Chapter 7
MITA

Melbourne   **5–12 March 2018**

The raid on our home in Biloela at dawn was something we hadn't imagined would happen. Even when I recall it now, it feels like a movie or something that would happen in Sri Lanka. It is too hard to believe that it happened to us here in Australia, an ordinary family with very young children living in rural Queensland. But it did.

The flight we were forced onto that morning arrived in Melbourne late afternoon. We were driven in a van for fifteen minutes to MITA

HOME TO BILOELA

in Broadmeadows. As our vans passed through several gates, MITA looked like a maximum-security prison to me. I know they call it a detention centre, but it was as secure as a jail, with high wire fences and security cameras pointing in all directions.

They made us stay in the office to complete all the paperwork. Nades asked the officers if we could speak to his migration agent in Sydney and my caseworker back in Brisbane, and if the paperwork could wait till the next day; it had been an exhaustingly long day, especially for the children. The officers insisted that the paperwork needed to be done straightaway. They took mugshots of us, as if we were criminals. Then they allowed me to make one call using a landline and I called my sister in India, without my mobile phone it was the only number I could remember. I explained our situation to her. She didn't know what she could do to help, but promised to notify someone in Australia.

It was the early hours of the next day before we were finally shown a three-bed unit. Inside were four meal boxes, which contained roast chicken, rice and salad; they had been sitting on the table for God knows how long.

Nades and I couldn't believe it. Did they genuinely not know that this type of food was not suitable for an eight-month-old baby and a two-year-old toddler? Or did they just not care? I had no breastmilk that day, having had no food or any liquid. We asked for fruit, even for just one banana, but they told us that fruit was not included in the 'deportation menu'. So we mashed the food with our fingers and fed it to the girls.

After only a few hours of sleep, they woke us up at 7 am the following day for medical check-ups. Then they asked us to sign some documents. These were in English; one of the officers read us

MITA

the deportation statement. All we understood was that, by signing, we were agreeing to be deported.

I was desperate to let someone outside know that we were being held in detention. I asked to use the phone so we could contact our friends in Brisbane or Biloela. But the officials told us that we could do so only after we had signed the documents, not before. Seeing no way out of this, I told Nades that we should sign them because, even if we didn't sign these, they were going to bundle us up and throw us onto a plane like sacks of potatoes. We had to let someone know of our situation.

Soon after we signed the forms, a guard handed us a piece of paper with our friend Vashini's name and phone number on it. She had managed to track us down and had called a few times. Over the next two days, the guards continued to let us know that she'd called but they wouldn't allow us to use a phone. I was so angry that they hadn't kept their promise that I called them names and cursed them. The guards told me that they were just carrying out orders.

When they finally gave me access to a phone, I called Vashini first. Hearing her familiar Tamil voice brought me great comfort. She was disappointed that we'd signed the deportation documents, but she promised to do all she could to help. Within hours, we had some important Melbourne contacts: Father Pan called to provide us with contact details for a lawyer he recommended, and Aran Mylvaganam from the Tamil Refugee Council called to say that he was alerting the media. When I spoke to the lawyer, Kajalini Ranjithkumar, on the phone she told me that she had had all our files transferred to her office and assured us that she'd be able to stop the deportation, at least temporarily. That news gave us some hope.

HOME TO BILOELA

Six days after the Biloela dawn raid, Kajalini came to see us. MITA made us both fill out a lot of paperwork before she could visit us on the Saturday. She told us that she would organise a court order that would stop us being deported, and Nades and I immediately felt relieved. Before she left, Kajalini asked us to call her mobile phone twice a day to check in so she would know we were still in MITA. We made sure to call her every morning and every night for the next two and a half days.

On the Tuesday evening we knew our lawyer would begin to wonder when we would call for the nightly check-in but we couldn't call her. The Australian government had already put us on a plane for deportation.

Chapter 8

THESE ARE MY FRIENDS AND THIS IS WHAT HAPPENED

On that Friday night, as her pub dinner was going cold, less than five days after the family had been taken, Bronwyn sent her friend and fellow social worker Angela Fredericks a text. She needed a favour.

Early the next morning the two women met for breakfast before a rural health conference they were both attending, where Angela was set to promote her new business as a self-employed social worker.

What Bronwyn was banking on was that Angela would be free to speak to the media because she was now working for herself. Bronwyn explained what the Tamil Refugee Council had said about where Priya and the family were being held, and that they had emailed her some suggestions on kicking off a grassroots campaign to hopefully gain some media attention. Bronwyn asked if she would be willing and able to front the media.

Angela didn't know Priya and Nades well. She'd only met them once when organising a translator, but Bronwyn didn't have to ask twice. Angela was on board and ready to start immediately. With that, a third woman joined the race.

The pair went to the conference and, instead of launching Angela's business, set about transforming the stand into a 'Help Priya and Nades' table. Angela printed off photos of Kopika and Tharnicaa and both women settled down to write the story of the family's background and ties to Biloela.

The timing of the conference couldn't have been better. In attendance were many well-connected locals who knew Priya and her family, including Mayor Neville Ferrier, who, although he spoke to Bronwyn and Angela that day, didn't reveal the warning he received from the stranger months earlier.

Bronwyn looked up midmorning and saw a news crew from the ABC had arrived to cover the conference. She suggested Angela go over and make friends with them. Neither of them had any idea that what they would do that day would form a template for a campaign that would take over their lives for the next four years.

Having caught the interest of the reporter, Angela hustled Bronwyn to one side to quickly drill her on what she needed to know before recording an interview. Angela Fredericks had a background in theatre, so knew how to remember her lines.

'We did the first TV interview that weekend and I remember sitting in the courtyard at the school where the conference was. And I had Bronwyn and I'm saying, "Okay, give me all the names." And she was basically just downloading the stories and all the information so then I could just launch into saying, "These are my friends and this is what happened."'

Angela recalls they also started a group chat with other locals who wanted to help. 'We started a group message and someone on there said, "Is there a petition we can sign?"'

These are My Friends and This is What Happened

It was a good call.

Not knowing where to start, Bronwyn googled petitions and found the Change.org website. Angela realised the process would require some writing so she volunteered to do that on the Saturday night after the conference. By the next morning, Angela had launched an online petition.

Meanwhile Vashini saw what was happening back in Biloela via Facebook messages, and she suggested they share the petition on the local online buy/swap/sell pages. The reaction was strong and immediate, and Bronwyn began to believe more locals would join her and Angela in speaking up for the family. 'Everyone was saying, "What the hell? That's disgusting. They were our people. How dare they take them."'

———

The Monday morning after the conference, exactly one week after the dawn raid, Bronwyn's phone started ringing and did not stop. The press release by the Tamil Refugee Council had gone out, with Bronwyn's name as the Biloela contact.

It was all on. This race was now being run in public and there would be no backing down from what that exposure could mean for the Biloela locals, the family and the Australian government.

Priya and Nades and their little girls were about to become known nationally and, later, internationally, including in Sri Lanka, the country they feared being sent back to. If anyone in the government had hoped to resolve this situation quietly, as had been Mayor Ferrier's hope months earlier, that window of opportunity was closing. No one, except perhaps other refugees detained by Australia, had any idea how far the brinkmanship would escalate. Angela quickly realised she had to front the media, who hadn't stopped calling Bronwyn.

'I remember cancelling my clients for the day, setting up in my office and Bron came over and we just worked the media storm. Neither of us had any idea what we were doing.'

Three days earlier Bronwyn hadn't really known what a press release was, and now she was getting calls from national TV news shows. But for the inveterate community committee member the first call had, momentarily, been somewhat confusing.

'The call was someone saying they were from *The Project*. I'm asking, "Um, is this a local project I'm involved in? Which project is it, sorry?" and they're, "No, no, Channel 10, *The Project*." I was like, "Oh, hi, okay!"'

Bronwyn steered them to Angela but her phone kept ringing. 'I got off the phone, then the phone's ringing again; it's Channel 7. And so I was thinking, Jesus.'

The amount of immediate interest and quick progress heartened the pair. They gave themselves a moment to wonder if this whole baffling event could be resolved quickly, and everyone could get back to their normal lives.

Meanwhile, on Facebook their posts were gathering massive traction and the petition was going viral. It would go on to collect the signatures of well over half a million people—109 times the entire population of Biloela.

Chapter 9

ENGLISH TEACHER

Simone Cameron lived in Biloela from age seven to seventeen and, like many local teenagers, had to leave the small town to study after finishing high school. After university, she returned there, working in several roles. One was teaching English to migrants.

'I had some contact with one of the refugee settlement organisations and they were bringing people seeking asylum to Biloela to work at the meatworks. Some other migrant English teachers and I decided we would try to lobby the local TAFE for some funding for English classes for them. Initially we couldn't get the funding for people like Nades who were on bridging visas; we had to lobby for quite a while. But at the beginning of 2014, we were finally successful in securing funding and I started this English class for people on bridging visas. Nades was one of the students in that class.

'He was really busy working at the time. I remember seeing him more downtown in Biloela than I did in English class. In fact, the first time that I saw him and approached him about it was down in the Woolworths car park in Biloela, and I asked him if he wanted to join the class. What I remember was just this hardworking, smiley guy with very kind eyes.'

Simone had been in Biloela in 2005, eight years before Nades' arrival, when an earlier influx of migrant workers had arrived.

'It was quite a time of transformation for Bilo, because the meatworks had brought in large numbers of Brazilian, Vietnamese and Chinese workers. I can remember that there was a lot of unrest in the town. I remember people saying things like, "Oh, I just dunno about these Brazilian men, they're gonna come and take our wives." And I can remember one person who said, "Those bloody Vietnamese, they don't go to the toilet like we do!" But then five years later, I was back there and that all settled down by the time Nades arrived.'

Like many of the Biloela locals, Simone had a family member who had a job at the meatworks, too. It wasn't a workplace for the faint-hearted.

'Most locals in Bilo recognise how difficult the jobs are at the meatworks. Anybody who can stick a job out there is worth their weight in gold to Bilo locals. My younger brother did a stint for a few months, and he would tell stories of people starting their first day and they'd get to two hours in and they'd be "I'm just popping out to go to the toilet", and then they would just never come back! There used to be a rite of initiation for new people that they would take blood clots from the beasts that they were killing and they would put them in people's boots.'

English Teacher

By the time of the dawn raid on Priya and the family, Simone was two states south of Queensland, living in Melbourne with her husband and two children. She was three weeks into her studies to become an immigration lawyer.

It was only a matter of hours after Angela and Bronwyn launched the petition that a friend in Biloela sent it to Simone. When she opened the link, she was startled to see Nades looking back at her.

After signing and sharing the petition on her own social media, Simone immediately started talking to other family members who were also horrified by the brutality of the raid, including her cousin Melissa Sweet, who ran a well-respected health blog called Croakey.

She suggested Simone write about the family and their place in the Bilo community for the blog and, somewhat reluctantly, Simone agreed. She didn't know Bronwyn, Angela or Vashini and hadn't written an article before, but she quickly realised—in another example of small-town efficiency—that Angela used to work with her mother in Biloela. So at least it would be easy to track her down. All four women would soon be in semi-constant contact.

'I wrote the article and at the same time thought I could probably ring the detention centre and see if the family wanted me to come and visit them. But I can remember putting it off for a couple of days because I thought, How silly, it might be that they'll be really upset, and won't even remember me. Would it be weird if I rang? But I did ring.

'I can remember just trying the landline. Sometimes you get the Serco guard who'd be, "Yeah, I'll get them to call you back." And they might call you back . . . And you just learned quickly to pick up any phone call that came from a no-caller ID location.'

HOME TO BILOELA

Nades was surprised to hear from his English teacher but encouraged her to make a booking to come and see them in the detention centre. The family knew no one else in Melbourne.

Simone had worked with refugees but she had never been into one of Australia's notorious immigration detention centres, so had no idea the application to visit would be a lengthy process that could take at least seven days, if it was approved at all. She also had no idea that by the time she got in to see the family, they would have been dragged all the way to Sydney, then Perth and then back to Melbourne again, in an attempted deportation.

Chapter 10
THERE AND BACK AGAIN

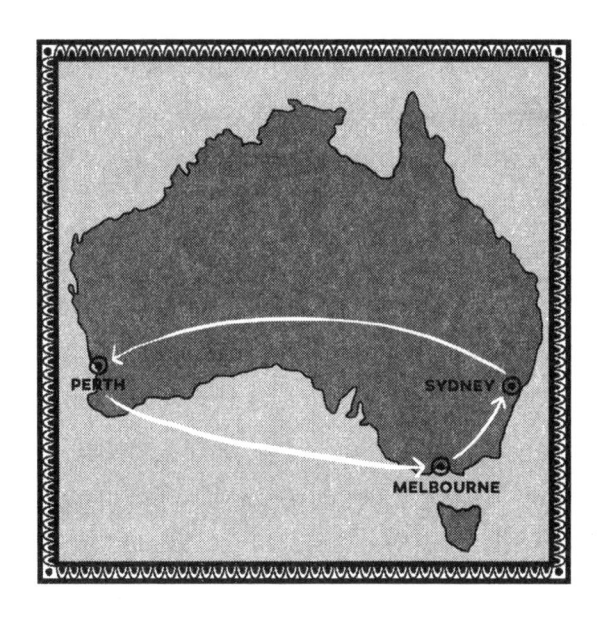

Melbourne 13–15 March 2018

Just over a week after we arrived in Melbourne, I was feeding Tharni her lunch and Nades was helping Kopi put her shoes on, when suddenly what looked to be more than fifteen Serco guards marched into our cabin with an ABF officer. We were shocked and confused.

The ABF officer started reading the deportation notice. 'You need to come with us immediately,' one of the guards said in a commanding tone. 'If you don't cooperate, we'll handcuff you if we need to.'

But before I could understand what they were saying, two female guards grabbed both my arms. I tried to tell them that a court order was going to arrive any minute to stop the deportation.

'I want to speak to my lawyer!' I demanded. 'What you're doing isn't right!'

But they hurriedly marched Nades and the children out while they held me back. I saw that Kopi had a sock and a shoe on one foot and a thong on the other. I heard Tharni crying.

'Let me go with my family!' I pleaded. 'My babies are crying. Let go of me!'

But they didn't care. They forced us into separate vehicles; this time the children and Nades were together in one, and me in another. I screamed and begged to be with my family. Nades, too, was pleading with the guards, and the girls were crying out for me. I could see the fear in my children's faces. But it was like the guards couldn't hear us. They showed no signs of noticing our distress.

After a short drive, our vehicles arrived at Melbourne Airport. We were driven into the holding shed near the tarmac and held there for an hour or so. I was praying that the court order would arrive soon. But then I saw them get Nades and the children out, and march them onto the awaiting charter flight. I was screaming at them to let me go, but they held me inside the van for a good fifteen minutes. I was terrified that we'd be taken to different locations.

Then they pulled me out. I was relieved when they led me onto the same plane, but they put me into a seat that was several rows in front of Nades and the children. I protested. The children couldn't understand why I was not sitting with them and kept calling out for me. Nades was trying to calm them down while trying to question the guards.

I asked the interpreter to go and get the immigration officer on the flight. 'You can't deport us,' I told him. 'You could lose your job for deporting a family with a court order!'

But instead of interpreting what I said, the interpreter told me just to do what I was told and not to make a scene. That set me off even more.

'Don't tell me how to run my life!' I shouted at her. 'You should be doing your job ! We don't need your thoughts!'

The plane took off. The female guards didn't let go of my arms the whole time. My head felt like it was about to explode. Whenever I tried to speak, they kept telling me to be quiet and sit down. But I didn't shut up. I kept asking to be allowed to speak to my lawyer; I knew she would be waiting for us to phone her for the daily check-in. Tharni and Kopi were still calling out for me.

'You are making a huge mistake,' I told them. 'Our court order is probably in effect now and you are going to look like fools!'

Within two hours, the plane landed in Sydney. I asked to speak to my lawyer again and this time the immigration officer handed me a mobile phone. Luckily, I remembered Kajalini's phone number by heart. She answered and I told her we had been put on a plane. Kajalini immediately asked to speak to the immigration staffer and I passed the phone back to him. Kajalini had asked for his email so she could send through the paperwork to him directly.

Just then, around 25 men were escorted onto the plane; they were all Sri Lankan detainees from Sydney's Villawood Immigration Detention Centre. One of the young men had his hands cuffed and his feet shackled. The guards were making fun of his behaviour by re-enacting the scene when they had handcuffed him. If Nades had been without a family and a community behind him, he could've easily been one of these men, deported without a sound. It was a frightening thought.

The doors shut and the plane began to move. My heart dropped to my stomach. I felt my chest tighten and I couldn't breathe. I wanted to speak to Nades, who was sitting with Tharni and Kopi a few rows behind me, but the guards wouldn't let me move. I kept shouting for the officer to check his email. 'How can you be so heartless? You spoke to my lawyer, check your emails!' I kept repeating. 'You can't deport us!'

As the plane took off, my mind was racing, playing all kinds of scenarios if we returned to Sri Lanka. Nades would be killed or taken prisoner there, I knew that. He was a wanted man because he'd been forced to be a Tiger in the past. My children would have to grow up without a father and I had no means of bringing them up on my own. I could also be imprisoned and raped. Surely the Australian government couldn't deport us back there.

All that Nades and I had endured over the past few years had been in vain. I felt like crying, but I held it in. I wasn't going to give the guards or the immigration officials the satisfaction that they'd broken me.

We'd been flying for about five hours, when suddenly the captain announced that we were preparing to land. I knew that we couldn't have reached Sri Lanka in five hours. This gave me a little hope.

The plane began to descend and landed in Perth. A woman in business clothes got on and spoke to the immigration officer on the flight. Then, to everyone's surprise and to my great relief, the four of us and our entourage were ushered out of the plane and into the

There and Back Again

airport—this time, without force. The plane left soon after that, for Sri Lanka. I was too relieved for my family to give much thought to the fate of the Tamil men on board.

'Why did you do that to my family?' I asked the immigration officer once we were inside the terminal.

He laughed at me. Then, as if I wasn't there, he started telling the other officers how I had been making a scene on the plane. Maybe he assumed my English wasn't good enough to understand him. Certainly, the interpreter wasn't saying anything. The others laughed. That made blood rush to my head.

An ABF officer came over and told me that we'd be kept at a hotel in Perth that night while our court order was being checked. Tomorrow, this same plane would return from Sri Lanka after deporting the detainees. If our court order was valid, the plane would take us back to Melbourne; if not, it would take us to Sri Lanka.

By the time we were taken to a hotel in Perth, it was one o'clock in the morning. The girls were asleep on Nades' shoulders, completely exhausted. They gave us a couple of food boxes, which were again unsuitable for our children. We were so tired that we fell asleep without a shower or a change of clothes.

The next afternoon we were back on that plane to Melbourne. Our court order was indeed valid but our lawyer believed the processing of her application had been delayed by a public holiday in Victoria.

After Kajalini had got off the phone to us in Sydney she had called the night registrar of the Melbourne Court and explained that we were being deported. Kajalini had asked if the court needed to be convened to stop our plane, which was already in the air. The Judicial Registrar had told the department's lawyers and Kajalini to come to an agreement and the department had immediately agreed to land our plane in Perth.

When we arrived at the MITA facility for the second time, Serco treated us like new arrivals. All our waiting at the front office previously for hours was for nothing; all our paperwork needed to be done from scratch.

I was looking for our luggage. Serco guards had loaded all our suitcases and boxes on that first flight to Sri Lanka, when they tried to deport us. But now I could only find a couple of the boxes and no one would tell us where the rest had gone. They contained almost all our belongings, including several silk saris that had been given to me as gifts at our wedding and photos of the children. These had been packed by the police officers during the dawn raid in Bilo just over a week ago. When I complained, the guards came into our unit and began searching through all our things.

When I asked them what they were looking for, the guards said that they wanted to make sure that the boxes weren't in our unit. I was so angry I shouted at them to go and check their surveillance video, which should show what they did with our luggage. 'You're always filming us when we're getting on a plane and off! What's the use of all that footage?'

The next day the guards returned and said there was footage of all our luggage being loaded onto the plane, but that was all.

'What does that tell you?' I yelled. I was frustrated by their stupidity.

I filed a complaint at the front office and estimated the value to be $8000. To investigate my claim, an officer from Sydney arrived by plane two days later, and spent the day asking me various questions about what was in the lost luggage. I couldn't believe it.

There and Back Again

Why spend all this money to get someone from Sydney? Was there no one in Melbourne capable of investigating this?

But nothing came of it, so I complained to the Commonwealth Ombudsman. After all that, they agreed to pay us $2179, which we were told was the maximum amount anyone could claim. So, all that time asking us about what was inside the boxes was just a waste of effort. I wasn't bothered about the money; I was upset that Serco and ABF had lost these items, which were of sentimental value to my family. Till this day, I haven't claimed that money.

I was in daily contact with Vashini. She told me that the Bilo community was doing everything they could to get us back home; Angela, a social worker I had met through Bronwyn, created an online petition and that was getting a lot of signatures. They were organising a vigil at the park in Bilo. Simone, Nades' English teacher, who was now living in Melbourne, had written an article about us and a lot of people were sharing it.

I was speechless; I couldn't believe the contrast between the Australian people and their government.

Chapter 11
VIGIL

Back in Biloela, just moments after hearing the court action had successfully stopped the deportation, Angela got an unexpected call from Priya's brother in India. He hadn't yet heard the legal outcome and was terrified for his sister and her family.

'He phoned me, beside himself, saying they're on a plane, they're being sent. And I just remember him pleading with me and it took me straight back to sitting with families in ICU when you're telling them, we've gotta turn off the life support. It was the same fear, they're gonna die. Fortunately, by the time he phoned me we'd already heard, things were already happening to stop it. So I could reassure him that we were doing everything we could.'

For the social worker who barely knew the family and had been doing her friend Bronwyn a favour in fronting the media for just over a week, it was a galvanising moment. 'I still feel like that was the spark that, for me, sustained the whole thing 'cause it was just the moment that made me go, okay, there's no choice in this.'

Meanwhile, Simone had been speaking to her cousin Melissa who had made another extremely useful suggestion: that Biloela supporters hold a vigil to demonstrate their support for the family.

'I talked to Angela about a vigil and she said, "Oh, that'll be difficult. That won't take off here. People won't turn up to a vigil."' But Bronwyn, too, had been told by refugee advocates that she needed to keep momentum up with a vigil. 'I was sitting in one of my kids' bedrooms, noticing they had spilled red cordial on the floor, and I was thinking, How can I do this? I'm working full time, I have five kids and all kinds of financial constraints.'

Feeling overwhelmed, Bronwyn also took the temperature with Angela as to whether locals would actually come to a vigil. Luckily, Angela was wrong, and it would be the first of countless vigils she would speak at around Australia.

Simone asked local women Marion Meissner—her high school English teacher—and Jacinta Jackson—a quality assurance officer at Teys meatworks—if they could assist. They promptly organised a vigil to take place at Lions Park in Biloela on 14 March, nine days after the dawn raid.

Lions Park also, appropriately, happened to be very close to Priya's Rainbow Street home, and she and Nades had often taken the girls to play and meet friends like Bronwyn there.

Simone's mother was on hand to livestream the late afternoon vigil to the newly established Home to Bilo Facebook page. In it, a group of around 80 locals can be seen sitting on the ground or standing in the shade of a small gazebo, all listening quietly and intently to the speakers in the warm autumn twilight.

Tucked behind a collection of small candles and handwritten notes can be seen the smiling family photo of Priya, Nades and the girls that was used on the petition and in thousands of subsequent news stories. In the livestream footage, Bronwyn can be seen walking behind one of her children as they place a note on the display. She remembers being surprised but pleased by the turnout, which included hospital workers, meatworks staff and other locals who clearly had a connection to Priya and the family.

In an unusually still and serious atmosphere, the voices of the speakers carry clearly over the park with no microphones or amplification. Their only competition comes from the local birdlife.

Angela can be heard telling the crowd, 'The government have to pay attention.' Much later she would reflect that being able to explain the success of the previous day's court injunction was a useful moment for her to inspire the locals who showed up.

'At the rally, that was very much "we got them off the plane, you know, we can do this" and I think that very much empowered people that the fight's not over.'

The fight hadn't even really begun, but the group of core supporters was about to increase, as the rapidly growing petition had caught the eye of someone else in Melbourne.

Iain Murray was an experienced campaigner with a day job fundraising for universities. He'd heard about the family via Aran Mylvaganam of the Tamil Refugee Council.

Vigil

'Aran gave a speech at a rally for refugees ... I saw the video of that, we didn't know each other very well, but hearing him tell that story, I could tell he was really affected by the brutality of the raid. And I think, the fact that there were kids involved, I was shocked.'

What Iain, a chronically but usefully online individual, also noticed was that the shares of the press release and petition on social media were extraordinarily high. 'I can't remember exactly, but it got shared some phenomenal number of times.'

This very much caught Iain's attention. He thought there must be something in the combination of the informed urgency of Aran's message, backed up by the women from Biloela speaking out and demanding the safe return of the family to their small rural town, that showed a genuine groundswell of support from rural Queensland.

After years watching Australia's treatment of refugees, what Iain saw in the response from the women from Biloela was an opportunity to tell Priya and the family's whole story.

'Few of us really understand that much about how the legal system works and it was important that we weren't limited to telling a story about the law because, ultimately, this wasn't a story about the law. It was a story about right and wrong.'

Iain quickly found Angela's Facebook profile and messaged her. He wanted to contribute money to help promote the petition but if he was going to do that, he also had some ideas.

'I think I said to Angela that if the petition is written in the same language that you have been using on your personal Facebook page, the same language that you would use when talking to a friend, that's what's gonna help people connect.'

Everything was now moving apace. In Melbourne, while helping organise the Biloela vigil, Simone noticed there was another vigil being organised, this time in Melbourne by the Refugee Action Collective (RAC). She messaged the organiser, Lucy Honan, and, with endearing naivety, asked if she could attend. Lucy quickly realised who Simone was and where she was from, so not only asked her to attend—she wanted her to speak.

Simone wasn't exactly brimming with confidence. This would be her first time speaking publicly about the family. But she agreed. As awareness spread, a vigil was planned for Sydney on the same day.

'On my way to the vigil, this guy called Iain messages Angela and I, and says, "Are you going to the vigil? Can you just tell people not to do the chanting, that they shouldn't do the chanting, they should try singing? And maybe they could sing 'I Am, You are, We are Australian'?"

'And I was thinking, Who's this guy? And who the hell am I to go "Let's not chant, let's all sing a song!"'

In the space of one week Simone had written her first ever article, made her first application to visit a detention centre, discovered she didn't have to RSVP for a vigil that she was now speaking at, and was learning from an experienced campaigner about low-key crowd control and strategic messaging. For someone only three weeks into her studies to become an immigration lawyer, this was quite the immersive experience.

It was only after the vigil had ended that Simone met Iain Murray for the first time.

'Iain and I, and the two friends that I came with, were standing there chatting for like, half an hour afterwards. He had so many solid suggestions. And he's saying how impressed he was by the style of advocacy we were using, and I was thinking, Who is this guy and where did he come from? So I said to him, "You've got so many good ideas, do you think maybe I could start like a group chat so that you and Angela and I can chat some more?"'

With that, Iain Murray joined the core group of supporters in the race to save the family from deportation.

Iain, like Bronwyn, had been involved in working with a wide variety of organisations and committees for years and he preferred the efficiency of small groups. 'I've always found that small groups with high levels of trust are the easiest to work with when it comes to stressful social-change work. We were just so lucky that the particular combination of people that were involved early on just had a natural affinity. And there can be terrible, terrible conflict in groups working for social change. And it's understandable because the stakes are so high, and particularly around refugee stuff, it's really, really hard work for anyone. It's hard emotionally. But with a smaller group of people that have had an opportunity to get to know each other and where there's high levels of trust, it's amazing what you can do.'

The Home to Bilo campaign team was up and running.

Chapter 12

INTO DETENTION

Because she was living in Melbourne in March 2018, Simone Cameron would be the first person from Biloela to get into the detention centre to see the family.

While she didn't know exactly what to expect, she thought her work in the refugee sector would help her to deal with going into the facility. It didn't. She also thought she had successfully booked a visit to see the whole family. She hadn't.

'It was pretty horrific, that first visit. I was just sitting there waiting and waiting for about half an hour for them to come in and sort of looking around ... But when only Nades arrived so very late, he was quite upset. And the reason why was because I'd stuffed up the application form and they wouldn't let Priya and the girls come to the visit with him. So he said, "Okay, well I won't go." But then he changed his mind, and he came alone.'

Into Detention

What Simone was experiencing in extreme close-up was the infuriatingly byzantine processes that visitors to Australian immigration detention centres have to go through. By 2018, I was deeply familiar with them, as a journalist developing a particular interest in the onshore centres incongruously tucked away in Australian suburbs.

At the time of Simone's first visit to Nades, I had been going into detention every week for 18 months, and had started to publish news stories about the living conditions for those detained in the Australian mainland centres, as well as the access issues for those wanting to visit. Like Simone, I had also been surprised by the level of security.

In late 2016, the Melbourne centre already reminded me of a medium-security prison, with its high fences and razor wire. Set back and therefore unseen from the road, beside an army barracks in the semi-industrial suburb of Broadmeadows, MITA is a 25-minute drive from Melbourne's central business district. But the facility's anonymity was more complete than any prison. Only the large number of staff arriving and leaving in uniform carrying transparent plastic shoulder bags, and the vast collection of white vans used to ferry detainees around, were clues to what lay just back from the main road.

In 2016, the centre accommodated most of its residents in dozens of basic demountable cabins. Separate to the main centre, but still in the grounds and surrounded by the same high fences and locked gates, was a separate series of basic motel-like units for family groups allowing them to live in the same unit while sharing a bathroom and a kitchen—not that anything like normal family life was achievable. Guards could still enter whenever they chose and in the kitchens there were no knives allowed. Families had to try to prepare meals with basic plastic cutlery. This was where Priya and the family would be held in Melbourne.

By 2018, a large new area called MITA north had been built to accommodate detainees who had convictions, though there was no clarity on how ABF staff decided who was housed where. Over the next five years I would hear of and speak to plenty of detainees with a range of criminal convictions being housed in areas alongside non-criminal asylum seekers, including the children.

Human rights lawyer Alison Battisson, who represented one of the other infants in detention, refuses to even call these facilities 'detention centres'.

'The places where Priya, Nades, Kopika, Tharnicaa and my clients, baby Isabella and her mother, were held bear all the hallmarks of a prison. The only reason these places are not called prisons is because that would make them illegal under Australian law. Prisons are places used to punish people. Under Australia's constitutionally enshrined separation of powers, only the judiciary can sentence a person to imprisonment because it is only the judiciary that has the power to punish. The executive and legislative arms of government cannot act to deny a person liberty as a form of punishment.

'Though it should be obvious, immigration prison is no place for a baby or child. It is no place for a lactating mother, or anyone trying to provide care for their child. These are dangerous places— each month there are approximately 65 recorded assaults. These occur in the same prisons holding children. And these are just the assaults that are recorded. Drugs are also a serious issue in immigration prison, including those that held the children. There is evidence that drugs are brought in by visitors and government contractors. Ice is prevalent in immigration prisons, and that causes violence. Uncontrolled, manic violence. I can think of no worse place to have a baby.'

In 2022, when I asked ABF directly to detail numbers of deaths and assaults in their detention centres over the period the family were detained, they refused, citing the confidentiality of 'operational matters'. But their own annual report for 2020/2021, freely available online, shows that between 2017 and 2021 there were a total of 71 'major disturbances', 196 sexual assaults, 15 deaths and 1015 cases of self-harm.

The department's own statistics make it crystal clear that an Australian detention centre is no place for children to grow up, but that was exactly what was about to happen.

Chapter 13

THE CHILDREN

When Priya and the family were shifted to the Melbourne detention centre from Biloela in March 2018, I was especially worried about the children. When they arrived, I thought they were the only children there, but barely ten days after they arrived from Biloela, a pregnant Vietnamese woman who had been taken into detention gave birth. Mother and daughter would live in the Melbourne detention centre for the next two years. That infant, baby Isabella, would become Kopika and Tharnicaa's beloved playmate for the next year, but only after I reported on the fact that the families were being kept apart by guards, only seeing each other through windows.

The government's assertions that they had got the children out of detention were clearly untrue, but when I first started reporting on the children in the centre, the media staff from Home Affairs and ABF would attempt to insist—via their answers to my official questions—that the infants and children were actually not living in the detention centre, because they were held in a part of the centre called, highly euphemistically, a 'residential precinct'. But that area was also called an APOD—an 'alternative place of detention'.

The speciousness of this argument was almost amusing. There was nothing alternative about it. It was like renaming Alcatraz a 'seaside residential precinct' and therefore pretending it was not a prison. Lawyers would tell me that, by using the term 'APOD', the government could convert any kind of building into a detention centre, including hotels and motels—something they subsequently and regularly did.

In the APOD the families had no freedom of movement and were, in fact, even more isolated from the medical office in the main centre than most of the other detainees. To take their children to see a nurse, Priya and Nades would have to get a guard to arrange a van, and then multiple guards would escort them through multiple gates. If they had been allowed to simply walk it would have taken two minutes. They also had to go through this process every time they had a visitor.

While Simone had dealt with asylum seekers before, the environment at MITA was entirely and disturbingly new.

'I remember walking out of there and ringing Angela and crying, because of just the absolute lack of decency, just treating people like prisoners. The likelihood that any small mistake would be seized upon and used as a way to stop you from visiting.'

While Simone didn't see Priya and the girls on her first visit, she did see baby Isabella in the visit room, which was the only place her mother and the baby could see Paul, Isabella's father. Simone was shocked to see a tiny baby in detention.

'I saw her and she was a brand-new baby, on my very first visit, because I remember that was another shocking moment. And I was thinking, What the fuck is happening here? Why is there a newborn? What is this place?'

―――

To visit the family, Simone had to start an online account with ABF, then go through approximately nine pages of detailed declarations for each family member she wanted to visit. There were PDFs to attach, and she had to register proof of her ID to even get the visit approved.

It is impossible to know where she made a mistake in her first application, because there was never any explanation.

She was by no means the first visitor to be flummoxed by the system. Her experience demonstrates that if an Australian-born English speaker with high computer literacy struggles, then of course others will, too.

Over the years I observed two groups for whom these strictures made visiting if not an impossible then at least a highly unpredictable venture—those without the necessary computer skills, and asylum seekers who didn't have enough ID.

The former were seriously disadvantaged when it came time to go through multiple complex online steps, and the latter, if they were still one of the thousands of refugees on temporary visas, were often hamstrung by a lack of recognised documentation—a very common problem for persecuted minorities and people who have had to flee conflict.

The Children

If an applicant gets past the online process, then they get the chance to experience the true conditions of detention.

Upon arrival, you push a button on an intercom set into a 6-metre-high metal fence topped with razor wire. You provide your full name, state your reason for being there, and are hopefully allowed in. The reception area itself resembles a worn-out 1990s corporate building. Only upon sighting the large metal detector surrounded by uniformed guards does it become clearer where you are. The next part of the process is often far more difficult than the exhausting online application.

First, you need to make sure you have brought enough ID to be allowed to register for your booked visit, even though the department has gathered all of that from you already. Then you are put through the metal detector and a drug-testing process.

The metal detector is turned up so high that it pings at even the suggestion of an underwire bra. A hip replacement is enough to send it into space.

I became very aware of the detector's sensitivity because I had sustained multiple fractures in my right leg a decade earlier, and the plates and screws in my knee tripped the detector like a cheap car alarm. Guards that knew me would end up yelling at the ones that didn't, 'It's just Rebekah's leg!' Eventually I would have to get a letter from my GP that I carried in my wallet for the next three years, stating that I have the metal in my leg, so that my visits would not be declined. Other guards would mutter to me that it was dialled up too high on purpose. My leg never set off the detector at the airports.

If you got past the metal detector, next was a drug test. This system was introduced early in 2018 and has also been highly successful in keeping visitors out.

The guard asks for your permission to take a test and, upon your approval, swipes a plastic wand with a testing strip across various points of your clothes. The paper swab is then processed in a scanner. Like the metal detector, this machine seems to be dialled up to its peak.

Every week I would see the most improbable people test positive for that most unlikely of substances, fentanyl—a powerful synthetic opioid analgesic similar to morphine, but up to a hundred times more potent.

One week it would be the senior Salvation Army chaplain testing positive for trace amounts of fentanyl; the next it would be a nun or retired local mayor. While I may have been occasionally amused at the situation I found myself in—having to explain to a senior church member that they had tested positive for fentanyl, the drug implicated in Michael Jackson's untimely death—the reality of testing positive was a denied visit. Which meant the person detained did not see their family member, friend or chaplain.

Again, certain guards muttered about the machine's problematic proclivities and many of us developed techniques to avoid getting a false positive. I had read about problems with the same machines used in prisons overseas and saw that hairspray, perfume and drycleaning fluid had been indicated as possible contributors to a positive test result.

To dial down the likelihood of a positive test, I kept several changes of clean clothes separate and made sure I hadn't taken anything for drycleaning. On visit days I changed into clean clothes at the last minute. One day, after I had been at the hairdresser, I did test positive.

At that stage, guards would carry out a second test. On the day I failed I was lucky enough to be dealing with a reasonable guard

The Children

and explained that I thought it was hairspray on my shoulders and asked that he test a different area instead. I passed and was allowed in.

Another day I had a firm discussion with a guard who went to swipe the bottom of my shoes.

'Why would you test there? My shoes walk through God knows what on the street to get in here.'

He capitulated but I knew it was a matter of time until someone would be less reasonable. After that I also left clean shoes in my car, meaning I had a complete change of clothing set aside just to get into detention.

I was able to drive to MITA for my visits, but as usual, it was those who could least afford it who were messed around the most. People who had travelled hours by public transport would be told by the guards, after testing positive, that they probably touched something on the train or the bus, before they had to turn around to take the same lengthy journey home, without seeing their family member.

It wasn't just getting yourself into detention that was made difficult. If Simone had wanted to bring the kids a toy or some fresh fruit, she wouldn't have been allowed. By 2018, any food allowed in needed to be non-refrigerated, in commercially sealed, expiry-dated wrapping.

One Christmas Eve I tried to bring a colouring book for one of the children and was told that the item didn't meet the criteria. Another day, a particularly zealous guard told me the baby food I was wanting to take into one of the toddlers was not allowed. I had read the rules extensively and knew that the food met the criteria. There was some back and forth before another senior guard, who knew me and knew by this stage that I was a journalist, simply looked at the zealot and shook his head. I was let through with the food.

If you passed all the other requirements, then you were allowed in. But you had to leave all your personal belongings including your keys, phone, wallet and the ID you'd needed to enter in a locker. Occasionally I would try to bring a pen and paper in, but even that was often disallowed.

Everything in the process was unpredictable and stressful, and often seemed to be based on the discretion or mood of whichever guards happened to be working that day. It was a great example of the constant overreach and emboldened corporate personality of Serco, the huge private company that staffs the detention centres.

I saw this up close when I first started reporting on refugees. In 2017 I attended my first court matter for a refugee from MITA. The court was open and all kinds of people were waiting for any manner of minor appearance before the duty judge. The appearance was not a trial or a significant court date, just a standard appearance in which both sides agree to a date in the future. It's the kind of thing that takes two to five minutes.

As such, the court was not cleared and at least 40 or 50 people sat around me in the public viewing area waiting for their own matters. On the way into court the refugee appearing, a small woman in her fifties, had given me a little wave as she was being escorted past by four Serco guards. Half a minute later, one of the guards came up into the viewing area, sat down next to me and asked for my ID. I raised my eyebrows and we both smiled at each other. 'Under whose authority are you requesting my identification?' I asked. The female guard, who was about the same age as me appeared slightly puzzled, but replied, 'We just have to get the ID of anyone they know.' I asked again, 'But under whose authority are you requesting it? You work for a private contractor. You're not an officer of this court.' She shrugged and smiled and kept holding her hand out. I reached into my bag, got my ID and said, 'Just as a fun fact, where I come from, this would constitute an illegal search.' She noted down my details on a clipboard, handed back my driver's licence, and rejoined the other guards.

This was what they call a 'learning moment'.

It was one thing seeing the behaviour of guards inside a facility like MITA, but this was overreach at an entirely different level. It was a useful lesson early on in my time writing about refugees, as it was the kind of behaviour I would see again and again, not just from Serco, but from the government itself.

Chapter 14

UNDER GUARD

MITA   **March–December 2018**

We spent the next seventeen months in MITA while our case was at the Federal Court and then at the High Court. We were there indefinitely, literally locked up inside the cabin. We were isolated from other detainees within MITA. For the first three months, Serco guards stayed with us day and night. They'd sit at the dining table and log our behaviour throughout the day: the family is watching TV; the family is talking to each other; the family is eating, and so on. This meant that we had no normal family moments.

The guards brought us boxes of food three times a day and took us to IHMS (International Health and Medical Services) for a check-up once a week but this wasn't even an outing; the office was inside the main centre inside more gates and fences. Living like this stressed me out and I often felt like breaking the doors down.

After three months of living with us, Serco decided to remove their night duty and lock us in from 6 pm to 6 am instead. During those hours, we couldn't open the door from the inside. In the mornings, they'd unlock the door without knocking and do a headcount, in case a family of four somehow managed to slip out through the locked door into the fortified compound and escape. They did this no matter if we were asleep or in the shower.

Kopi's third and Tharni's first birthdays came and went inside those four walls. Friends or family weren't able to see how we had to live—people who might celebrate with us and perhaps bring a camera to take photos of that special day. My poor children were growing up knowing nothing of the world outside, without feeling the sun on their skin or the sand on their feet. They couldn't play with other children, and I worried they would forget what it was like to live a normal life in a community, surrounded by friends and family who showed them love and care.

At the end of June, more than three months after arriving at MITA, we received mobile phones because of a Federal Court order that all boat arrivals in detention should be allowed to have them. After that, I was able to speak to Vashini and Angela regularly, and I started taking photos of everything.

There was a Vietnamese woman and her toddler at MITA while we were there, but they were also kept in isolation, despite both her and me requesting that the children be allowed to play together.

By now, a few friends and supporters in Melbourne had begun visiting us, including Aran, Brad, Umesh, Rajini, Rebekah, Chandra (who had arranged my marriage to Nades and was now living in Melbourne), Simone, Angela and several members of our Bilo community. But for them to visit MITA was no simple procedure; there was so much paperwork to complete for each visit by both the visitor and us.

As well, there was no saying when Serco would reject these applications, as it seemed to be rather random. Sometimes they'd reject our application to receive the visitor; at other times, they'd reject the visitor's application. Sometimes it seemed like they'd send visitors home because the metal or the drug detectors were set off by a buckle or by someone standing nearby. They didn't care if the visitor had taken a day off work or travelled many hours to get there. I'm sure it was harder to visit a refugee in a detention centre than an inmate in a maximum-security prison.

But, whenever the stars aligned, we were allowed to meet the visitors in the visit room of the main centre and even then we were patted down by staff after being transported across the centre. It was never explained to us what the guards thought we could possibly take from one heavily guarded compound to another. Chandra and Rajini brought us clothes, toiletries and limited amounts of pre-packaged food, but we weren't allowed to take these foods into our cabin and the clothes and toiletries were all checked by guards. Sometimes they brought their children to a visit, so my girls would have playmates for two short hours. Simone and Aran updated us on all the legal stuff and the increasing support we were getting

Under Guard

from all over Australia. Once the visitors left, we'd be thoroughly searched before being taken back to our cabin.

As we waited, from time to time I would remember my early life in Sri Lanka, when the Indian army joined the fight against the Tamil Tigers and our young lives seemed suddenly in such great danger.

Chapter 15
WAR

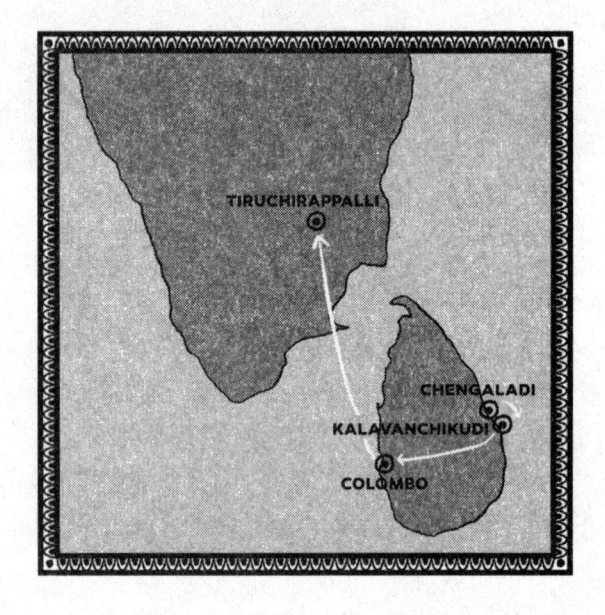

Chengaladi   **1988–1989**

Moving to Chengaladi was an obvious choice; Appa had set up a shop there several years before, when we moved out of Ampara. It was a beachside village, known for its long, beautiful, uninterrupted coast, and yet we were prohibited from going anywhere near it. The Sri Lankan Navy ships were stationed all along it.

At this time, I was in Grade 5 and I didn't like Chengaladi. My brothers felt the same, but we had little choice. We understood that our survival depended on living there, but our education suffered. I lost all motivation to learn.

We were also unlucky. Soon after our move, the conflict escalated in Chengaladi also. The Tamil Tigers infiltrated the jungles of the east after losing the Jaffna peninsula to the Indian Army. Indian and Sri Lankan soldiers patrolled our neighbourhood in their armoured vehicles and jeeps. Artillery shells rained down at all times of the day. Sometimes they'd start shelling when we'd just sat down for lunch or dinner, and we'd carry our pots and pans and run to a neighbouring village, not wanting to leave our food behind. We couldn't dig trenches or bunkers in Chengaladi, because the east coast soil was just fine sand.

Whenever the Tigers attacked one of the Army camps, the soldiers took revenge on the civilians. They'd fire indiscriminately as they drove by in their jeeps, killing innocent people and animals on the footpath going about their business. They'd raid our high school and take some of the boys away—many of them were never seen again. So, every time the soldiers came near the school, word would spread around the village and all the parents would come running to grab their children before the soldiers could. Amma did the same thing.

During one raid, a military helicopter was hovering very low over our school grounds. When I came running out of the classroom with everyone else, I saw a sari float up in the air in the turbulence created by the helicopter. It turned out to be Amma's. When she heard the Army was at our school, she had loosely thrown a sari over her nightie and run out of the house. It would've been improper for her to come out of the house in her nightie, even if it was to save her children.

HOME TO BILOELA

One time, while I was at school, the soldiers executed a man in our backyard, beside our well. He had been chased through the neighbourhood until he was cornered; then he was shot, at point-blank range. Appa had to inform the man's family and ask them to collect the body.

Amma worried that this was a bad omen. 'How could we live in a house where a man was killed?' she'd ask and answer it herself, 'We need to move.'

Appa wasn't keen on the move, but over the following weeks dead bodies started to show up along the main road, hanging on the electricity cables or tied to lampposts. The bodies were always at a prominent intersection located between the Catholic Church and the local MP's house. It took us a while to understand that the Tigers were doing this as a warning to those who worked with the enemy. Traitors will be executed and hung in public, they were saying.

One morning, my brothers and I set out for school and, within a few minutes, came across a body tied to a lamppost. Startled, we fled back home and told our Appa as we tried to catch our breath. Appa calmed us down, saying that we had nothing to worry about, and then he walked us to school by a different route.

Another time, our teachers dismissed us early from school. They told us to hurry home and they warned us to be careful. My brothers and I walked cautiously, only to be confronted by a terrible scene. A few armed young men, who we thought were Tigers, had a man kneeling on the side of the road, with his arms and mouth bound by pieces of a sarong. Suddenly one of them pulled out a machete and hacked the man's head off in one sweep. As the head rolled onto the ground, my brothers and I screamed and ran all the way home. That scene shook me to my core. Even when I think of it now, my blood runs cold.

For a while after that, Amma walked us to school and back, but it proved too much for all of us. So we moved back to Kalavanchikudi the following year. Appa took a job in the capital, Colombo, at a shop that sold old wares. He came to visit us every three months.

Back to Kalavanchikudi 1989–1995

Not long after we moved back, our neighbourhood became a warzone. In 1990 the Tigers attacked both Kalavanchikudi's police station and military camp at the same time, killing hundreds. Heavy bombing pounded our village, damaging homes, hospitals, shops and temples. Several innocent people were killed. We could see burning bodies along the side of the road. Many young men were disappearing, either arrested by the Army or joining the Tamil Tigers.

My sister was born that year. Although I was fourteen by then, I was very naive. I hadn't noticed Amma's growing belly and I was startled to find her holding a newborn baby when I came home from school one day. It was my neighbourhood friend who told me that I now had a baby sister (a *thangachi*, as we say). I remember being surprised and embarrassed.

My culture was to blame for this lack of understanding because young people weren't allowed to listen into adult conversation or ask questions. We didn't have television or access to books or the internet. These days, when my little daughters tell me about their teacher's pregnancy, I am amazed how much they know. Anyway, I quit school after that and stayed home to help with the household chores. Amma was busy with my *thangachi* and with fulfilling her sewing orders, which were drying up fast as the fighting went on.

HOME TO BILOELA

Over the next few years we learned to live with expecting the unexpected. The fighting increased in the north and east of the country. Every day brought with it more uncertainty. One time, a few days of ceasefire was declared. So Appa decided to sell the large sacks of rice husks we had harvested and began loading our bullock cart. But suddenly, out of nowhere, an artillery shell came whistling and landed right beside the bullock cart. The bullocks took off in one direction and Appa ran for dear life in another. Fortunately the shell didn't explode. During another ceasefire, soldiers turned up at our house in search of my *anna*. As usual, he jumped the fence and disappeared.

The military didn't stop their activities just because a ceasefire had been declared, so we never stopped being alert. It didn't help that our house was on a main road where the Army regularly patrolled. Whenever the soldiers interrogated Amma about my *anna*, she would defend her son, screaming at them. Because of this, the soldiers kept tormenting her, both verbally and physically. They even shot at her once. Luckily the bullet missed, but they shot and killed our two dogs who were barking at them.

One time they managed to catch my *anna* at home and Amma lost it. She wailed, screamed and threw herself at them, trying to free her son from their grip. She held on to my *anna* and refused to let go. So they beat her up and split her skull. Afterwards, she needed eight stitches. Fortunately, my *anna* was released after a day in detention; I thought that was because the soldiers were scared of Amma coming at them again.

One night, when the bombing got close, we grabbed whatever we could and ran out of our house. We crossed the river and took refuge in the church in the next village. We lived there with several other families for over a week, until things settled down. That side of the river was controlled by the Tigers but where our house was, on the east of the river, was under military control.

We heard that our house had been damaged, so we decided not to return and Appa found a house on the Tigers' side of the river for us to live in. But we found no peace. Every minute of the day was lived in fear of being killed or taken away. If we managed to cook a meal, we didn't know whether we'd have the opportunity to eat it, if the Army showed up or if fighting erupted. We had no electricity, no firewood or running water. The families often burned bicycle tyres to cook meals. The strong smell of burning tyres permeated the food and made it revolting but our only other option was starvation.

During this time, I learned that the soldiers had burned a few young men to death a few miles away. They were garlanded with burning tyres. One of those men's families had been talking to my family about me marrying him. Although I didn't know him well, I felt heartbroken. I thought I'd never get married.

Although my life in Kalavanchikudi turned out to be a nightmare, I was fortunate to grow up with an extended family of aunties, uncles and cousins and have some wonderful memories. My heart sinks with sadness that my children won't see the house I grew up in, the school I went to or the pond we swam in. My Australian children have to create their own extended family here and start building good memories.

Colombo 1995–2001

One morning, the first artillery shell for the day fell next to our house and exploded. We were all hurt in some way. There was blood and dust everywhere. The pain in my hip was so bad that

I thought I was going to lose my leg or something. We were all taken to hospital, which was full of injured people.

My family's injuries were not as serious as those of many of the other people there. The staff treated my wound; they said one piece was deep inside my pelvis, but they could do nothing about it because they had to treat cases that were more serious. There wasn't enough staff or medicine or painkillers to go around for everyone. I was in a lot of pain; I could barely walk or sit down without yelping. Since Appa was working in Colombo already, my parents decided to take me to a hospital there. I didn't realise it at that time, but my parents were planning to use this trip to escape the country.

So, two days after we'd returned home, we departed from Kalavanchikudi, leaving my aunties and cousins behind. Since my birth, I had been living with them, so leaving them was tough. We didn't know when, or if, we'd ever see each other again. My youngest aunt begged my father not to separate the family. As we drove off, I watched her run after the car behind the fine dust rising from the dirt road, with tears streaming down her face, until she could no longer keep up. I feel my heart squeeze in pain when I recall that scene.

This was my first trip to a big city, let alone a capital city. I was amazed by the fancy shops and restaurants, tall buildings and fast-moving cars, but I didn't like Colombo at all. It was too crowded, dirty and smelly. I preferred the open spaces, tall trees and the fresh air of my village. Colombo felt like hell to me.

We took a unit in Torrington Flats, a housing commission estate. It was a terrible little place. We weren't used to being stuck in a flat, but we had to stay there so I could get treatment. I had

War

to wait for weeks to get a bed and undergo surgery. As it wasn't easy to access painkillers, I lived in pain the whole time. Even after the surgery, things didn't go smoothly; I suffered complications post-surgery because the stitches unravelled before healing. I bear the large scar from that surgery to this day. When I became pregnant with my first child, Kopika, the pelvic pain returned.

As my health began to improve, my parents tried to find ways to go anywhere overseas. Many Tamils were fleeing to Europe, Australia and the Middle East. All the hope for peace had disappeared after the Indian government withdrew its Peace Keeping Force some years before this. The Tigers had become very powerful from all the support they were getting from the Tamils abroad. They had captured most of the north and east. Intense fighting was going on there all the time. So, for the next five years, my parents and my *anna* tried to find a country that would take us. Finally, not having much success, my parents devised a plan to visit India on tourist visas and claim asylum. There, Appa thought, we'd be safe among the Indian Tamils. But the Tamil Tigers had assassinated the Indian prime minister Rajiv Gandhi in 1991 and, if we had known what life was like for Sri Lankan Tamils in India as a consequence of this, we might've thought twice.

So in 2001, when I was 25 years old, we left for India by plane. Once again, we were fleeing. This time we were not just leaving our home, but our homeland.

My brothers and my sister and I were very excited to be going to India. We had grown up watching Indian Tamil films, where beautiful women and handsome men sang and danced in colourful clothing in front of amazing backdrops. We expected beauty and good food in India, but, more than all that, safety. We thought that our lives would be normal; no more living like second-class citizens. My parents promised me that, once we were settled, we'd organise to get our relatives over as well.

Unfortunately, none of this happened. The hardship I endured over the next ten years in India made me often wonder if I would've been better off continuing to live in the warzones of Sri Lanka. At least Sri Lanka was my birthplace, a place where I had some happy memories.

Chapter 16
INDIA

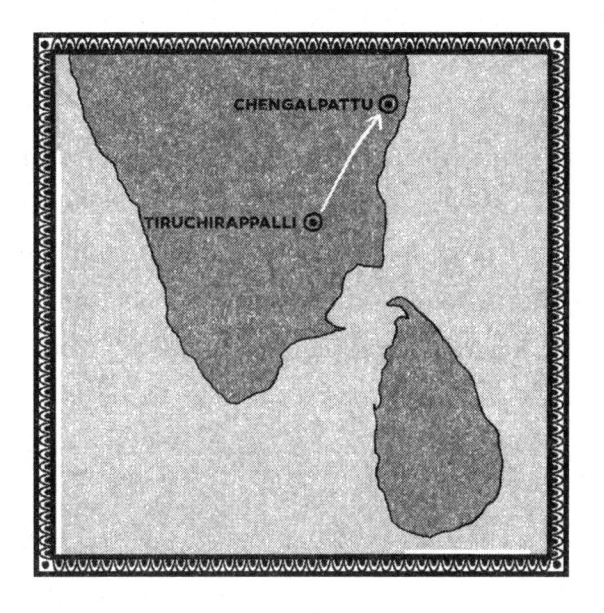

Tiruchirappalli   **2001**

Our plane landed in Tiruchirappalli, Tamil Nadu. On arrival, we joined the large group of asylum seekers waiting to be registered. It was a chaotic scene—no orderly queues, everyone pushing and shoving, and the police yelling as sweat poured off everyone in the midday heat. There were a lot of questions to answer and many forms to fill in. I couldn't understand the Tamil spoken by the Indians; it sounded like an entirely different language to me.

Once we were all registered, we were kept in their disgusting 'Intermediate Camp' for a few days. It looked like a prison. The Q Branch of the CID (the Criminal Investigation Department of the local police) controlled everything there. They treated Sri Lankan Tamils worst of all. Whenever they spoke to us, it was as if we were subhuman; they demanded bribes for everything, made up false accusations, used violence as punishment and harassed the women like they were their property. They beat you up if they didn't like the look of you, and there was no arguing your case with them.

We didn't want to live under these conditions, so my brothers tried to find a rental house. But it proved impossible because no one would rent their place to Sri Lankan Tamils. The Indians branded us with two labels: 'refugees' and 'Rajiv Gandhi killers'. My parents tried to enrol my *thangachi* into the local school, but they faced rudeness and a lot of questions. It was soon clear that, as refugees, we had no legal rights and, as Sri Lankan Tamils, we received no sympathy.

At the end of our first week in India, Appa suggested that we move north, close to Chennai, to get away from having to deal daily with the Q Branch police. My brothers also had more chances of finding jobs in a big city like Chennai; they were now in their twenties, young men who wanted to get out and find their way in this new country, rather than endure living as refugees in camps.

Chengalpattu   2001–2013

We travelled north to Chengalpattu, once an ancient village south of Chennai. It was a bustling city, full of historic Hindu temples, set by the Palar River on the east coast. My brothers found jobs in

India

construction as labourers. Appa was homebound, being too old to undertake physical work, which was the only employment available for refugees. Amma took work from the local tailor; there is a very high demand for tailor-made clothes in India and, because Amma was a very talented seamstress, she kept receiving orders.

My *thangachi* was able to enrol in a high school, so all the housework fell on me; from dawn to dusk, I did the cooking, cleaning and washing. After everyone went to bed, Amma expected me to stay up and help with hand sewing: hooks on blouses, beads on saris and hems on salwar kameez. She was a tough taskmaster and never once considered how hard I had been working all day.

The twelve years I lived in India was like being under house arrest; this experience would help me cope with similar conditions later in Australia. I never saw any sights or went to the movies. Nades still teases me about that. Who lives in India, home to Bollywood and Mollywood, and doesn't go to the cinema? It's unheard of.

My *anna* didn't want Amma or me out of the house. If we did go out, he wanted us to dress like the local women and speak as little as possible. He worried that our Sri Lankan Tamil accent was too easily identifiable. My brothers had become fluent in the local lingo, having worked in construction for years. My sister was fluent, too, having gone to high school and then to college. Appa was of Indian origin, so the accent came easily for him. But my brothers made fun of Amma and me, calling us 'fresh off the plane' because our accent didn't change. If people found out that we were Sri Lankan Tamils, it would mean abuse on the streets or a demand for money, or being refused service at a shop or, worse still, being kicked out of our rental home.

So I stayed indoors, mostly doing housework, and I only went out to the markets to buy fresh vegetables and to the local temple on Fridays, with Amma and my *thangachi*. I felt very lonely, but *thangachi* had her own life with friends at the college. She was out and about most of the day.

Our Indian neighbours didn't mingle with us; maybe they didn't like us foreigners, or thought that we were of a lower caste. The only time the old woman next door spoke to me over the fence was to check if the electricity or water supply was switched back on for the day. I lived like a frog in a well, not knowing much about the world outside.

As a woman heading towards my thirties, I was without a love interest or a husband. This made people treat me even worse; if my neighbours saw me in the mornings as they stepped out of their homes, they would turn around and go back inside. Then they'd wait till I was out of sight before setting out again. I heard them mutter out loud that seeing a spinster first thing in the morning would bring them bad luck that day.

I wasn't spared by fellow Sri Lankan refugees either; they'd invite my family to a wedding or their daughter's coming-of-age ceremony (an important ritual among our people) and specifically ask that I didn't attend so bad luck wouldn't befall the couple or the young girl. I couldn't go to the markets or the temple without other women asking Amma why her daughter was still single and whether I had received any marriage proposals, as if I wasn't there. No one spoke to me directly. I was deeply hurt by these acts.

I didn't lack suitors, mind you. A couple of my *anna*'s Indian friends were interested in me. But I wasn't going to marry an Indian man. Indian brides were expected to live with the husband's

India

family and obey his entire family for as long as they lived. I didn't like that idea—being born a woman was bad enough as it was. I only wanted to marry a Sri Lankan Tamil man.

Amma put the word out, asking her friends to find someone suitable in the local refugee camps. But nothing came of it. Whenever my mother brought up the topic of marriage, I used to ask her who'd replace all the unpaid housework I did if she sold me off as a wife-maid. She'd answer, 'Your brothers' wives', and we'd laugh. But Amma reminded me often that I was getting old, well past marriageable age, and I'd struggle to have children because I was reaching my mid-thirties. I was very fortunate to meet Nades when I was 38 years old and to naturally conceive two children after that.

Meanwhile, I busied myself by going from one household chore to another: cooking, cleaning, washing for eight adults and raising my *anna*'s two children. This way I didn't have the time or the energy to dwell on thoughts about the state of my life, but it seemed no one else did either. Having always relied on others to make decisions for me, I now found myself forgotten. A decade had passed since I arrived in India with my heart full of hope and my head full of dreams, but my life was not much better than the one I'd left behind.

True, I wasn't living in fear of death anymore, but I felt like I was slowly dying inside. Beauty and youth had already passed me. Sadness often came in waves and at those times I'd feel hopeless about my future—that I'd continue to live like this, with no one to love me. If I died, my family would only miss my cooking and my cleaning up after them.

When these dark thoughts came to me, I'd tell myself that I didn't survive a war to be a nobody; there was a better future for me somewhere, with a husband and children. This fantasy helped me sleep at night. In the reality of the morning, though, I didn't see a way out of my situation; we were forever branded *akathigal* (refugees) in India and reminded of it in every interaction with the locals. We could never feel safe or permanent. We had no access to medical treatment, or chance of legitimate work. For heaven's sake, I couldn't even leave my house whenever I wanted to.

Through all this, I never felt resentment towards Amma for making me work this way or towards my sister for receiving the education that I missed out on or to my *anna* for being married with children. I was truly happy for them, but I wished that I was as happy as they were. So, when I turned 37 in April 2013, and an opportunity came to get on a boat to Australia, I wasn't going to question it.

Chapter 17
THE BOAT

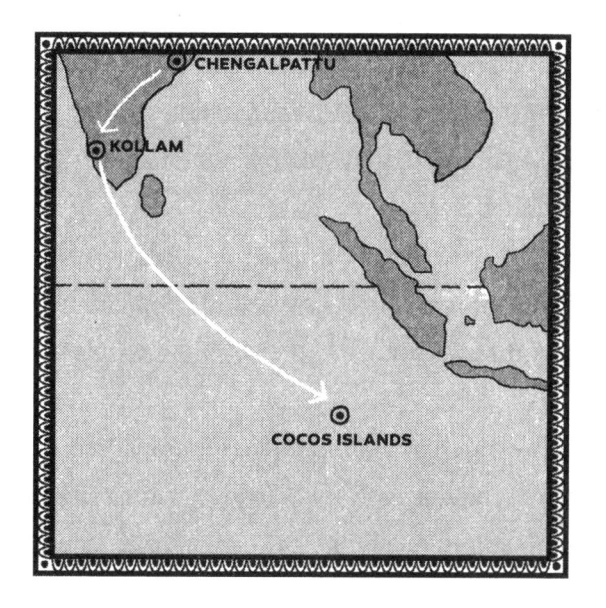

Kollam   **2013**

I never imagined that I'd leave India. It happened out of the blue. In my culture, it's the male child who gets all the good opportunities first, so no one was going to send me to America, Europe, Australia or the Middle East. During the years we lived in India, my *anna* and *thambi* tried to go to anywhere that would take them, but they failed each time for one reason or another.

One day, my *anna* announced that he had secured two spots on a boat heading to Australia from the west coast of India, leaving in two days. After some discussion with my parents, he decided that it would be *thambi* and me; he himself wouldn't go, because his children were too small.

'Once you're settled in Australia you can sponsor us all over,' he said.

I often wonder if he knew how dangerous the journey was and if it played a part in his decision. I, of course, had no idea and had no say. My *anna* was the decision-maker in the family now; what he said, went. I was excited at the chance to make my miserable life better. I was also terrified. In my 37 years of life, I hadn't lived a day without my family.

I told myself not to get my hopes up; it might turn out like our trip to India. But Amma was encouraging: 'You can find a husband in Australia and build your life there,' she said, her eyes shining with hope.

I didn't know much about Australia. I had learned in school that it was a large continent with lots of bush, kangaroos and camels. I knew nothing about its people, culture or what everyday life was like there. I just hoped that life would be better than in India or Sri Lanka. I wanted to be able to live freely, without fear of getting caught, raped or killed; to have my own family and friends; and to go out shopping or to the movies. I had lived my best years in hiding, as a nobody. My youth and beauty had gone to waste. I had nowhere permanent to live, no income, no identity and no one to love me.

I believed things could only get better. But, unbeknown to me, it would get way worse first.

I don't know how my *anna* had organised the voyage to Australia and I didn't care to find out. He had said that the less I knew

The Boat

the better. When the day arrived, I promised my family that I'd bring them all to Australia as soon as I could. I didn't know of the epic battle I had ahead of me to settle myself in Australia.

So my *thambi* and I boarded the train to Cochin. I had a larger bag packed with toiletries, a few sets of clothes and a blanket. In my handbag, I had a set of clothes, a few bars of chocolate, dates and anti-motion sickness tablets. The journey took us about thirteen hours through some of the most scenic and historic parts of Tamil Nadu, but I was in no mood to enjoy it. *Thambi* and I hardly exchanged words during our entire journey. We were sick with anticipation. Once we entered Kerala, the scenery changed; with its waterways, luscious greenery and coconut palms, Kerala reminded me of the eastern border of Sri Lanka where I grew up.

From Cochin railway station, we were instructed to get an auto-rickshaw to an address in Kollam on the west coast. When we reached the house, we found several men, women and young children, all Sri Lankan Tamil refugees waiting to take the trip to Australia. We didn't know anyone there. As the sun was beginning to set, a bus arrived at the gate.

Five men appeared at the door, casually dressed in sarongs, T-shirts and rubber slippers. It was clear from their accents that these men were Sri Lankan Tamil refugees also. It was only when they started telling us about the trip that I realised they were the people smugglers. Everyone was checking Christmas Island on their smartphones. Someone whispered that these men had bought a boat off some Indian fishermen for the trip.

One of the smugglers ordered the women and children to get on the bus. Another bus was coming for the men, he said. We didn't think this was unusual, because in India the sexes were often segregated on public transport. After a short ride in the dark, we were dropped off near dense bushland by the sea. As we got off the bus, some of the women asked after their husbands and sons they'd left behind in the house. The men assured them that they were right behind us.

It was getting dark now and I was frightened of stepping on snakes, lizards or insects as we followed the men through dense bushland. At that time, I didn't realise that Kollam was a popular tourist destination. We were kept well away from the beachfront and the harbour. After a short walk, we reached the shore, where several small wooden boats were moored. At a distance, I saw a medium-sized fishing vessel. There was no sign of the large ship that I was expecting to take us to Australia. I wondered if that ship was moored somewhere further away. Ten at a time, we waded through the water and got into a small boat, which took us to the fishing vessel. The men only allowed us to take our small bags with us; they promised us that the large ones would be loaded later.

'Throw your phones into the sea,' said a smuggler. 'Otherwise the government can track us.'

So, I threw my phone into the ocean like everyone else.

Once on the vessel, we were sent down into the hold, where normally the catch of the day would be stored. We were told to sit crouching on the floor; but with almost a hundred of us, it soon became very crowded with no room to stretch your legs. Among the passengers, there were twelve boys, seven of them teenagers. The rest were all female.

The cabin had no windows and the hot air stank of rotten fish, diesel and body odour. The floor was wet and dirty. It got so hot inside, I thought that I was going to faint. When someone asked to

The Boat

stay on the upper deck, the men told us that we could, but not yet. I wanted to escape to the deck also, but we had to stay put for now.

Suddenly the boat lurched and began to move. One of the women shouted, asking for her husband. Panic set in as we realised that our men weren't on our boat and neither were our bags. Now all the women started to scream asking for their husbands, brothers, sons and fathers, but the smugglers simply ignored us. Some women begged them to stop the boat, asking to be let off, but we all knew that this wasn't a bus to get off when you wanted to. The children began to cry also, and I could barely look at their frightened faces.

I was sick with worry about my *thambi*. Was he following me on another boat, or was I going to Australia alone? I had not been anywhere on my own, not even to the local markets. Now I was on a boat to an unknown country where I knew no one. I prayed to Goddess Durgai Amman to let me see *thambi* in Australia when I landed and promised to do an offering to her with her favourite sweets.

As the boat began to speed up, the noise of the engine and the huge waves crashing against the boat drowned out the women's voices. Soon the cries stopped as severe seasickness took over the passengers. Almost everyone was vomiting all over the floor we were sitting on.

Over the next fourteen days, we faced harrowing conditions at sea. Most of the passengers, including me, suffered from severe seasickness the entire time. The men allowed us onto the open deck on the second day, so I managed to scramble up. I stayed there, lying on the floor and spewing stomach juices. Huge waves crashed onto the boat and drenched us with icy cold sea water while the sun burned our skin. The salt water made my eyes sting. I could barely open them without seeing the entire vessel revolve around me. The men offered us handfuls of boiled rice, but no one had any appetite. I couldn't think about anything or speak to anyone.

The toilet on the boat was a hole at the far end screened by pieces of cloth for privacy. There was no fresh water for anything other than drinking. Because I was being frequently drenched in vomit and sea water, when they dried, my clothes began to itch and smell badly. I changed into my two spare outfits twice in the two weeks and discarded what I had been wearing into the sea.

Back at home, I used to be very hygienic, refusing to share a drink or food even with my own family. Amma used to get angry at me, saying, 'Don't act as if you're the queen.' Now on the boat, someone offered me a jug of water. As I took a sip, someone else yelled out: 'Don't drink it, that's our vomit jug!'

One time, severe winds and giant waves nearly capsized our boat. It was so scary. I thought that I was going to die. Many passengers were crying and praying loudly. Most of them didn't know how to swim. I could, having swum every day as a child in our waterhole back in Kalavanchikudi, but where was I going to swim to? There was no land anywhere near that I could see. Without our phones to track us, who would even know if we drowned? It was one of the worst experiences of my life.

Even today, the thought of getting on a boat makes me sick and brings back all the bad memories. When we were living in Perth Community Detention in 2021, our friend Angela wanted to take us on a ferry to Rottnest Island. She convinced me that the children would love the quokkas, and they definitely did. But when I got on

The Boat

the boat, I couldn't escape the feeling of terror or the seasickness even on that luxurious ferry. I never want to be near the ocean again. If anyone out there is thinking about getting on a people-smuggler boat to seek asylum, I beg you—don't do it.

Chapter 18
AUSTRALIA

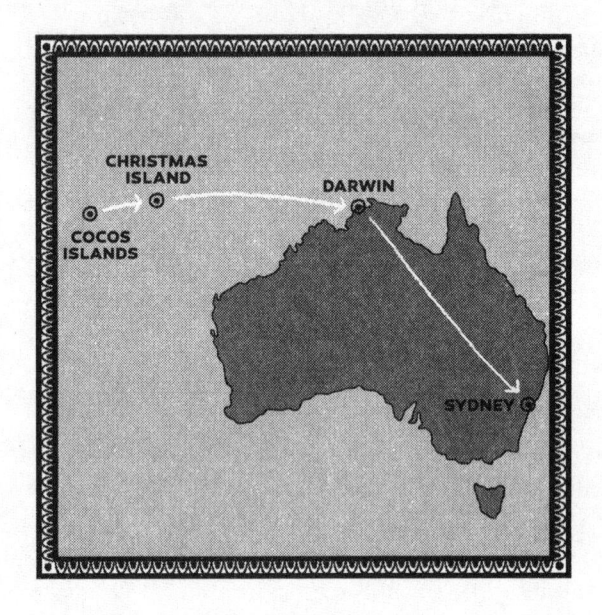

Cocos Islands   **1 April 2013**

Around ten days into our trip, the men announced that we'd be heading to the Cocos Islands instead of Christmas Island; the boat was fast running out of diesel and it was damaged badly, so we wouldn't make the extra distance. The biggest worry for everyone was whether the Cocos Islands were part of Australia. It would have been a great shame, after all we'd gone through, to end up just outside Australian territory. The men said it was, so no need to worry.

Australia

I didn't care where I got off; I just wanted to be on land. My seasickness hadn't got any better and our living conditions were only getting worse. I had no more changes of clothes, except for my salwar kameez, and there was very little rice or drinking water left. But we hadn't spotted land so far.

I remember Day 14 being a clear, sunny day. Late in the afternoon, suddenly one of the men shouted, 'I see a bird!' Excitement rippled through the boat. Everyone was feeling alive again, thanking their Gods: 'Nandri, Muruga!', 'Nandri, Anthoniyaaré!'

'You'd better not be making fools of us,' someone said out loud. 'It's the 1st of April.'

We saw some seabirds and then land formations at a distance. They were the Cocos Islands. Within minutes of us sighting land, a motorboat was speeding towards us. As it approached, we realised it was an ABF patrol boat. Like everyone else on our boat, I was happy to be caught by the Australians. I was thinking that this ordeal was over, and I was finally somewhere safe; my future was going to be okay.

By now four ABF boats had surrounded us, and some of the officers jumped into our boat. The officers, both male and female, were all *vellakkaarar* (white people). First, they handed us life jackets, then biscuits and bottled water. I wanted to laugh; we had survived two weeks on the deep sea in a broken boat without any safety jackets, and here we were nearly on shore and they were concerned for our safety. Then they towed our boat towards land.

With its sandy unspoilt beaches, swaying coconut palms and feral chickens, the Cocos Islands reminded me of Chengaladi. I hadn't imagined any part of Australia to be as remote as this. We were taken to a couple of small demountable buildings and given some fresh clothes, a large bin bag in which to discard the clothes that we were wearing and a small plastic bag for our valuables. I had nothing valuable on me, just a pair of fake gold earrings. Then they offered us warm food of cooked rice and lamb mince and some biscuits. Being a vegetarian, I ate plain boiled rice.

Later we were shown to our cabins, which had bunk beds made up with clean sheets. While it was nice to be able to stretch out and sleep, I struggled to fall asleep that night. I couldn't shake off the rocking motion of the sea, even though I was on solid ground now. I kept thinking about *thambi*; I wondered if he had made it to another boat, and if he was alive and heading to Christmas Island.

The next evening, as the sun began to set, ABF told us that we were being taken to Christmas Island for processing. It took several trips in a small plane to take all of us there. When we arrived on Christmas Island, it was pitch dark; we could hardly see our hands in front of us.

We wondered why they'd waited till nightfall to transport us. I know now that the government would always pick the cover of darkness to transport refugees. It was easier to avoid media attention that way.

Christmas Island   April–August 2013

The Christmas Island detention facility was run by the security firm Serco. It was huge. There were hundreds of refugees there from all parts of the world, many from Iran. Once all the paperwork was done and I received a phone card, I rang home.

My family were happy to hear my voice. They'd been worrying for the past two weeks with no news from me. My *thambi* was back home as no one had come to pick up the men at the house in Kollam.

Australia

I became worried when I realised I was all alone in Australia. I didn't know anyone in this big country. After all these years waiting to be told what to do, it was all up to me now; there was no one to care for me or to protect me. I was going to have to fend for myself. It was a frightening thought.

I was on Christmas Island for five months. What I remember about it is all the waiting we did in those humid hot days—waiting in long queues at the single toilet block, waiting for food and waiting to find out your fate. There were so many cultures and languages inside the detention centre that we all kept to our own kind.

There were occasional dramas—suicide attempts, hunger strikes and pregnancies from illicit affairs among detainees, as well as between detainees and the guards. Some women made it their mission to seduce the guards, who they thought might sponsor them. But we Sri Lankans stayed quiet and tried to avoid drawing attention to ourselves, not wanting to ruin our chances of permanent visas.

For the first time in a long while I had a lot of free time, but this only made me feel lonely, sad and depressed. I kept reminding myself that this was temporary and I was now in a safe place, with hope for a bright future. I relied on my companions—three young single Tamil women and a married mother of two, called Chandra—and considered them as my new family.

Soon stories spread that many detainees at the facility were being deported. This scared us all. Every morning we worried that it was our turn to be sent back home. Some of those who had arrived on the boat with me started leaving the detention centre one by one. We had no choice but to wait to be called in to learn our fate.

Days passed this way. My waiting came to an end one evening; I was called into the office. Feeling sick in the stomach, I approached the official, my heart pounding heavily. I held my breath and silently prayed to Durgai Amman not to let me be deported.

Before the interpreter could translate for me what had been said, I heard the word 'Darwin' come straight out of the official's mouth. I nearly screamed with happiness.

Darwin September 2013–February 2014

The following morning, I was put on a charter flight with other refugees and brought to Darwin. Although I was only going from one detention facility to another, the threat of deportation had vanished from my mind. I felt that, if they were planning to deport me, it would've been easier to do so from Christmas Island. They wouldn't have allowed me to enter mainland Australia.

I told myself that my future was now safe. But I was wrong, so very wrong.

The detention centre in Darwin, although it looked like a maximum-security prison, was paradise compared to the Cocos and Christmas Island facilities. It was massive; every detainee had their own room, and families had cabins. There was also a lot more to do here; you could take English lessons, yoga and gym classes. In the evenings, I went for walks with my new friends, keeping to the Sri Lankan side of the compound. Over the next few weeks, I watched hundreds of people arrive at the detention centre and hundreds leave. Most of those who left had received their bridging visas to live in Australia.

I lived in hope that my day would come. When it finally did, in February 2014, I had been in the Darwin detention centre for nearly five months. I was given a four-year bridging visa, valid till 4 March 2018, without the right to work. However, there was a new problem:

now I was free to go anywhere, but I had nowhere to go. I knew no one in Australia and was too frightened to make my own way into this big country, and I could barely speak English. So, when one of the older women I had befriended suggested that I come to Sydney with her, I readily accepted.

'Auntie' was in contact with her friends, who had come on a boat a few months earlier and now lived in Western Sydney. When she and I arrived at Sydney Airport we were led through a back door, where we found several immigration caseworkers and Red Cross vehicles waiting for us. We were assigned a caseworker. He came with us in a Red Cross vehicle to an address in Mount Druitt.

Sydney   February–September 2014

Auntie and I arrived at a small two-bedroom house in Mount Druitt, where a young couple lived. Auntie and I shared a bedroom. Our caseworker helped us with all the paperwork: opening a bank account, registering with Centrelink, obtaining a health and travel card and access to other services. Money was short, because we had no work rights and an agency fee was deducted from the Centrelink payment. After paying my share of the rent, some groceries and the mobile phone bill, I was left with $20 or so, which I saved.

Without a disposable income, I found life in Sydney to be very limiting; I couldn't go sightseeing or shop for clothes. Other Sri Lankan women commented that I looked 'fresh off the boat'. Twice a week I attended English lessons at the local community centre, but for the rest of the time we had little else to do other than cooking, eating and napping. Sydney's summer heat hung over us like a heavy blanket. I wanted to get out of this rut, but I didn't know how.

HOME TO BILOELA

As the weather began to cool, the two young Tamil refugee women I had befriended on Christmas Island arrived in Sydney. With them, I moved into a place in Blacktown. Lacking a work visa, I was no better financially, but sharing a house with single women in similar situations lifted my spirits a bit. We continued to wait for our permanent visas and for our lives to begin.

I was unprepared for my first winter; I didn't have warm clothes or blankets. The cold was unbearable. The house we lived in had just one portable electric heater. So I used a voucher my caseworker gave me and went shopping at the Salvation Army shop; I bought myself some warm clothes, proper shoes and a blanket. Despite all this clothing, I still shivered through the cold. Most of the time I couldn't feel my fingers and toes.

One time when I called Amma, she brought up the topic of marriage again. 'It's been five months since you were given a bridging visa and nothing has changed for you,' she said, sounding disappointed. 'You can't live on your own forever. You have to marry a man with a permanent visa.'

Chandra, my friend from Christmas Island, was now living in Brisbane community detention with her family. After I repeated my conversation with Amma to her, she made it her mission to find me a husband in Queensland, so I could live closer to her.

Chapter 19

MEETING NADES

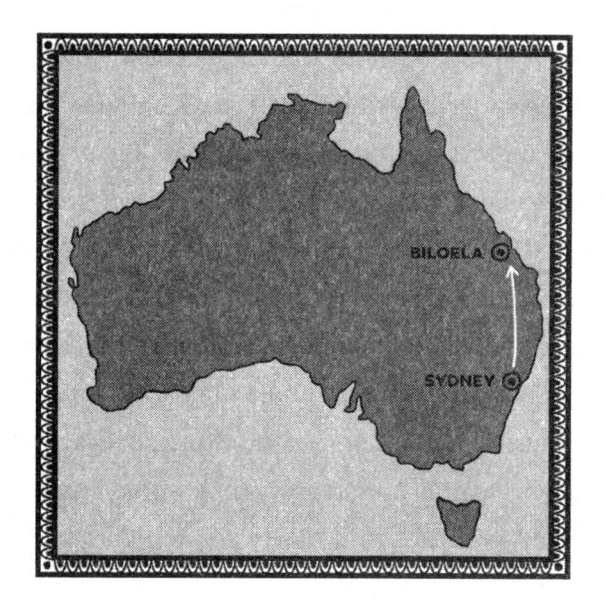

Biloela   **September–December 2014**

The first time I laid my eyes on Nades was at the altar during our Hindu wedding ceremony. I hadn't even seen a picture of him before that. I know this may shock many outside our culture. But we couldn't be more perfect for each other; he's introverted and quiet, and I'm the opposite of that.

I had spoken to him over the phone in the weeks leading up to our wedding and I felt certain that he had the qualities that I wanted in a man: respectful, hardworking and wanting a family of his own. He was also born and brought up in the beachside village of Kaluthavalai, the village next to mine. How we hadn't met before, I don't know. But there was one problem—he didn't have a permanent visa. Like me, he had a bridging visa, but with a work permit.

A man with a permanent visa was a better catch, and Nades had previously been rejected as a suitor because of this. But when Chandra asked my permission to give Nades my phone number and also to get his horoscope, so it could be sent to my family in India, I agreed. This decision, to consider marrying a man without a permanent visa, would become a huge problem later. But at that time, we both felt that we had nothing to lose; we'd been lonely for a long time.

Nades was living in a Queensland country town called Biloela at that time. I didn't know where that was. When he made his first phone call to me, I told him straight up not to talk to me until our families got back to us with the compatibility rating of our horoscopes. They were consulting an astrologer that very hour. He said he didn't believe in horoscopes, only in the compatibility of hearts; if I liked him too, he'd marry me regardless of what the horoscopes said. That was good enough for me, and I liked him already. While we were chatting, my sister rang with the verdict: our horoscopes were 90 per cent compatible, but it came with one condition: we needed to be married by the end of September because, by December, Nades would run out of good luck.

The very next day we set our wedding date and organised the wedding invitations. Within a week, I received a parcel from Nades with the printed invitations and the wedding sari. I was no longer feeling lonely, but hopeful and optimistic about my future. After all, in my late thirties, I was going to get married.

Meeting Nades

Around this time, I met a lovely Tamil woman during one of my evening walks in Blacktown. On hearing the news that I was planning to get married, 'Bubby Auntie' and her husband assumed the roles of my parents, organising the ceremony and the reception. I'm forever indebted to their kindness.

The Sri Lankan community in Western Sydney was well organised and many people gave us assistance. But Nades bore all the expenses of our wedding. When I saw him in person for the very first time at the Yaarl Function Centre in Pendle Hill, near Parramatta, I was very happy. He seemed healthy and well. I was never concerned about the physical attraction between us because I accepted that Nades was my destiny. Our wedding took place without either of our families in attendance. But because of our many friends and their generosity, it was a beautiful traditional ceremony.

I arrived in Biloela on 13 September 2014 as a married woman. Bilo, as it is known locally, is nothing like Blacktown; it is a small farming and mining town with hardworking, friendly locals who make eye contact with you and say 'Good morning' as they pass you by. A small shopping area and lots of large green open spaces, with only two major roads.

Nades was worried that I might be bored in a quiet place like this, but I assured him that I loved the slower pace of life and hearing the birds instead of the traffic noise. Being a country girl myself, I really hated living in Sydney. I learned that Biloela meant cockatoos in the local Aboriginal language, and there were plenty of those strange, noisy birds about. Anyhow, my first impression of Bilo was a good one; I thought to myself that I wouldn't mind spending the rest of my life here with Nades.

We moved into a five-bedroom house Nades and four other Sri Lankan men were renting. The men were like brothers, all having arrived in Australia by boat, with no one but each other. They worked hard during the week; on the weekends, a few more Tamil men from nearby Rockhampton would turn up. They'd go fishing for some barramundi at the dam or pick up fresh roadkill or catch a wild chicken, deer or pig. They'd cook the slaughtered animal with Sri Lankan herbs and spices. Then they'd have a slow long lunch, play cards late into the evenings and listen to Tamil movie songs. They didn't drink, smoke or gamble. They'd split all their expenses evenly between them and no one argued.

Nades told me that we could move out if I wanted to, but I enjoyed seeing Nades happy in the men's company. During the week, though, I was lonely. Nades was working two jobs, six days a week. I'd wake up late, pray to Durgai Amman, cook my vegetarian meals, tidy the house, pack lunch and walk up to Woolworths to see Nades in daylight.

―

People always ask us how we ended up living in Bilo. Nades came to Biloela in December 2013 after a friend and a fellow boat arrival told him about the jobs going at the meatworks in Biloela. Around fifteen Sri Lankan men were already working there. After his arrival, he worked as a cleaner at the meatworks in the morning and as a trolley pusher at Woolworths in the afternoon until late evening.

Meeting Nades

In his little free time, he attended English classes. Nades doesn't mind hard work.

Nades and I have a lot in common. We are both Tamil Hindus, from the same neighbourhood, and even born in the same year. He, too, had a carefree childhood, growing up in a large farming family. But, unlike me, he enjoyed the privileges of being a son, the youngest of eight at that. With four older brothers and two sisters, no one expected him to do housework or any work at all. One of his sisters drowned in the river when she was a toddler. Nades wasn't particularly interested in school, but enjoyed sport.

The war came to him when he was about twelve years old. He experienced the same things I did: hearing gunshots, seeing exploding artillery shells and dead bodies. As the fighting increased, the Tigers began recruiting young boys. Nades was fourteen then. I often tease him that he only became a Tiger to escape schoolwork. But in all seriousness, the Tigers became Nades' family for the next fifteen years. He knew nothing except being a militant engaged in combat, protecting his comrades and surviving attacks and the harshest conditions of the jungles of eastern Sri Lanka.

During that time, he witnessed unspeakable violence and experienced immense tragedy. He even carries pieces of shrapnel in his body from those years. But the worst memory of all for him was losing his father. It was only after he left the Tigers and returned home that he learned that his father had died four years earlier, asking for Nades on his deathbed. It still upsets him to talk about it.

The reason Nades left the Tigers was because he didn't agree with the infighting that had recently begun and the senseless violence that they were expected to be part of. As he was nearing 30, his mother and brothers thought the best way to help him settle was to marry him off. While they were in talks with a young woman's family, the CID (Criminal Investigation Department) came looking for him. After that, luckily for me, no family wanted their daughter married to him. In the ceasefire that then existed, he managed to get to Colombo and organise a passport, tickets and visa through an agent.

The only country that would give Nades a tourist visa was Qatar. When he got there, he got a temporary job at a car showroom as a driver. They expected him to drive around seventeen to twenty hours a day every day without much of a break for very little money. But when his visa expired, they immediately replaced him with another new arrival. He had nowhere to go but to return to Sri Lanka.

Over the next few years, Nades lived in hiding because he learned that the CID, the Army and the Tigers were all looking for him. Sri Lanka at that time was a very unsafe place for anyone, let alone for a young and fit ex-Tiger. He tried to go overseas again and got a visa for Kuwait. But it was the same story: he wasn't able to stay there past his visa, so he was forced back to Sri Lanka.

A couple of years later, he got a visa for Qatar again. But when he landed there, he found out that there was a case filed against him, falsely accusing him of scratching one of the cars at the showroom. Although this issue had been sorted out before he left his job, the case file hadn't been closed. So the authorities wouldn't let him into the country and he had to come back to Sri Lanka. He continued living in hiding.

So, when the chance came in April 2012 to get on a boat to Australia, he immediately took it. He and 98 other Sri Lankans left the west coast near Beruwala, arrived on Christmas Island fifteen days later, and then transferred to Scherger Immigration Detention Centre near Weipa in Queensland. Unlike me, he doesn't suffer

Meeting Nades

from seasickness, so I often argue with him that my journey was tougher. But he can't stomach pumpkin anymore, from it being the only food in the jungle and on the boat, so we call it even.

After four months in detention, Nades was released on a bridging visa that also allowed him to work. He went to Sydney and found work in Western Sydney at a Sri Lankan shop for $12 an hour. But in September his protection visa was refused. He appealed against the decision through a migration agent in Parramatta, who was a fellow Tamil from my village, Kalavanchikudi.

It's tough living in Sydney on a temporary, low income like that. So, when his friend told him about a Bilo meatworks job with better pay and low living costs, Nades was happy to move. It was to be a life-changing decision but, of course, he didn't know it at the time.

Within a year of arriving in Bilo, things would change for Nades: he would lose his right to work and the right to live in Australia. By then, he was also a married man, with a baby on the way.

Rockhampton and Biloela   December 2014–March 2018

Nades was so excited by the pregnancy; he announced it to everyone as soon as we had a positive test without waiting for three months. We were both very thrilled to be expecting a child this late in life. But our joy would soon be spoiled.

One evening, after a relaxing Christmas break, we were having dinner when the phone rang. Nades was due to return to work the next morning. A co-worker called to inform Nades that he no longer had a job because his work permit had expired. Nades contacted his migration agent in Sydney. The agent confirmed that Nades' visa application had been rejected after a High Court appeal. The only option left was to appeal to the Immigration minister. The minister was Peter Dutton. The astrologer had been right: it was December and Nades was running out of luck.

Instead of enjoying my miraculous first pregnancy, I became very stressed and worried about our situation and our future. Nades had no visa, no health care and no income—it was as if legally he did not exist. I still had my bridging visa, but I knew that even though we were married, it wasn't enough to keep Nades safe here in Australia.

I remember those endless, hot, humid summer days being filled with worry and the nights when I struggled to sleep. Without health care, I worried about him becoming sick or being involved in an accident. Without him working, we had to rely on my Centrelink payment and a small income from me catering for private Sri Lankan gatherings in Rockhampton. This was hardly enough for one person to survive on.

Despite this, Nades stayed positive. He kept telling me that, as good people who worked hard and didn't break the law, we had nothing to worry about. 'Unlike Sri Lanka, Australia is a fair country. That's why we came here,' he'd often remind me. I desperately hoped that he was right.

But the Australian immigration officials kept calling him daily to sign something so they could book his flight back to Sri Lanka. Nades refused, saying that he was going to be here for his child's birth and watch her grow up; he had an unwavering belief about that. They'd also call me to convince Nades to sign the document. Anytime an unknown vehicle drove by our house, we worried, expecting immigration officials to arrive. I became highly anxious.

One day in January, I began bleeding. Frightened, Nades drove me to the hospital. Fortunately, the scan showed the baby was still

Meeting Nades

fine, but the doctor ordered bed rest for me till I passed twelve weeks. Not long after that, I was diagnosed with gestational diabetes. Then suddenly, at the beginning of May 2015, my waters broke. The baby wasn't due for another nine weeks.

I was transferred from Biloela Hospital to Rockhampton Hospital and kept under observation. I was terrified for the health of my baby, but Nades kept telling me that everything was going to be fine. I could tell that he really believed that.

Just over a week later, I was induced and gave birth to a baby girl. Although eight weeks premature and weighing just over 2 kilos, we were so happy that she was healthy. We named her Kopika, after our family astrologer back in India told us to choose a name that began with K for good luck.

I was discharged after four days, but Kopi was kept at the hospital for another three weeks, attached to all kinds of machines and fed by a tube. Nades and I stayed at the Red Cross Rockhampton accommodation across the road and visited our baby every two hours so I could express breastmilk and feed her, even throughout the night. We were new parents in awe of our baby but, with no support, we didn't know what to expect.

It was about this time that Nades began to complain that he couldn't see very well. We put it down to lack of sleep, but it turned out he was losing his sight due to cataracts in both of his eyes.

On returning to Bilo, we took Kopi to St Joseph's Catholic Church across the road, because there was no Hindu temple in Bilo. We believed it was important to get her blessed. After that, I started to go there often to pray and meditate. The priest Father Thadayoose and the locals were very welcoming, and would come over to me and chat. I was beginning to feel that I belonged in Bilo.

HOME TO BILOELA

We decided to find a place of our own. We didn't think it was right to bring a newborn into a house where working men needed their sleep. It was hard to find a rental with three of us on one Centrelink income, but eventually we found a little semidetached house. It was a tough time, neither of us knowing much about newborn babies, while in a new country with no family support. We couldn't buy anything new, not even for our baby. So, I was grateful when Anglicare offered support, including counselling. The local hospital also supported us with the newborn.

This is how I met some wonderful Biloela locals—Jenny, Bronwyn, Margot and Marie, who became family to me, Nades and our children. Since we had no money for Nades' cataract operation, Marie and her husband Jeff paid for the surgery and gave him the gift of vision. Bronwyn and Margot supported us in so many ways that I can't list them all here. Nades and I must've done some good in our previous lives to deserve all this good karma. Because of this community support, Nades and I were able to focus on Kopika. Nades was a very much hands-on dad. He did most of the housework and looked after Kopi to give me some rest.

When Kopi was two weeks old, the Immigration department called us and asked us to come to Rockhampton. There they told us to sign some documents to apply for a Sri Lankan birth certificate for Kopi. Her current birth document states her nationality as Sri Lankan and Australia as her birthplace. They made us wait till late afternoon with the new baby, but Nades and I refused to sign anything.

The day after Kopi's first birthday, the phone rang with some happy news. Nades' visa had been extended for another twelve months while Mr Dutton was giving the matter consideration, and

Meeting Nades

Nades could start working legally again. Biloela meatworks immediately offered him his job back. I remember Nades smiling at me, saying, 'Why did you worry so much? Australia is full of good people.'

'How could you always be so optimistic?' I asked him.

'If you were like me and had stared death in the face many times, you'd be, too,' he replied.

In October the same year, I became pregnant with my second child. We were thrilled that Kopi would not grow up alone. But this pregnancy was not worry-free either. At the twelve-week scan the doctor was concerned that the baby was underweight and not thriving. I felt bad that all the stress I was going through was causing this. Nades, as always, remained optimistic that our baby would be perfect.

She sure was. We named her with the unusual spelling of Tharnicaa (instead of Tharunica) as suggested by the astrologer. She was born healthy in Rockhampton in June 2017, but her birth wasn't easy. She had to be pulled out using forceps and this caused complications for me, including uterine prolapse.

We returned to our quiet lives in Bilo, working hard and raising our two little girls with the support of the wonderful community. My bridging visa was going to expire on 4 March 2018, but I didn't worry. My caseworker in Brisbane was taking care of it. After all, the government had allowed us to live and work in mainland Australia for four years now, and we had two Australian-born children. Surely, I thought, they wouldn't deport us to Sri Lanka.

Chapter 20

FIRST WINTER

After Priya and the family were returned to detention in Melbourne following the aborted deportation attempt, their first winter in their new city was approaching. They would never see much of it, aside from its detention centre and airport hangars, but Melbourne was the furthest south either Priya or Nades had been in Australia.

Locked in their unit in MITA, their days were punctuated only by guards allowing them outside for one 30-minute session to let Kopika and Tharnicaa play on the small playground within the compound, and the visits from Simone and Aran in the detention centre visit room.

Like every other asylum seeker who had arrived by sea, the family would be without their mobile phones for another four months. This meant they were reliant on waiting for any call—be it Vashini's daily call or their lawyer's—to be patched through to their detention unit. This made their isolation in the midst of a city of five million people almost complete.

First Winter

By 2018 this was clearly part of the Liberal National government's plan. And it was an effective strategy. It's very hard to report on something you can't see.

With the combination of strictures around visiting and no mobile phones allowed for boat arrivals, onshore detention was only reported on by a handful of journalists. They, in turn, were reliant on refugees as sources, most of whom did not have phones, so reliable reporting on the sector became an even more complex undertaking. Overlaying all of this was the fact that the department was not exactly inviting the media into detention with open arms.

With public and editorial awareness mostly focused on the asylum seekers held in the offshore camps (Manus in Papua New Guinea and Nauru in the Pacific), the detention centres in the suburbs of Australia's capital cities had, on the whole, been able to escape scrutiny. This was despite these centres costing over $300,000 a year for each and every asylum seeker held there.

―――

While I hadn't had a plan for when I would start concertedly publishing stories about detention because I had a reasonable amount of work doing regular news and political reporting, I wasn't in a hurry to make a decision. One of the factors on my side in being able to pick my moment was that the department didn't exactly know I was there. I had the unanticipated benefit of having a different birth name to my publishing name. All the ID I used to get into detention was in my birth name.

In effect, this meant the department would have had to put two and two together to establish that a middle-aged New Zealand journalist had been quietly and regularly visiting a detention centre every week since 2016. And I was fairly sure they hadn't.

So when Priya and the family arrived, I was publishing a handful of stories about the changes to visit rules, but I didn't immediately seek to make contact with the high-profile family from Biloela. From the outside it looked like this family had as much media coverage as they needed, so much so I—wrongly, as it turned out—thought the government would release them into community detention as soon as possible to avoid the public relations bonfire of being responsible for locking up toddlers while multiple ministers insisted there were no children in detention. I also had concerns about being banned from the facility, because I had seen this happen to other people.

But any reticence I had about identifying myself and explicitly exposing my access disappeared very quickly when I discovered, by chance, a very disturbing piece of information. There were other children in detention.

During one of my regular visits, a couple of refugees I knew well said to me, 'There's a boy here, he's like you, a New Zealander.' When I managed to track him down via a refugee with a phone, the NZ teenager told me he was being held in a unit with a Lebanese teenager who was even younger. He said neither of them was being taken to school, and essentially they just passed their time playing PlayStation watched over by a social worker. They both told me a separate staffer showed up for an hour a day and gave them photocopied handouts to fill in—this was their education.

I had heard this from other people in detention. Unlike prison there was no clear and meaningful access to education, and there was no clear date of release. Not only were Kopika and Tharnicaa in

First Winter

this centre alongside baby Isabella, but there were also two teenagers. The more I heard, the more incredulous I became.

———

Just weeks after my first stories on the NZ teenager appeared, he won his appeal at the Administrative Appeals Tribunal (AAT), meaning he would be released. But I was beginning to understand there were key differences and major inequities faced by asylum seekers who went through Australia's humanitarian program. Because, while the boy may have faced being returned to New Zealand, an outcome that would have been deeply unfair for a child with no contacts or support there, he at the very least would have been deported to a country in which he was essentially safe.

The same could not be said for Kopika or Tharnicaa. There was, disturbingly, never any clear answer from the Australian government on what guarantees were in place for the safety of the two little Australian-born girls if they were deported, despite it being an absolutely fundamental concern. Professor Damian Kingsbury, an expert in the political and security issues of South-East Asia, would say in 2021 on *Australian Story* that if the family were deported back to Sri Lanka, both girls would most likely have been placed in state-run orphanages, while their parents would have been detained for 're-education'. His opinion was clear: they all faced substantial risks and danger.

I was beginning to understand that asylum seekers who arrived by boat were a group so thoroughly demonised by successive Australian politicians that the mere mention of their method of arrival was enough to stop any further rational discussion. It was simply and automatically assumed by many people that they were hopeless cases and therefore undeserving of decent conditions while held by Australia.

Seasoned campaigners would tell me later that the term 'boat arrivals' had become so poisoned by various politicians that they'd made a conscious choice in referring to people like Priya and Nades as 'maritime arrivals' to try to dial down the acrimony.

The word 'illegal' was weaponised in the same way. In fact, it had been Scott Morrison in 2013 who ordered officials to start using the word to describe asylum seekers who arrived in Australia by sea. This was a false description in 2013 and remains one today. Under both international and Australian laws, any asylum seeker has the right to seek safety regardless of their method of arrival. Arriving by sea and seeking asylum is not and never has been an illegal act, no matter how many times a politician says so.

Simone Cameron had her realisation about how limited the family's legal options were almost as soon as she joined the campaign. The mother of two had started her law degree just a few weeks before the raid in Biloela.

'As the campaign continued and I learned about the family's experience with Australia's refugee policy, and my studies progressed, I began to understand the limitations of the law. In the campaign team, because of my studies, one of my core responsibilities was to try to make sense of the legal appeals within the group, and then work out a way to communicate complicated legal concepts in a language that the broader public could digest.

'The starkest realisation, early on, was that there was no legal solution that would keep the whole family safe. Nades and Tharnicaa could not be named in Priya and Kopika's appeal, and so even if that appeal succeeded, we would still need ministerial intervention for Nades and Tharnicaa to be able to remain in Australia. When Tharnicaa's appeal came later, the success we had with that was not going to directly assist the rest of the family. The solution was always going to come from a combination of legal appeals and political pressure. The risk of one family member being without a legal appeal was that they could be removed from Australia. And indeed that was what we later found about Nades, that the department was making assessments about him in 2018 for possible removal from Australia, even while Priya and Kopika's appeals were ongoing. I was stunned that this policy could separate families and there was no recourse.'

As I began to understand more about the changes to immigration law in Australia, I would reach many of the same conclusions as Iain Murray. This wasn't a story about law, it was a story about right and wrong.

Now that I was out in the open as a journalist with access and knowledge of onshore immigration detention, it was time to start reporting on exactly what detaining children did to them.

Chapter 21

ANGELA'S SPEECH

In May 2018 Angela Fredericks flew the 1800 kilometres from Biloela to see Priya and the family in the Melbourne detention centre. Bronwyn was desperate to see her friends but simply couldn't afford the costs of such a trip.

Angela met and stayed with Simone Cameron for the first time. Simone was able, to some degree, to prepare her for what her first visit to a detention centre would be like. It would be Angela's first face-to-face meeting with the family since the single time she had briefly met them in her role as a social worker, years earlier in Biloela.

'Technically it was my first meeting with the family and I went and got stuff to take in to them because when you go to someone's place for the first time, you want to make a good impression, so I remember getting activity packs for the girls.'

Angela caught the train to the far northern suburb of Broadmeadows, then a taxi to the centre with her small bag of gifts for the family.

Angela's Speech

Like every other visitor, the social worker from Biloela had to stand at the huge gate, press the intercom button, then wait for a response.

'My first impression was "Oh, I am actually visiting a prison." And then seeing the guards and everything. There was another family visiting a refugee dad and I saw kids and I just felt sadness for those young children who were obviously seeing a parent in there and having to go through metal detectors.'

Once inside, the guards told Angela she couldn't bring in the playdough for Tharnicaa and Kopika. She was stunned. While visitors were allowed to bring in packaged food with expiration dates, Angela was finding out firsthand that you couldn't bring in anything that was a gift—even if it was as innocent as playdough for two locked-up toddlers. When Kopika and Tharnicaa came to the Melbourne detention centre's visit room, the only provision made for them was that sometimes there was a small container of coloured pencils beside the hot water urn for tea and coffee. Over the years I would notice that most of the pencils were broken or unsharpened.

'I am actually such a rule follower, I don't want to do anything to get in trouble. Once I got into the visit room, the tables were like prison, with your designated tables to sit at. I just waited there for them.' From her table Angela could see Priya and Nades walking through the main detention centre to the holding room where they would be frisked and wanded every time they had a visit.

'It was like greeting old friends. I wanted them to know, "You may be in Melbourne but we are still going to get to you."'

Nades immediately tried to make them comfortable, steering her and an emotional Priya into plastic chairs while he made them tea in disposable cups. 'He was straight into making me as welcome as possible, just like he always would later, too.'

It was the first of two trips Angela would make all the way from Biloela, two states to the north, to see Priya and the family while they were locked away behind the high fences, barbed wire and endless security checks of the Melbourne detention centre.

Iain Murray is the very definition of a quiet backroom organiser—not a seeker of the limelight. 'It's years since I have done any kind of media interview myself and I've heard myself on the radio enough to know it's not my thing. But writing is my thing and what I was able to offer was an ability to recognise when I heard something that would be powerful when written down or used in social media.' In reality and actuality, Iain offered far more than just writing skills to the campaign. In his very first conversation with Simone, his suggestion that she influence those attending the vigil to sing a benign but still patriotic Australian song showed his clear strategic thinking. Iain had tapped into the messages Bronwyn had given Aran and the Tamil Refugee Council that 'these are our people and we want them back'. But he also, even at that early stage, knew that concerned vigil attenders singing played directly against the Liberal National Party narrative of chanting angry protestors. The other element that Iain knew would be priceless against Canberra rhetoric was the country women from Biloela getting themselves to the big city where their friends had been imprisoned.

The rapidly assembled Home to Bilo campaign team had already benefited hugely from Angela's ability to effectively front the media and speak plainly about what was at stake. This would be invaluable because Bronwyn, another gifted communicator, would be stymied

Angela's Speech

from speaking publicly for another eighteen months due to her role with Queensland Health.

But Bronwyn's decision the week after Priya and the family were taken from Biloela in the dawn raid had paid off. In asking her friend Angela to speak up for Priya, Nades and the kids, Bronwyn had anointed not just a proxy, but someone as impassioned as her about the injustice the family were facing.

By May 2018 Angela had already done dozens of media interviews, and her message to the rest of Australia about what Biloelans thought was crystal clear and cut through the government rhetoric. Later, in an op-ed, I would point out that the plain-speaking, no-nonsense women from Biloela were shaping up to be 'Ocker Kryptonite' for Prime Minister Scott Morrison. He and Home Affairs Minister Peter Dutton couldn't paint these women as 'inner-city, latte-drinking lefties' because they weren't. And that was the edge they had over both men. Authenticity.

On that same trip Angela first met Priya and the family, Angela and Simone would both speak at a rally for the family outside Melbourne's Federal Court.

Wearing an Akubra hat and surrounded by supporters holding meticulously cut and coloured cardboard cockatoos and large photos of the family, Angela would make a powerful speech that Iain Murray would use as a template for the Home to Bilo campaign.

'That speech would really be my guide for the next four years; everything Angela said in there, everything she laid out, was the message of the Home to Bilo campaign.'

HOME TO BILOELA

In footage of the event Angela, in a dark blue blouse and jeans, her hat pushed back off her face, stands confidently in the tepid Melbourne autumn light. Her voice can be heard above the sound of council lawnmowers because schoolteacher Lucy Honan had brought along a microphone and amp. Visible in the crowd are family groups, private school students in uniform and women from the group 'Grandmothers for Refugees' in their own uniform of purple T-shirts.

Angela's speaking style is off the cuff, like an affable tent preacher. She breaks complex legal language down into understandable bites. Many of the politicians responsible for what had happened to Priya and the family would have done well to take note of her technique.

'Look, I am so overwhelmed by the show of support. In coming down here today I had some of my close friends, who were farmers out in Biloela, who said to me, "You go tell those city folks that we want that family back." They said, "These are our friends."'

The small crowd cheers.

'Biloela, we are a community that has been built by migrants. So after the Great War, the first war, we had hundreds of migrants from Eastern Europe who descended on our town and who toiled our fields.

'And today we still pay recognition to the refugees from Russia, from Greece, from parts all over Europe who came to Australia for a better future, a safe future. Our town would not be where it is without them, and that is still true today. Today we rely on our migrants to keep really important industries like our meatworks actually operational.

'In Biloela we welcome anybody who wants to join our community and be part of it. And that's exactly what Priya and Nades did when they arrived in our small town four and a half, five years ago. Nades, straight from the start, he was out there pushing trolleys

Angela's Speech

at Woolworths. He was then down at Vinnies, St Vincent de Paul, helping and volunteering.

'In the time they've been there we've watched them—they went and got married at our local courthouse, then went on to have two beautiful girls who are Australian born, their birth certificates say Australia. Does that not mean anything?

'They then continued, so every weekend "What's on? What's happening in the community this weekend, let's go, let's be there, let's show our support." It's the small things.

'You know Priya, she was so thankful to the hospital staff who helped with her deliveries, she would bring up curries to the hospital to show her thanks.

'These are people with just beautiful souls. They want to be here, and more importantly we want them here. The town of Biloela, we wouldn't be where we are without these people.

'So today, today as they face the impossible task of our legal system, which I myself, I've studied [at] university, English is my first language and yet I don't understand it. I sit and go through the policies and they don't make sense to me. And that's what so many people say to me: "Where is the common sense? Where is the common sense and the compassion?"

'So today as they face court, all of Biloela is behind them, I know the 97,000 people across Australia and the world [who signed the petition] are behind them, and regardless of the outcome today, I want us all to know who actually has got power in this situation, because we don't and nor do Priya and Nades.

'The person with the power is Peter Dutton. He has the ability to stop this; he has the ability to pick up the phone, pick up his pen, and put an end to this. He is there to represent the people. This is how our society works, we elect people to represent us, and we are saying, we the people are saying, we want this family home to Biloela.

'And so today, I ask you to please, throw up your voices, throw up your prayers, speak to the universe, to anybody, speak to your local politician, tell them what we want. Because they are there to do what we want, and to represent us.

'So, I really want to just finish with the words that really did touch me when I spoke to the people back home. And it's a very simple message and I want Peter Dutton to hear us. "We want our friends back!"'

Angela's speech clearly touched the small crowd who had gathered outside court buildings to show support to the family from Queensland. Iain Murray was taking note.

After Angela's speech there was another address, this time from Priya. But because, at this time, Priya still wasn't allowed a mobile phone, the only way for her to communicate with the crowd that had gathered was for Simone to read out a written message.

'I've been through lots of stuff in my life. I came from an unsafe country, a country which persecutes Tamil people. Finally, after so much uncertainty and pain I found peace and happiness in Biloela, a small town in central Queensland. Biloela is the place where my life really started.

'My family lived in Biloela for four years. Nades is a wonderfully supportive husband. Our two girls, Kopika and Tharnicaa, were both born in Biloela. They are Biloela kids.

'Biloela is such a good community. The people are very friendly

Angela's Speech

and they always have a smile on their faces. They give you a warm welcome from the heart. I feel very lucky to have such good people around me.

'My husband Nades worked in the meat factory in Biloela. He loved his job, he loved the people he worked with and they loved him.

'Thank you, Australia, you gave me a safe and peaceful life. And I want to thank you for that. I feel proud to live here because Australia is a good country that gives safety and freedom to its people, to live their lives in the way they want to.

'Biloela is my home, so please let us stay here.

'Thank you, from Priya.'

Chapter 22
AT THE MINISTER'S DISCRETION

Any asylum seeker who arrived in Australia by boat after 2012 faced a difficult path to even having their plea for asylum assessed. Part of the difficulty was in the language deployed to describe them.

It wasn't just Immigration Minister Scott Morrison ordering officials to start using disturbing new terminology such as 'illegals' to describe asylum seekers yet to go through any assessment process.

Morrison's ramped-up approach to language went further. Going into the 2013 election he appeared on the ABC and said, regarding the arrival of asylum seeker boats, 'This is a war against people smuggling and you've got to approach it on that basis.' Once in the seat as the Immigration minister, Morrison went further and gave the Australian government's asylum seeker policy a new name: Operation Sovereign Borders.

Priya and Nades arrived in 2013 and 2012, respectively. After short stints in immigration detention they both passed rigorous security and health checks and were given visas to live in the Australian community temporarily. Understandably they thought they were finally in a safe place, but they had arrived in an Australia that was at war with itself.

With Morrison now in office very busily portraying immigration core business as something that suddenly required military trappings, the more acute battleground was the language Australia would use to describe anyone seeking asylum. Under Morrison changes were made, and in departmental language an 'irregular maritime arrival' became 'illegal maritime arrival'. A 'client' became a 'detainee'.

What the Home to Bilo team were discovering as they did interview after interview was that years of political rhetoric had indeed affected the way media told the stories of asylum seekers. Iain and Simone would, in an attempt to even an unjust playing field, write a fact-check document that journalists and interested parties could be directed to. The fact check would live permanently online at www.hometobilo.com/facts.

———

In Biloela a secondary support group was more formally organised when Bronwyn observed the enormous demands the campaign was placing on her friend Angela.

When media approached with requests for interviews, the support group for the core team could assist. Nearly all of these people would be locals who were friends of Nades and Priya and wanted to do anything they could to support the family but also knew the campaign team were all volunteers—now more than a year into an unimaginably difficult endeavour. One such person was

Brenda Lipsys, a retired teacher and poultry farmer Nades and Priya had regularly bought chickens from.

'It was nice to be able to say to politicians, "I'm not just someone who jumped on the bandwagon, I know this family, they supported my farm business, them and other Sri Lankan families." It was good to be able to call certain politicians, actually call their offices. You never got them on the phone, mind you, usually you always spoke to the people in reception.'

Out in the isolated quiet of the chook farm, Brenda began keeping a close eye on Facebook and reading more news about asylum seekers. 'I didn't know when I first got into this that refugees were held offshore. I knew a tiny fraction of what I know now. The more you read and more you find out, the more flabbergasted I was and because I used to be a teacher, educating is a big thing for me. I like to think I am a pretty reasonable person and if I can be horrified by what the government was doing, it's just a matter of making sure people know about it, and if they are horrified, too, then they might write a letter to a politician or pick up a phone.'

Brenda didn't know any of the core campaign group, but Simone had noticed Brenda's comments on the campaign's Facebook page. She was impressed by her calm even-handedness in her online comments, especially what she had to say about her customers and friends Priya and Nades. Angela arranged to meet Brenda for a coffee when the farmer came to town. Brenda was more than happy to join what came to be known as the support-support group.

'The group here in Bilo, which is just so passionate, they just couldn't get things past us, and when politicians were telling fibs, we were calling them out and it was really great to be able to inject personal things into what I wrote or into what I was trying to get across to any politician I was ringing up.'

———

Alison Battisson is a Sydney-based human rights lawyer working specifically with refugees. Her clients Huyen Thu Thi Tran and her Australian-born daughter Isabella were also held in the same unit of MITA with Priya and the family. As Alison explains, for people such as Priya, Nades and Huyen, the barriers to even seeking asylum if you arrive in Australia by sea start immediately.

'It is a little-known fact, but under Australian law, a person arriving via boat cannot apply for a visa. Any visa application will be deemed "invalid" until a portfolio minister personally invites the person to apply for a specific type of visa. This leads to years of delays for people waiting to be invited to apply, and sometimes it never happens. People fall through the cracks and inconsistency creeps in as some people are invited and others rot in detention waiting for their turn.' More than a decade after arriving in Australia, Battisson's client, Isabella's mother, is still waiting for that invitation.

Carina Ford, the Melbourne-based immigration lawyer whose eponymous firm would take on Priya and the family as clients in late December 2018, about ten months after the raid, had by then been practising for fourteen years. By which time it was impossible to ignore the heightened predicament of clients who had arrived by sea.

People like Priya and Nades and Alison's client Huyen simply couldn't make an application for a visa—and this is intentional. There is a barrier to any maritime arrival applying for a visa and to be able to apply, a person must request a 'bar lift' from the minister.

HOME TO BILOELA

As Carina explains: 'The bar-lifting mechanism was deliberately put into the Migration Act, in relation to this cohort of people; it was put in so that someone could not lodge an application that was considered valid. Effectively it was done so that the minister alone would determine when a person could apply for a visa and also when they could stop applying for a visa and what type.

'So, unlike a person who arrives by plane, who can lodge a protection visa because there is no bar unless you've lodged one before and had it refused, someone who arrived by sea can't do that because the Act said your application would automatically be considered invalid unless the minister lifts the bar. That's why it's called lifting the bar.'

The bar-lift mechanism includes the bewildering variety of visas that asylum seekers who arrive by sea can apply for. These include bridging visas, like the one Priya had, and was in the process of applying for an extension to, when she and the family were taken in the raid.

At the time of the dawn raid, there were always other options the Australian government could have taken, instead of putting Priya and the family in harsh detention centres. Many, if not most, asylum seekers continue to live in the Australian community once a visa has lapsed while they go through the various next steps, so it wasn't as if the government didn't have a choice. By 2018 the act of detaining whole families was provocative and unnecessary.

Carina, speaking to me in 2022 and reflecting on the raid of Priya's Rainbow Street home in Biloela, would remark on how deeply unusual the raid was in and of itself.

At the Minister's Discretion

'There are many people in Australia who are unlawful in the sense of having a lapsed visa at certain times. What makes this case unique is that their visas had expired at midnight and then they were detained in that early morning raid. *That just does not happen.* I deal with lots of cases where people are unlawful and living in the Australian community for years. I have one where a man has been unlawful for twenty years. So why this family? People often miss their bridging visa deadline and the approach would normally be to contact them and say you need to come in and regulate your status. It was even more unusual because they lived regionally and there were two small children involved and there were so many other families who had already gone through that process and who are still in Australia now, and they have not been detained. Many people have gone right through the appeal process right to the end and have not been removed [from the community].'

Alison Battisson and Carina Ford would both contact the United Nations on behalf of their clients because Australia has signed and ratified the United Nations Convention on the Rights of the Child (CRC). As Alison points out, Australia has undertaken to enact laws and to treat children in accordance with the articles of the CRC.

'This includes a prohibition on the arbitrary detention of children (the mandatory nature of Australia's Migration Act, in which a person without a visa must be detained, is directly contrary to this prohibition) and treating the best interests of the child as a primary consideration. Anyone familiar with the story of these families knows they were arbitrarily detained and the best interests of the child were not a primary consideration. If they had been, not only would these families have been released much sooner but they would never have been locked up to begin with.'

HOME TO BILOELA

The United Nations would subsequently request that the Australian government release both families—to no avail, despite Australia being a signatory to the convention.

As Carina points out: 'The minister has the power to release anyone who's in detention under section 195. The minister also has the discretion to grant a visa to any person. In this case, what I constantly said to the media, at the end of the day it rests with the minister because the minister can grant a visa.'

Somewhat notoriously, Minister Peter Dutton used this ministerial discretion when he overruled advice from a senior ABF official and allowed a French nanny to escape deportation after being lobbied by AFL boss Gillon McLachlan. But there were literally thousands of other times he did the same thing and it didn't make the news. Between 23 December 2014 and 31 August 2018, then Home Affairs Minister Dutton intervened to grant 4129 discretionary visas, a rate of roughly three a day during his tenure. Peter Dutton was the Minister for Immigration and Border Protection when the dawn raid occurred in 2018, while simultaneously being the Minister for Home Affairs, the over-arching mega-department that houses ABF.

But there was another man who had the power to release the children, and that was the prime minister himself. After the 2022 election, it would be revealed that PM Morrison had secretly signed himself into a handful of portfolios including Home Affairs, giving him all the powers of that position.

Carina wasn't impressed: 'He actually did have a say in the Immigration portfolio despite at the time saying he didn't. He could have been the one that could have intervened, but at the end of the day, we just couldn't get traction with any ministers.'

At the Minister's Discretion

But the handful of ministers with 'God Powers' weren't just saying no to Biloela, they were saying no to members of their own party. It would be Simone Cameron, writing an essay for her law studies, who would discover that at least eighteen serving senators and members of parliament had written to the Immigration minister asking for the family to be released. This included senior members, such as ex-Liberal Prime Minister Tony Abbott, deputy Prime Minister Barnaby Joyce, and deputy leader of the Liberal Party and Minister for Foreign Affairs Julie Bishop. Startlingly, the department itself also advised the minister that the family should be released. But none of these approaches had any effect.

Asked how many times over four years she would routinely ask the department in writing to release Priya and the family from detention while their legal matters played out, Carina Ford says she would have made that request hundreds of times.

Chapter 23

DISTURBING BEHAVIOUR

In late August 2018 I was shown a concerning medical report from the Royal Children's Hospital in Melbourne. The family had finally been referred by IHMS medical staff to a medical service provider not employed by ABF. The doctor who wrote the report noted that they were not aware that there were any children who had been detained long-term in Melbourne prior to this referral.

After six long months locked in MITA, for Kopika and Tharnicaa a hospital trip under guard would be the first time either toddler had left the detention centre since the aborted deportation attempt in March.

The family were driven to the Royal Children's Hospital in one of the dozens of anonymous white vans used to shift detainees, and accompanied into the hospital by three Serco guards. In the notes about the consultation, Priya explains to the doctor that there is one guard in their MITA unit at all times—despite the unit being surrounded by fences, barbed wire, CCTV and even more guards.

Disturbing Behaviour

The doctor's notes made sobering reading. Kopika had started to bite her own hands in frustration. Tharnicaa stared out the window constantly, had language delays and was notably quiet for a fourteen-month-old. One of the issues noted for both girls was that in detention there was no playgroup, no early childhood education—no contact with other children at all.

Both girls had significant sleeping issues but, as Priya and Nades explain, this was almost impossible to rectify given guards would do regular headcounts through the day and night, disrupting the entire family's sleep. There is little advice even the best paediatrician could give to the mother of a toddler who is woken constantly by strangers in uniform shining a torch in their face.

In the same period I was also shown a report on baby Isabella, living with her mother Huyen just metres away from Priya and the family. At six months old, she was exhibiting disturbingly similar behaviour to Kopika and Tharnicaa.

Huyen would tell me Isabella would squeal in excitement when she saw Priya and the girls outside on the small playground in the compound. But she would be told by guards that they weren't allowed to go outside until Priya, Nades and the girls finished their allotted 30 minutes.

The punitiveness of separating toddlers from each other took my breath away. Huyen, an asylum seeker who had arrived by sea like Priya and Nades, had been living in the Melbourne community when she was taken into detention. She was four months pregnant and married to a man with a visa. Her husband lived and worked just fifteen minutes from the centre but would have to book a visit and pass all the usual tests to see his wife and baby in the visit room every night after he finished work.

HOME TO BILOELA

As with Priya and Nades, there was never any privacy. No one was allowed into the unit to see the families, not even their lawyers. Only the guards and cleaners. By August 2018, Priya and Huyen had not been allowed to see each other inside the compound but both women told me the exact same story. For months Serco guards had sat inside their respective units 24/7 making notes about exactly what they were doing and neither of them knew why. Huyen would say to me, 'I have no one to help me with the baby, I can't even take a shower without my baby and they just sit there. Why? No one can tell me why.'

In my subsequent news story I would mention various behavioural concerns and vitamin deficiencies of the little girls. The doctor noted that Tharnicaa's blood tests showed a vitamin D deficiency and, after six months locked indoors for nearly 24 hours a day, it was hardly surprising.

I began regularly submitting questions to ABF asking, among other things, exactly what early childhood education arrangements the department was making for the preschoolers if they weren't taking them out of detention to any actual playgroups, preschools or kindergartens. I would never receive any meaningful answer.

Within ten days of my stories being published, Huyen told me that there had been one major change—she and Isabella were allowed to see Priya and the family. Finally, after nearly seven months, Kopika and Tharnicaa would have a friend, and the two families could be proper neighbours. For the first time since she was taken in the dawn raid from Biloela, Priya would have the benefits of a female friend who understood exactly what her day-to-day life was like in detention.

So, in early September 2018 inside the heavily guarded Melbourne immigration detention centre, a very small and very exclusive playgroup of three tiny girls was started.

While the campaign group was working steadily on what else could be done to increase petition numbers, there were two significant additions to the core support team.

In September 2018 a new staffer would join Change.org. Melbourne-based Nic Dorward, a highly experienced and astute campaigner with a canny ability to interpret the political landscape, would effectively join the Bilo campaign team.

'I remember thinking instantly it was an incredibly powerful story. It had all the hallmarks of a really powerful campaign. You had at the heart of it a singular story. The story with these two little girls, this family. It really heightens the emotions and makes it even more powerful. In those early days I was so impressed by the scope of what the campaign was already doing.'

While he worked on countless other projects, in Nic's four years at Change.org the Home to Bilo campaign would dominate his time: 'There was no other campaign I worked on with that intensity. At peak moments it was 24/7 but there was no other option. It was just too important.'

Up in Biloela, Bronwyn would occasionally, half-jokingly, refer to Nic and campaigner Iain as 'our Southern Belles' when either would make suggestions that felt unachievable or too 'city'. Both men would take it on the chin, always acknowledging that without Bronwyn, Angela, Vashini and Simone there would simply be no Home to Bilo. Both men also had enough experience to know how unusual it was to get a supporter who could do a tidy eight-second sound bite, let alone a whole group of them. Nic knew very well what the emotional outcomes could be for people who threw their entire lives into a cause, because he saw it every day.

'You always have a bit of work to do upfront to earn the trust of campaigns, and people like the Home to Bilo team, the petitions started by people who are deeply invested in something because they are either personally impacted or they know someone who is. In those instances, people can be very protective, they're protective of their campaign, they're protective of their friends or family members, they're protective of their story. And you can understand why, so an important part of my job is to show I am capable of giving some good advice that they might like to take into account, that I am someone who can be trusted not just with their campaign but with their stories. It was always about the story of the people involved, Priya and the family.'

Meanwhile those core supporters faced a pressing issue. By December 2018 they needed a new lawyer. Kajalini Ranjithkumar had been acting pro bono for Priya and the family and had successfully seen off two deportation efforts. But she had signalled to the campaign team that she wouldn't be able to continue representing the family past December, so there was a void that urgently needed to be filled.

Many asylum seekers must look for any lawyer who will represent them pro bono, but by the end of 2018 the Home to Bilo campaign was in a unique position—there were funds available to employ a law firm. The group had been collecting donations from Australians horrified by their government's treatment of Priya's family, and Angela had been amazed by people's generosity.

Disturbing Behaviour

'It was sort of like a poker machine. When we'd set up these crowd-funders and then were watching the figures just go up, we'd be messaging each other saying, "Oh my gosh, it was at this level and now it's at this level." So you'd have these huge lows where you felt like the human race is just terrible, then you'd have these moments when you thought, There are beautiful people out there. People were putting in $1000 at a time. There was this beautiful old woman who used to phone my house and she would post me $20 at a time when she could afford it. And another woman who always sent me a cheque because she didn't trust the internet, and she'd send me a little slip of paper and a self-addressed envelope with a stamp on it to post back to her acknowledging I'd received the cheque.'

At the very end of 2018, the campaign team put a call into Carina Ford, the highly experienced Melbourne-based immigration lawyer, to see if she would represent the family. Carina was very aware of the government's legal style: at great expense to the Australian taxpayer, they fought cases that could have been settled much earlier with fairer outcomes. Refugee lawyers I interviewed called this style of engagement 'fighting it up to the court steps', and the cost to taxpayers never mattered.

By the time she came on board for Priya and the family, Carina had seen this with her own eyes. She had spent that Christmas Eve in a Melbourne court fighting for the medical transfer of a group of seriously unwell refugees: 'Around the same time I took on Priya, Nades and the family's case, I was in court fighting for the medical transfer of a client off Nauru. I remember thinking, This is so ridiculous. This huge group of us—eight or nine cases, all connected. All these extremely unwell people and here we are, a courtroom full of lawyers fighting over whether someone should get medical treatment. It all seemed so wrong. And in the end, all of them got transferred [to Australia] because they all needed help.'

As Ford says, the medical transfer case was a good primer in dealing with the Morrison-led government and seeing exactly how far they would take matters. But she could never have predicted that she was about to become known nationally as the lawyer for a family that the Coalition government simply refused to back down on: 'By then I think I had the experience, and I knew it could be tough, but what I probably didn't know was the length of time it would take. I did know when you take on more controversial cases, you could be in for a long time. You've got to be willing to understand that it's not going to go away overnight, and that it's going to need a bit of a battle to get it moving forward.'

For the rest of 2018, stuck inside the detention centre, time passed painfully slowly for Priya and the family. Various court dates came and went without the minister blinking. Around them, Priya and Nades would see a steady stream of other asylum seekers being released—often at the discretion of the minister—but they were, on the whole, cases that had never had any media coverage, and that genie was now firmly out of the bottle for the family from Biloela. Media coverage was one of the only tangible ways they had of countering the political rhetoric.

With Priya and Huyen now both having smartphones, both women became adept chroniclers, regularly calling to show me the prison-like conditions in which they were trying to raise their children.

Disturbing Behaviour

With fully caged verandahs, the units looked like basic motels that had been retrofitted to become prisons. The kitchens could theoretically be used, but were only stocked with cheap plastic picnic cutlery, which was largely useless for cutting up anything. It looked to me to be much like a kitchen in a prison or a mental health facility: anything that could have been turned into a weapon had been removed. Both women would tell me they weren't supplied with cleaning products and had to wait for cleaners to come around the units to properly clean up the spills their small children made. A single bottle of dishwashing liquid was all they were given.

Food was a frequent issue. With no ability to shop or reliably choose what food they wanted, Priya, Nades and Huyen were delivered basics to cook with but both families would often show me photos of fruit and vegetables that looked well past their best-by date. Many others in detention would send me similar photos.

When they had first been detained, they explained they had been given meals transported from the centre's main kitchen, and those had often been cold and greasy by the time they were delivered. They now had the ability to cook their own meals, which was a small step forward, but they still couldn't properly prepare food for their children. As any parent knows, children's tastes change rapidly as they start eating solids and, unbelievably, at the end of 2018 neither family had the ability to even put some vegetables in a blender and make decent baby food.

On one visit, when a guard attempted to stop me bringing in baby food that met all of the criteria, I ramped up my questions to the department about the reality of conditions. I also spoke to my colleague Helen Davidson at *The Guardian*.

Helen was highly experienced in reporting on immigration and detention in Australia and would become a good friend. On this occasion she said, 'I'll do something on the food, and how about I interview you?'

Helen published a story that featured my interaction with the guard who tried to block perfectly legal baby food. Within a matter of days both Priya and Huyen were given blenders for their kitchens. This was a small victory, but the fact remained—these were asylum seekers and their Australian-born children. Why were they being treated like criminals?

———

In 2023 I submitted questions to Serco asking:

'Are Serco staff responsible for communicating to catering staff that there are new detainees arriving in the MITA APOD who will require meals and/or grocery supplies?

'Can you explain how detainees are consulted about their dietary requirements when they are in the MITA APOD, which is somewhat removed from the main centre?

'Can you explain if Serco staff are responsible for noting and then alerting catering staff about the dietary requirements of infants, toddlers, children, diabetics and vegetarians detained in the MITA APOD and unable to communicate with catering staff?'

In response, Serco stated through their lawyers that:

> Serco is contracted by the Australian government to deliver a range of services, such as facility security, welfare and engagement, catering, cleaning, transport and escort, and facilities management

services across Australia's onshore immigration detention network.

Serco provided the family with a selection of fresh food daily, which was selected and ordered by the parents to meet their self-catering needs. Mr Murugappan and Ms Nadesalingam were responsible for cooking meals and making dietary choices for their children.

All detainees are provided appropriate food and beverage while in Serco's care, including when required during transport and escort tasks.

Chapter 24
THARNICAA

MITA   **January–August 2019**

The seasons changed but our lives in MITA stayed the same. We did have a new lawyer who had taken up our case. Her name was Carina Ford. But I was beginning to lose hope. I felt like I was inside a dark tunnel and could see no way out. It was hard to stay positive while living a life in limbo, especially with two young children confined in a small space and being watched all the time. I thought that I was going mad. I was struggling to stay a good parent when

Tharnicaa

I myself had no control over my life. I couldn't pretend, even for five minutes, that I was okay for the sake of our children. I couldn't play with them for more than a few minutes or concentrate on anything. My children's suffering made me feel guilty and this was eating at me.

I was often in tears because I didn't have enough milk to feed little Tharni. Getting formula milk was not easy either. But it was Kopi who showed the effects of detention first. One day, looking through a children's book sent in by one of our friends, Kopi asked Nades for a bicycle, pointing to a picture. 'Appa, can you buy me this bicycle? A red one. Like this. For my birthday?' Another time she asked me if I could make her string hoppers and *sodhi*, a Sri Lankan dish. In times like that, both Nades and I didn't know what to do.

One time I saw Kopi rolling up a piece of paper and pretending it was a cigarette. That scared the hell out of me. She had been watching the Serco guards smoke outside our windows. From then on, I had the front window shut. I didn't take the kids outside when the guards were there smoking.

As months rolled by, Kopi started to behave strangely. We noticed that sometimes she was talking to herself or pulling out chunks of her own hair. At other times, she was still biting her arm. She was also becoming aggressive towards us and her baby sister. One day, I tried to discipline her for screaming, but Nades told me to stop. He reminded me that Kopi had only experienced the real world outside until she was two and a half years old. She was now stressed from being locked up.

From that day on, Nades started to play with her and Tharni, often becoming one of them. He'd be rolling on the floor, playing hide-and-seek or imaginary hopscotch, and shouting with excitement like a four-year-old! He got the visitors to bring colouring pens and paper, and spent time drawing and painting with the children, telling them Tamil folk stories that kept them mesmerised. Over time, I started to see a difference; Kopi was somewhat becoming her normal self again, and so was Nades.

But Tharni was not doing so great. She was growing up in the confines of a cabin with limited sunlight, poor nutrition and stressed-out parents. First, I noticed cracks appearing in her front milk teeth and soon they began to discolour. I asked for her to be taken to IHMS. It was located inside MITA, but a few minutes' drive away. The doctor there said this wasn't unusual in baby teeth and nothing to worry about. But over the next week, her front two teeth started to dissolve.

IHMS organised a trip to the Royal Children's Hospital. There the doctors found both children were low in iron and vitamin D. The hospital staff looked after us very well and the doctor in charge there wrote a letter to MITA requesting that we be allowed to cook our own meals. They also said that Tharni's teeth needed treatment sometime soon.

Back in detention, some officials from some Commonwealth department came and interviewed Nades and me about Tharni's condition. It was like watching the same movie again; they asked us so many questions and recorded everything. As usual, nothing came of it and we never heard from them again.

―――

Whenever Tharni cried that her mouth was hurting, we'd ask the Serco guards to take us to IHMS. At IHMS, the doctor would give her some pain relief syrup and sometimes antibiotics and send us back to our cabin. If Tharni cried in pain in the night, we had to wait till the morning to see a medical officer at the IHMS. Nades and I asked IHMS medical staff several times for permission to take Tharni back to the Royal Children's Hospital, but they told us we were overreacting and kept giving her pain relief. We weren't allowed to have any medication in our own possession, even for the children.

This kept going until after her second birthday. One night, Tharni started vomiting. Because we were locked up inside our cabin, we banged on our door several times, but no one answered. It dawned on us that there was no one outside, guarding our cabin. So we tried the landline several times, calling the reception, but no one answered the phone either. We didn't know what to do; it was a tough, sleepless night for Nades and me, taking turns to comfort little Tharni, who was vomiting and crying all night, and trying to call the front desk.

The next morning at 6 am, when the guards came in for a headcount, we told them about Tharni's condition. She was limp and not readily responding to us. Two hours passed before they brought in the nurse, who checked Tharni and administered pain relief syrup. We asked that she be taken to the hospital for a proper check-up. We were worried that she was seriously ill. The nurse agreed to organise transport and left.

We waited all day, but no one showed up. I kept ringing the reception, but still no one picked up. Tharni was lying terribly still with another high temperature, Kopi was crying and we were stuck within the walls. I was going crazy with worry and anxiety over my child. As 6 pm approached, my frustration boiled over and I flew into a rage. I took the landline phone and the computer that were in our cabin, and smashed them on the floor. Honestly, I can't even remember doing it. The computer was not connected to anything; it had been sitting there for show.

It worked. The sound immediately brought all the guards into the cabin. The guard in charge came very close to me, as if he was about to hit me.

'Don't you dare come near me!' I screamed.

'You've damaged government property!' he angrily shouted.

That made me so mad. Here was my baby, almost lifeless, and all he cared about were objects.

'If you had taken my daughter to hospital when I asked you to, this wouldn't have happened!'

Finally, Serco transported us to the Royal Children's Hospital. But it was too late. Her top front teeth were so bad that they told us they would need to remove all four of them. This made me very upset. She was already so skinny and couldn't eat many solid foods and we couldn't simply go grocery shopping for the food she could eat. What made it all worse was that they didn't remove the teeth immediately; we had to wait months while Tharni struggled with more infections. We weren't told why there was a delay but eventually she had surgery. Nades and I had to make the decision on who went with Tharni and who stayed to look after Kopi, as she couldn't be alone in detention. This was another time I thought about the basic rights we lost when we were taken from Biloela.

―――

In early 2019, almost a year into our solitary confinement, they began to bring in several refugees from Nauru and, with that, our lives improved. Finally, we were given fresh fruit and vegetables to cook for ourselves and allowed to wander around the compound. There were now several children in detention, and they set up a spare room for them with a whiteboard and a few other materials. To be able to see and talk with other people helped us a great deal.

Kopi turned four in May and Tharni, two in June. My friend Chandra tried to bring in a cake from a shop for Tharni, because Serco hadn't allowed her to bring a homemade cake for Kopi's birthday. But they didn't allow this one either; they said the box wasn't sealed properly.

Just a month before Tharni's dental surgery, she had an incident with the whiteboard in the activity room. While she was playing, the whiteboard fell on her head; there was a visible bump on her head and she seemed unsteady. I wanted to take photos of the activity room and the whiteboard, but Serco wouldn't let me in, saying it was closing time.

We were terribly worried about her. We were still waiting for her dental surgery and knew she was still considered underweight by doctors. It was hard to believe something else had gone wrong. Several hours after the board hit her head, she started vomiting. We asked guards to get her to hospital. It felt like we waited hours; Nades and I were beside ourselves waiting for guards to organise staff to transport us.

Eventually we saw a doctor late at night. Tharni was kept for observation till the next day and released back to detention. But the following day, she couldn't walk properly. We managed to convince the guards to take her to the hospital again. The doctors explained that it was from the concussion she had suffered; they asked us to watch her over the next few days. Nades and I were very worried that our child might not recover, but fortunately, a week later, Tharni was back to her normal self.

During this time, some officials from some department—maybe it was Child Protection—came and interviewed Nades and me separately for three to four hours each, then again together. They asked so many questions and recorded everything. But nothing came of it and we never heard from them again.

After the whiteboard incident, the children were allowed to attend a community playgroup once a week, accompanied by a parent and several Serco guards. But this only happened twice. While the children played with other children from the local community, the guards stayed and watched. I hated going on those occasions. I couldn't interact with the other adults freely because I felt that the local parents looked at us as if we were criminals.

Going to the court for my case hearing caused me similar embarrassment. At the court two guards would hold on to both my arms and march me in from the van. People passing by would often stare at me, like I was a criminal. I knew that I didn't deserve this, and the general public didn't know any better, but it didn't stop me from feeling humiliated every time.

I was so upset over these months, our second winter in Melbourne in MITA. An extra Serco staffer was allocated to monitor me as they thought I was being overly emotional. That made no sense to me; of course I was emotional, I was a mother in distress over her child.

I was then firmly encouraged to visit a mental health nurse. She was kind and understood why I was so upset. After that, I was taken 'off watch' and the extra guard was removed. Serco was now allowed to entrust us with the recommended doses of children's pain relief medicine so we could administer it ourselves but even this would be temporary.

Every step inside MITA to parent our girls was a battle to be fought, and I was becoming exhausted. The only thing that stopped me from going mad was Nades and the support we were getting from the wonderful Australian community.

By mid-August Angela's petition had gathered over 100,000 signatures. Simone, who had moved to Malaysia, visited again on her return with her family. Many people from all around Australia were supporting the Home to Bilo movement, started by our community. Even some of Prime Minister Scott Morrison's own MPs were speaking in support of us. People were holding vigils in Biloela and Melbourne. All this gave me something I hadn't had much of till now. Hope.

Chapter 25
THIS IS NOT A PLACE FOR CHILDREN TO BE

Huyen texted me late one weekend night and said she had seen Priya struggling to feed Tharnicaa, who seemed to have a very sore mouth and a temperature.

I wondered if it was a brutal bout of teething and suspected IHMS weren't exactly in the habit of handing out Bonjela to soothe gums, since they wouldn't even give the parents a thermometer, and it was difficult to convince them to dispense even single doses of pain relief. That presented me with a problem. My stories for *Crikey* were often behind a paywall but, if this was as bad as it looked, this story needed to be widely accessible. It was less than a month until the general election. I texted Helen Davidson again: 'I think I have something for you. Tharnicaa seems to be very unwell, can't eat.'

Days later Helen would publish a story featuring horrific photos of Tharnicaa's blackened teeth and swollen mouth. I immediately thought of the medical report that outlined Tharnicaa's vitamin D deficiency the previous year.

Dozens of media outlets followed the story with their own. Photos of Tharnicaa's tiny swollen face and painfully decaying baby teeth were everywhere. There was suddenly acute national interest in the family and the coverage began to erode the government's constant talking points that the family weren't held in a harsh detention environment, simply because they chose to call it something else. More Australians were beginning to understand that the family were completely denied any scrap of autonomy, evidenced by the fact that they had not been allowed to take their youngest daughter to a dentist for months on end. Helen was mystified by the continued political obfuscation.

'I do remember how farcical it all felt, that there continued to be this idea that there were no kids in detention. The semantics and games played with jargon and official definitions were just so intense and confusing by then. It made it impossible at worst, or discouraging at best, for someone not inside the Australian immigration bubble (of detainees, activists, lawyers, journalists, social workers, etc.) to make heads or tails of even something as simple as "Are there kids in detention?"'

Despite the national media coverage in May, Tharnicaa did not get her teeth extracted until months later, on 25 July 2019 at Dental Health Services Victoria. In a photo Nades sent me, he is holding his unconscious two-year-old daughter after the surgery, a heart monitor still in place, a bandage around her right hand from where a cannula had been, and her mouth visibly swollen.

The discharge notes said the patient was going home after surgery. She wasn't. The address registered for Tharnicaa was simply a post office box, not a physical address. It was the PO Box for the detention centre.

Chapter 26

THE PLANE

On 30 August 2019 I was at home in Melbourne, thinking I had finished work for the day, when I noticed a missed call from Priya. I typed back a message asking if I should ring.

The answer came vividly. In a videocall from Priya, I could see an ABF staffer reading a deportation notice to the family. It was a few unmistakable seconds. Then we were cut off.

I slumped against the hallway wall. Priya had also sent me a screenshot, but what that image didn't contain was the sound of Kopika's and Tharnicaa's little voices beginning to rise in the background as they were separated from their parents and surrounded by guards.

I immediately called Carina Ford to see if she knew anything. Even though it was dinnertime she answered and said she hadn't been told by the department that the deportation was imminent. Carina rang barrister Angel Aleksov and they started hurriedly

The Plane

organising an injunction against deportation. Carina, her husband and Nina Merlino, her legal colleague, would work solidly at their respective kitchen tables for the next 90 minutes, trying to find a duty judge to attempt to stop the flight.

In the detention centre, other detainees became aware that something was off. Huyen had had a visit from her husband; now she and Isabella wanted to go back to their unit, but the guards kept delaying her return. It was a dark winter's night and Huyen wanted to get her toddler into bed. Normally guards were waiting for the end of any visit, to escort the families into a van and drive them to the part of the centre where they were housed. Later she would call me to say, 'Oh my God, that's why they kept me over there—so that I couldn't do anything or tell anybody.'

Other refugees—those in the same section as Priya and Nades—suddenly noticed they had been locked into their units and couldn't exit into the common area. They didn't know what was happening, but they could hear the footsteps of many staff, the sound of scuffling and the cries of Tharnicaa and Kopika.

The surprise of the deportation notice wasn't just felt by Priya and the family. Vashini was completely unprepared for what was happening and tried to reach Angela and Simone as fast as she could.

'Priya was told that the department were not gonna do anything. She was told they had to do some paperwork before a deportation. So we thought we don't have to stress. Then suddenly, they come into her unit and say, "Okay, we are going to deport you." Priya was calling and she was crying and screaming. I could hear Kopika screaming and Tharnicaa crying. And I was like, "What's going on? Priya, what's happening?" And she said, "It's deportation, you need to let Simone know, this is happening."

'I called Simone, and said this is it, they're gonna try to deport. I was still on the phone with Priya, because I just wanted to see everything and hear everything, and I need to pass what's happened to Simone for the lawyers. I was watching literally everything. Priya was screaming, she was in pain. And you know, the officers, you could see they get angry and her shoulder hurts. And she was in pain and she wants to see the children. And they were separated, put in a different van.'

Simone was walking back to her apartment in Malaysia with her children when Priya tried to call her.

'I was just walking back to our apartment, standing at the lift, Priya kept calling me and the connection was bad. And I could just see her surrounded by people. And I was like, "Oh, sorry, the wi-fi is so bad. Priya, can I call you upstairs? I'll be upstairs in about five seconds." And then the penny dropped and I was like, Oh my God. And she wasn't saying much, but I was like, Oh my God. And then I just sort of like ran up, got into the lift and got upstairs.'

Simone quickly cancelled the dinner she was meant to be going out to with her partner and opened her laptop, her daughter Isabelle sitting beside her.

'Isabelle was old enough to get it, and she was there that whole night. She just sat with me that night, just over the laptop as we all just watched and spoke to Priya and Nades.'

Angela was at her weekly dancing and singing class when she got a voice message from Simone. 'She left me a voice message saying, "It's happening." I remember sitting in my car straight after class talking to her saying, "What's going on?" and her saying, "I was on the phone with Priya. I watched all the guards come in. They've got them." Immediately Iain and Nic said, "Okay, we've got to get out

The Plane

to the airport." I remember coming home and there was a lot of waiting, and that was the hardest thing, being so far away. 'Cause we had people down there saying they were heading to the airport but I was just sitting here and doing nothing.'

Bronwyn Dendle started sending messages from Biloela to anyone she knew in Melbourne, telling them to get to the airport immediately.

'Anyone I could think of who might have been in the state of Victoria got a message from me asking them to go to the airport and support this family. I had no idea which bloody airport because I am up in Bilo.'

In Melbourne I headed out to Tullamarine Airport, too, as did Nic from Change.org. We hadn't met yet, and we took different routes once we arrived there. Nic and others, including Aran and my journalist colleague Chris Woods, drove down a tiny road beside the end of a runway. Someone had spotted a Skytraders plane sitting outside a hangar with an unusual amount of white vans parked around it. Skytraders owned the private planes regularly hired by ABF to carry out deportations.

But as I was getting close to the airport, I had noticed that my phone was nearly flat. I had to make a decision: did I stand by a road beside the tarmac with a phone that was flat, or did I go into the main terminal and charge my phone and regroup?

The decision was made for me when Priya called from the van. She was surrounded by Serco staff. She had no idea where Nades and the girls were, but she could see she was parked in a hangar.

That was it. What I needed was a charged phone, so she could call me—she was already working her hardest to tell me exactly what was going on and I needed to be able to hear her.

I quickly told Priya her lawyer was working to file an injunction. What I wouldn't know for several hours was that Priya was now about to give all those guards a run for their money. If they thought that the third time she had been grabbed in the dark was going to go smoothly, they were wrong.

Years later she would tell me that the decision to separate her from her daughters and husband gave her an unexpected edge. Now she could physically fight against the staff hauling her onto the plane because she wasn't holding her children.

Sitting alone in a van surrounded by Serco staff on a cold winter's night Priya would fight with everything she had, while her lawyers were at their kitchen tables doing the same.

Chapter 27
I BEGAN TO SCREAM

MITA   **30 August 2019**

Towards the end of August, the courts rejected our appeal regarding the rejection of our visa applications. Our lawyer told us that we had time to appeal that decision and would do so soon. But a similar scene to what had happened eighteen months ago played out all over again.

On the evening of 30 August, Nades and I were having dinner with the children. Suddenly several Serco guards appeared in our cabin.

Then even more came in until I could barely count them all. There had to be well over ten guards standing in the tiny kitchen where I had just cooked our dinner, and I thought I saw more outside.

Then an ABF officer holding some papers walked in, with a translator. For a moment everyone stood still. It was like the calm before a storm, then the officer began reading off the paper and I realised with my heart nearly stopping that it was a deportation notice. I quickly rang Vashini and Rebekah to tell them what was happening while she was still reading. I barely had the time because guards started trying to move us out of the unit.

The girls were crying out and some of the guards were trying to talk to them while others blocked me from going to comfort and pick up the girls. They wouldn't let me near them, and too late I realised I had been separated from my family by a sea of guards.

Nades and the children were loaded into a van and the guards shut the doors of their van. I realised that I was being taken separately again, and I began to scream and struggle harder. They dragged me by both arms into another van and my trousers started to come undone. I kept screaming and struggling.

One of the female guards tried to take my phone off me. This time I had a phone and the right to use it, so as she tried to wrestle the phone out of my hand, I kicked her with all the strength I could muster. She loosened her grip and let go of me.

They managed to push me into another van. Once inside, I took some selfies for evidence. The guards tried to stop me, but I yelled at them: 'You are the ones filming us all the time, so here's a different viewpoint!'

When my van arrived at Melbourne Airport, I knew that Nades and the children were already inside a plane. He had sent me a

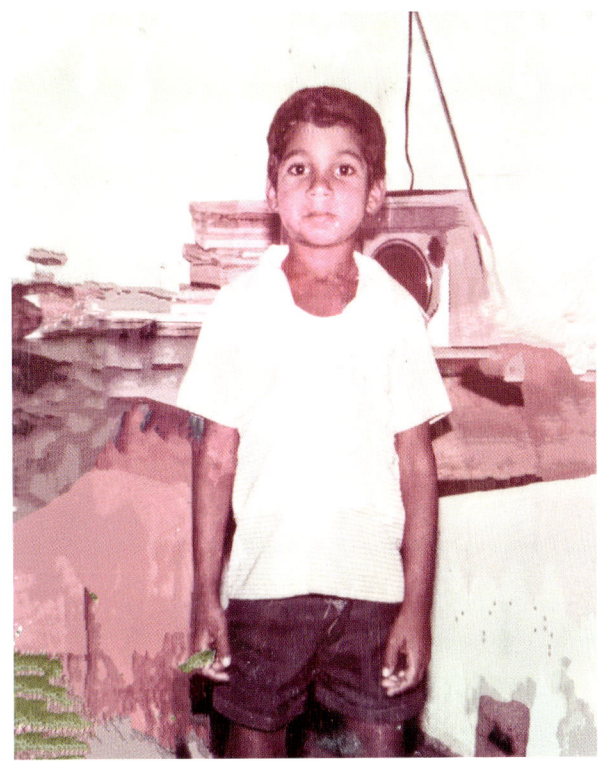

Priya (*left*) and Nades (*right*) as children in Sri Lanka, long before their separate journeys to Australia.

Priya and Nades met and were married in Sydney in 2014.

Priya and Nades started their married life in Biloela in September 2014. Baby Kopika arrived in May 2015, eight weeks premature.

In June 2017, Kopika's little sister Tharnicaa was born. Less than a year later the whole family was forcibly removed from their home and taken to Melbourne Immigration Transit Accommodation (MITA) in Broadmeadows in preparation for deportation.

After the family was taken to Melbourne, supporters began to organise. This rally was held in Sydney in April 2018. Iain Murray (*left*), managed communications for the campaign. (Zebedee Parkes)

Simone Cameron (*centre back*), who had lived in Biloela as a teenager and had taught English to Nades, was studying immigration law in Melbourne and became involved in efforts to free the family, visiting them several times during 2018. Pictured is a visit from 2019, when Simone and her daughter Isabelle (*left*) visited the family at MITA.

Rallies were held around the country in January 2019. This protest was at federal member Ken O'Dowd's office in Gladstone. It is said the local Gangulu people named Biloela after their totem, the white cockatoo. This hand-drawn cockatoo by Myfwangy Szepanowski became a motif for the campaign.

Rebekah with Kopika and Tharnicaa in the visitors room at MITA in 2019, just before the deportation effort that sent the family to Christmas Island. Rebekah first met the family on video calls once they had their phones back in June 2018.

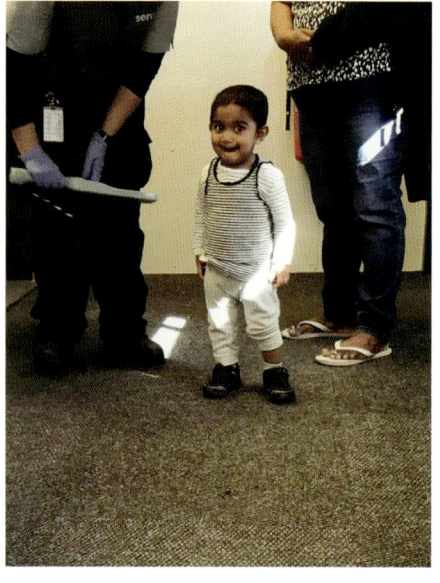

Tharnicaa and Priya at MITA, with a guard holding a metal detector, 2019.

The girls in the play area at MITA. At first they were only allowed outside to play for 30 minutes a day.

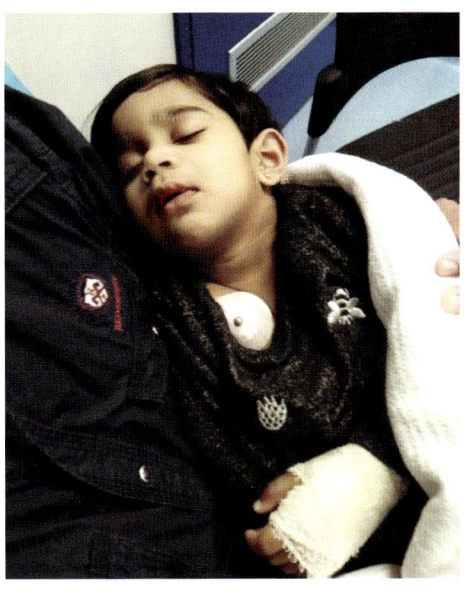

Tharnicaa after her surgery in a Melbourne hospital, while still at MITA.

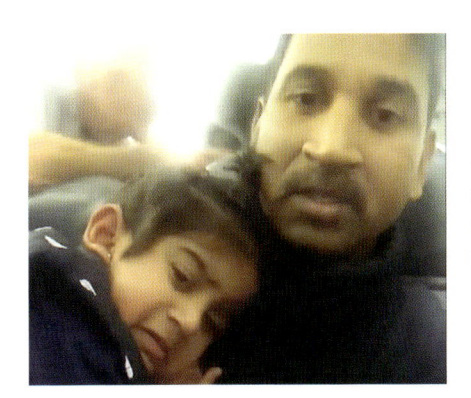

A distressed Tharnicaa with Nades during an attempt to deport the family from Melbourne to Sri Lanka via Darwin in August 2019.

In Darwin, Serco officers took the family to the airport. Swift action by Priya, supporters and the legal team thwarted the deportation at the last minute.

Angela Fredericks and Bronwyn Dendle deliver the national Change.org petition with 252,790 signatures to Parliament House, Canberra, in September 2019.

The girls in the detention centre on Christmas Island.

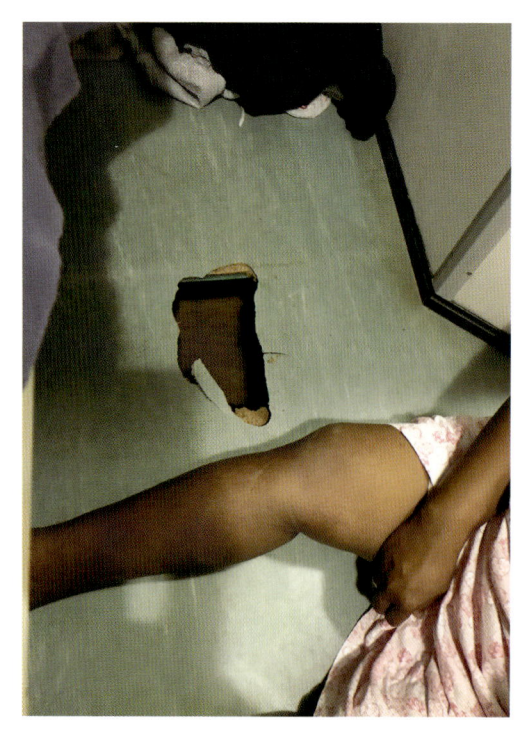

Priya was injured after her foot went through the floor in a poorly maintained cabin in the detention centre, September 2019.

The bed in the detention centre they all shared, July 2020.

Christmas Islanders held a vigil for the family in conjunction with many others across mainland Australia on 5 March 2021. Locals wrote messages to the family on cut outs of the Home to Biloela cockatoo.

The girls in costume for the Christmas Island school book fair.

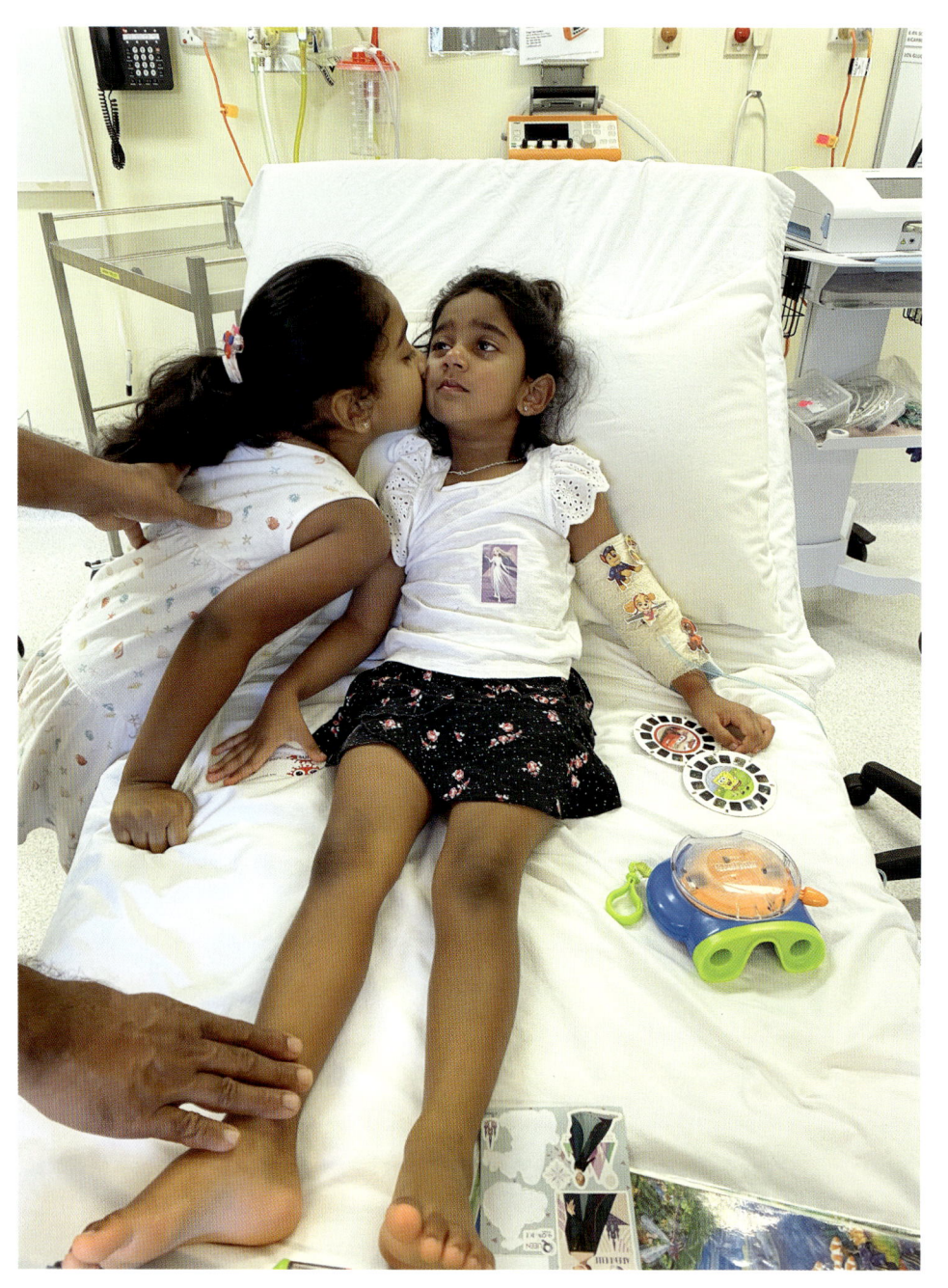

Kopika kissing her three-year-old sister Tharnicaa, who was in hospital on Christmas Island with sepsis and pneumonia, 6 June 2021. She had been vomiting for ten days with fever before she was airlifted to hospital in Perth. It was front-page news, and shocked the nation.

Kopika and Nades being farewelled by Robyn (*left*) and her daughters at Christmas Island airport. They had not been allowed to go with Priya and Tharnicaa to Perth.

Rebekah on a call with Priya and Tharnicaa in Perth hospital, 15 June 2021. The Serco guards had left once it was announced the family would be reunited and released into community detention. (Rebekah Holt)

Once released into community detention in Perth in June 2021, the family was able to grow fresh vegetables and cook their favourite dishes from home.

Angela and Kopika enjoying a home-cooked meal. After nearly three years in detention facilities, the family was at last able to enjoy living in a regular house, even if it was still community detention.

Mainstream media started taking more interest in the campaign. In July 2021 the Nine newspapers' *Sydney Morning Herald* visited Biloela and ran a moving article. The mayor, Nev Ferrier, is on the right. (Paul Harris / *The Sydney Morning Herald*)

The family were able to connect with the local Tamil community while in Perth, 2021.

At the Perth Shiva Temple, a Hindu temple in Canning Vale.

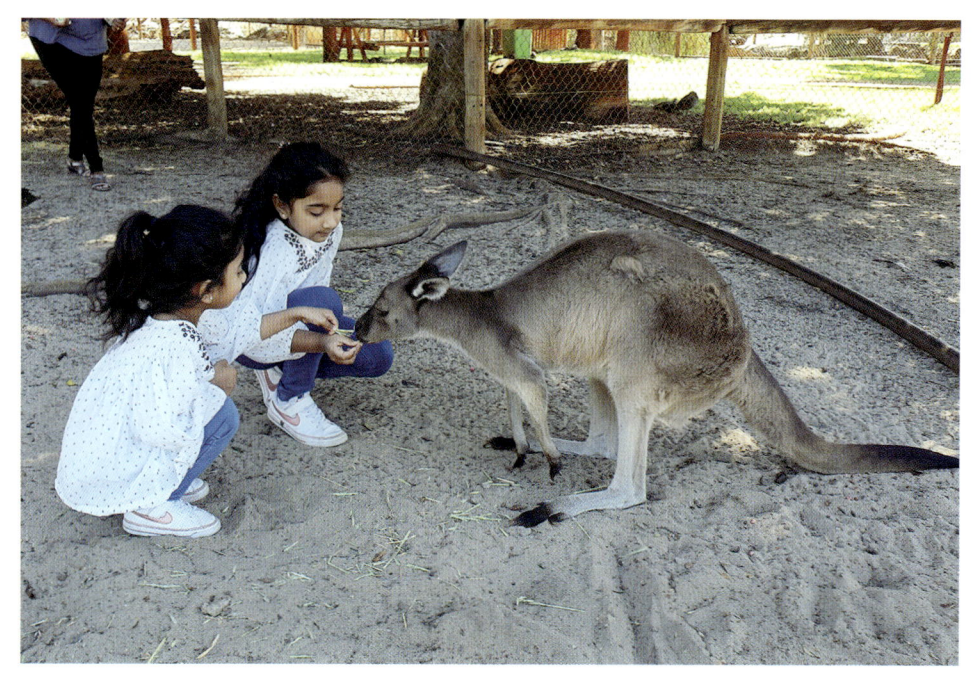

Visiting the Swan Valley Cuddly Animal Farm in Henley Brook. Although not allowed to move away from Perth, the family was able to live normally, and the girls could catch up on experiences they'd missed out on during years in detention centres.

Priya sewed the matching dresses for the girls that became such a recognisable element of the Home to Bilo campaign photos

Nic Dorward, Sally Rugg and Angela at Parliament House, Canberra. Nic, campaigns director for Change.org Australia, worked tirelessly on the Home to Biloela campaign. Over four years the petition amassed 600,000 signatures.

Angela Fredericks shared an update on **Bring Priya and her beautiful family back home to Biloela, Queensland** Check it out and leave a comment

PETITION UPDATE

Biloela family on Australian Story tonight

Friends, tonight at 8pm on the ABC's *Australian Story*, Priya and Nades will share the story of their family's three and half year battle to come safely home to Biloela in their own words.

Momentum had built from media coverage and the enormous response to the Change.org petition. After the family were released to live in community detention in Perth, ABC TV's *Australian Story* did a widely watched feature story, which aired on 20 September 2021.

In the lead up to the 2022 federal election, attention focused on Peter Dutton's role as Home Affairs minister in Scott Morrison's Coalition government. Labor leader Anthony Albanese had made an election promise to release Priya, Nades and the girls from detention.

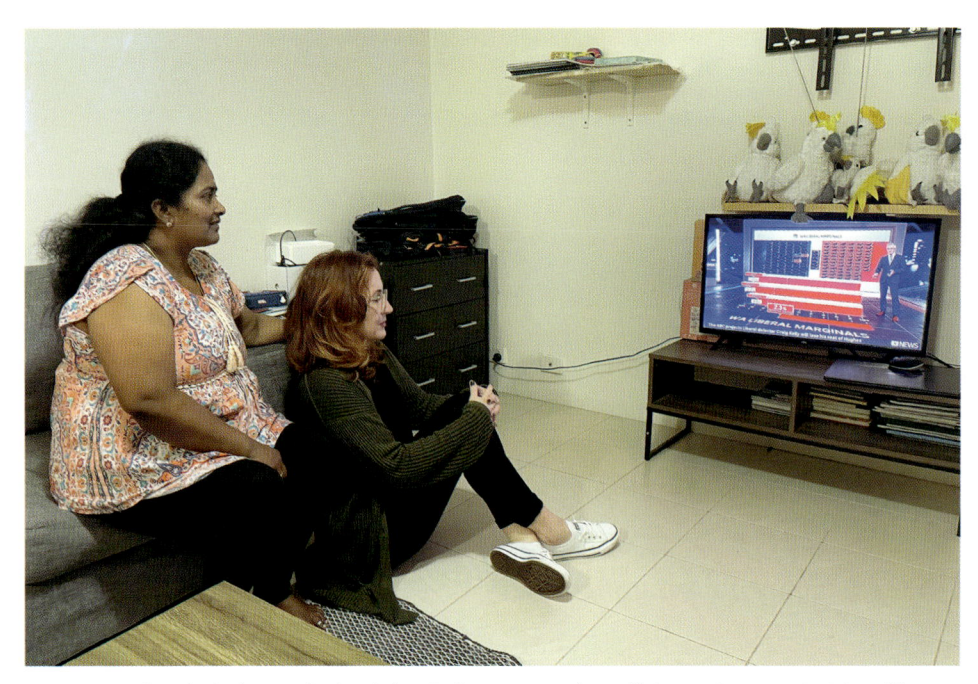

Priya and Rebekah watch the federal election results roll in on 21 May 2022, still in community detention in Perth. The family's future hinged on the result.

Huge smiles on the flight home to Bilo at last: (*clockwise from front left*) Priya, Vashini, Kopika, Simone, Tharnicaa, Nades and Angela.

Home to Biloela! Supporters gather to welcome the family back to Biloela on 10 June 2022. (© Mike Bowers / *The Guardian* / eyevine / Headpress)

New prime minister Anthony Albanese met the family in Gladstone in June 2022, demonstrating he had fulfilled his election promise. (Twitter @AlboMP)

Priya at Parliament House, Canberra, where she spoke at a rally seeking permanent visas for 31,000 refugees on 29 November 2022.

Tharnicaa and Kopika back at school in Biloela.

The family after a Tamil dance at Biloela's Flourish Festival in 2023.

I Began to Scream

text message asking where I was. He was worried that we might be deported separately. My mind was numb and I could not think properly but I could see I was in a hangar and just out the door was a large plane. Was that where Nades and the girls were?

As guards dragged me out of the van, several lights began to flash in the darkness. I realised that it was the media taking photos of me. I heard my name being called out by several voices and I knew that many of our supporters were also there behind the fence.

I was immediately shoved back inside the van by the guard who had hold of me, and I landed on the seat headfirst. Then she shut the door on my foot. I cried out in pain; blood began to stream out of my leg. Anger boiled inside me and I cursed the guards with all the obscenities I could think of. They drove the van closer to the plane and tried to smuggle me into the plane. Emboldened by the media and my supporters, I decided that I was not going to get on that plane if I could help it. I kicked, screamed and swore at them, and refused to give in to their strength.

For the next couple of hours, they tried every tactic. First, they talked nicely; then they threatened me. Finally, they tried to drag me by pulling me by my arm. I was not physically strong, after being locked up in detention for eighteen months. So I did my best to struggle and use my voice.

Suddenly I felt a sharp pain in my shoulder as we struggled. I had torn a ligament. Although it's been four years now, I still need to take painkillers and steroid injections. This is why you never see me carrying the children.

In the end, all the Serco guards standing around the van hoisted me up and carried me into the plane, like a *parava kaavadi* seen at Hindu temples. My trousers came undone and, by the time I was thrown inside the plane, I was only in my underpants.

Nades was in shock, seeing me like that, and the kids began to cry, calling for me. It was chaos. I yelled to Nades, who was trying to attend to the children: 'Quick, Nades. Film this!'

Nades then sprang into action and was filming as one of the female guards pinned me to a seat at the back of the plane. A male guard twisted my wrist and I yelled out in pain. But my other hand was free, so I got hold of one of the female guard's fingers and squeezed it hard. I wanted to give them back some of my pain. She yelped and jumped off me.

I continued to scream and swear at the guards. I know they were only doing their job, but it was hard to respect someone who just took orders and didn't think for themselves. Could they not see that we were ordinary people and not criminals? All we wanted was to bring up our two little daughters in peace.

Nades got all of this on film. We had to do it to protect ourselves because I knew it would be my word against theirs. As a female and as a refugee, no one would believe me. I had to have evidence.

Chapter 28

TULLAMARINE

Beside the runway, Nic was working to tweet what he could see happening while also live-streaming the unfolding events to the Home to Bilo Facebook page. In Biloela, after blasting messages at literally any person she could think of, Bronwyn was sitting alone in her kitchen glued to the Facebook live stream.

In the airport terminal I was huddled over my charging phone, still wondering if I should make the attempt to get to the side road where Nic, Aran and Chris Woods were stationed. Zach Hope from the Melbourne *Age* arrived and we introduced ourselves and both set up camp at a table beside an electrical outlet. I had already passed my colleague Gloria Kalache from SBS TV as I ran inside. She told me she would head to the roadside to try to get shots. This was understandable: as a TV reporter, Gloria needed footage.

In Malaysia, Simone was receiving a series of video calls from Nades who was already on the plane with Kopika and Tharnicaa.

HOME TO BILOELA

What Nades was about to quickly record on his phone and send to Simone would change Australia.

On the video from inside the plane, the girls are sitting beside their father looking both sleepy and occasionally anxious. Nades is telling Simone what's happening, but then all hell breaks loose.

The guards have dragged Priya onto the plane. When the girls see their mother being hauled down the aisle, dishevelled and injured, with her trousers hanging off her, they immediately and understandably start crying.

Moments later it gets much worse. Priya isn't allowed to sit with her husband and daughters. Instead she is forcefully, physically dragged past them. Both girls stop crying and start screaming, a sound many of us will never forget.

Nades stands and yells at the guards to let his wife go so she can sit with him. He is the gentlest man having the most appropriate reaction to what he is seeing. Both his daughters hang off him, plainly terrified, their faces caught in a rictus of fear. But still the guards insist that the family are not allowed to sit together.

It was a moment so palpably insane and cruel that it was almost impossible to process. But now it was also undeniable, because Nades had recorded it and sent it immediately to Simone Cameron. Soon Australia would see what was being done in their name as the footage of two little girls screaming for their mother was played over and over.

We were seeing what we had never seen.

As the plane started to taxi, Simone's ten-year-old daughter sat beside her in their apartment and watched as her mother held her own mobile phone up to the laptop screen to quickly record what she thought could be her last video call with Nades.

Tullamarine

'I had a tiny little bit more time with Nades still on the video call. It felt like I had my arms outstretched, but they were just slipping away and I couldn't bloody do anything. Especially not from Malaysia.'

On the line, all the way from Malaysia, Simone can be heard. Her voice is cracking, but she is still audible, reassuring Nades: 'We are with you, my friend, we are with you ...'

From their position next to the runway, friends and supporters could see the plane moving away from them, readying for take-off. Voices in the recorded live stream turn hoarse and urgent.

Watching in Biloela, Bronwyn could hear supporters yelling and screaming, but she could barely believe what she was seeing as the plane began to taxi.

Angela was watching, too, 'I remember the plane taking off. I was on the phone to Simone. And I could hear her daughter Isabelle in the background, just sobbing.'

Moments after the plane took off, inside the airport my phone rang. It was Carina: 'We got the injunction. They'll have to land.'

I immediately rang my colleague beside the tarmac, Chris Woods. I asked him to tell those gathered around that an injunction had been granted, and in the cold Melbourne night he did just that. Despair dialled back to something closer to hope, again. The hands that had been shaking the wire of the airport fence were released.

Up in Biloela, having just watched the live stream from Nic that showed the plane clearly taking off, Bronwyn was sitting by herself on the kitchen floor of her house, sobbing: 'I just thought that whole thing was for fucking nothing ... They're gonna be sent back there, and now with a target on their back because we've told the world about them. This is shit, the whole thing is shit and we are shit because of how we've helped put a target on them. I felt very alone.'

Five minutes after the take-off I called Simone and told her that Carina and the other lawyers had successfully gotten an injunction, so the plane would have to land in Australia. She was initially disbelieving. She later recalled her reaction: 'I was like, "What!?" And I thought, I can't handle this roller-coaster anymore, I want to get off please!'

Bronwyn would find out about the injunction when she texted Angela a simple, 'This is shit.' Angela responded, explaining that the plane was now legally compelled to land. The growing consensus was that Darwin was the likely location.

But no one knew for sure. Even though the injunction had been granted, the department had not communicated with the family's lawyer to explain exactly where her clients were being taken.

In 2023 I asked Serco to explain what their duty of care responsibilities are when transporting infants and children long distances, if they employed nurses to accompany detainees with medical conditions that may require treatment in particularly stressful environments, and what training Serco staff receive around transporting detainees who are exhibiting behaviour that indicates a state of high distress.

Tullamarine

They did not answer those questions. Through their legal representative, Serco refuted claims that Priya 'was inappropriately handled by any Serco officers during any transport and escort tasks'.

Chapter 29

'YOU CAN'T TAKE US OVERSEAS'

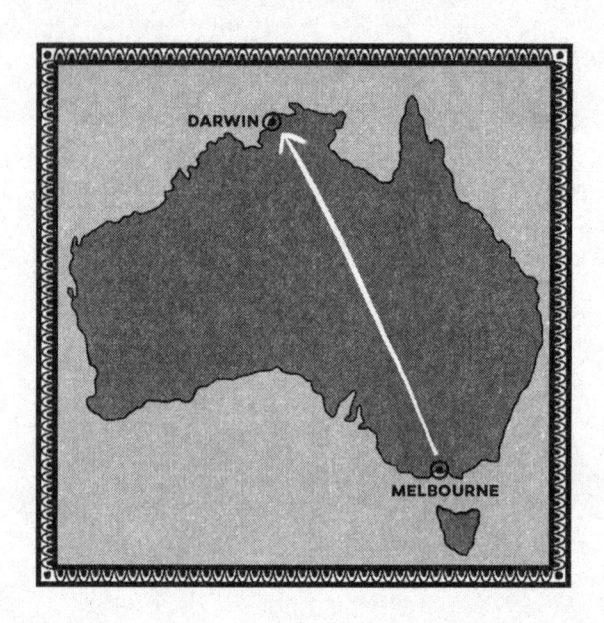

Darwin   30–31 August 2019

From his seat on the plane a few rows ahead, Nades tried to calm me down by telling me that things would work out. The kids were still crying. I wanted to sit with Nades and the kids, but the guards kept saying no. That only made me scream abuse even more. I didn't know how else to express my anger and frustration. Nades was trying to pacify our daughters.

'You Can't Take Us Overseas'

That day I decided that, even if I was paraded in public in my underwear, I wouldn't return to Sri Lanka. I'd do whatever it takes. But what was I going to do now? The plane was heading to Sri Lanka. I wouldn't let them get me off the plane. I'd fight to the end.

About four and a half hours later, in the early hours of the next morning, the plane began to descend. As it landed in darkness, Nades received a message from Vashini. 'Don't worry', it said. 'Your flight will land in Darwin, your lawyers stopped the deportation.' We were safe for now.

Nades was very excited. He read the message out loud to me because I was still being held at the back of the plane. I could hear his voice trembling. I felt a surge of relief, knowing we were not alone in this battle. The community of Bilo and many Australians were with us. I wanted to hold my head and cry. But I didn't.

We were escorted off the plane. It was warm, even at that time of the morning. The guards drove us to a motel close to the airport. It was not the cleanest place I've been to, but it was better than being any place in Sri Lanka.

When Nades saw me close-up, he was worried. I was black and blue, with bruises all over my body. I could barely lift my shoulder or move my hand. I also had a pounding headache.

After a warm shower, I felt a bit better. I had to put the same clothes back on because all our clothes were still being unloaded. Nades put the girls to bed and told them a story. Soon we all fell asleep from exhaustion.

HOME TO BILOELA

The following morning, the Northern Territory Children's Commissioner came to see us. We told her everything, especially about the treatment our children had received. How we had not been given time to pack or to feed them before we were dragged out of the cabin. How I had not been allowed to sit with them during the deportation flight, which was hard enough without that. No child should ever have to witness their mother being dragged in a public place in her underwear. She listened to us patiently for about two hours.

As soon as she left, Serco guards surrounded us. They asked us for our phones. We handed them over, thinking that it was temporary.

'You have to leave now!' one of them said. 'You aren't returning to your cabin.'

Aiyo! How much more of this Serco nonsense would we have to take?

'You can't deport us!' I exploded. 'We have a court order!'

'You are not being deported,' said the same guard.

'Then where are you taking us?' I asked. But no one would answer.

'Could we make one phone call to our lawyer?' Nades asked. They refused, saying that we were being taken to another Australian location, where phones weren't allowed. It was so confusing as our phones had been taken from us and returned several times that day. Then they marched us out to a van.

This time they kept us together and drove us towards the airport. As we were being driven, Nades, who was seated by the window, said to me that someone behind us in a car was taking photos of us. Nades couldn't tell who it was because the afternoon sun was in

'You Can't Take Us Overseas'

his eyes. So he made hand gestures to the man, trying to tell him that we didn't know where we were being taken. We decided that he was either media or a supporter. As we got to a gate, he got out of his car and called out Nades' name; he knew us! He gave us hope that evening when we felt hopeless.

Our van passed some military tanks and jeeps, so we realised we weren't at the airport. We were heading into Darwin's military base, and the man could no longer follow us. Without him, Australians wouldn't have known what happened to us that day.

We came to a stop in a compound. As we stepped out of the van, four female soldiers in full military uniform came over and frisked us thoroughly, even asking us to remove our shoes. This annoyed me so much. I wanted to explode, but I did my best to control myself. For the past two years we had been under the control of Serco every minute of our lives; what did the military think we were capable of smuggling into their base? They frisked us as though we were some kind of terrorists!

We were taken off to another part of the base accompanied by our entourage, which consisted of Serco guards, some medical staff, an interpreter and now several soldiers. Nades and I kept asking them what was happening to us, and where our belongings were. The only reply they gave us was that they didn't know, they were just following orders. Of course they were! It was frustrating to have to deal with people who didn't think for themselves; they always blamed all their actions on someone higher. Kopi kept crying that she wanted to go back home to Bilo. We had no answers for her.

The soldiers handed us some sandwiches and bottled water, and locked us up in a single-roomed cabin. Kopi and Tharni were exhausted, so Nades told them one of his stories again and he patted them to sleep.

That evening we were given permission to use their landline, so I called Vashini and told her that we were in a Darwin military base. She told me that ABF couldn't deport us while the court order was still valid. As always, talking to her brought me some peace. It was comforting to be able to speak to her in Tamil; trying to speak in English or through an interpreter was mentally tiring and at times frustrating. It added to my stress.

The same evening, we were packed into a van and driven a short distance. A small plane awaited us on the tarmac. I decided not to fight this time around, as we knew the plane was too small to fly to Sri Lanka. I hoped that they were going to fly us back home to Biloela, instead of to Melbourne again. Nades asked if he could speak to our lawyer again, but the guards said no.

As the plane took off, I asked the Serco guard next to me where we were being taken. She replied that she had no idea. I got mad at her. 'Why are you taking us somewhere if you don't know where you're going yourself?'

'I'm just following orders,' she replied.

I exploded. 'Why don't you think for yourself for once?' I shouted at her. 'Have you nothing inside your head?'

Nades tried to calm me down. 'Don't get yourself worked up. Wherever they're taking us doesn't matter now; they have to keep us in Australia.'

But when I saw that we were flying over the ocean, I became suspicious. 'Where are you taking us?' I asked out loud again. 'You can't take us overseas!'

Chapter 30

WE WILL
FIGHT FOR YOU

Vashini and Simone stayed up late to be ready to talk to Priya and Nades when the family were finally able to turn their phones on. As they thought, Darwin, in the far north of Australia's mainland, was where the plane eventually landed. Despite the injunction having been granted by a judge in Melbourne only moments after the plane took off, those in charge of such decisions in the Australian government kept the plane, and the family, in the air for over four hours.

The exhausted family were taken, still under guard, to a local motel where they could finally charge their mobile phones and call Vashini and Simone. Once again they had been dragged to the very edge of the vast Australian mainland and lawyers had acted fast enough to thwart their deportation.

Through pure chance, Iyngaranathan Selvaratnam, a Tamil doctor and about-to-be-activist, had also just landed in Darwin, planning to stay with his parents for a few days. The doctor, who everybody knows as Iyngaran, said: 'I remember everything very vividly. I had flown up that night. My flight from Sydney arrived at midnight, and I'd come up for a special festival at the Hindu temple. I'd left Darwin about two years before and I was just coming back for the weekend. When I got off the plane I started getting messages from Aran Mylvaganam at the Tamil Refugee Council, who I'd met through community radio. So I sort of knew him not super well but well enough, and he was reaching out to see if I knew anyone in Darwin. And I was like, "Oh look, I've literally just got off the plane."'

As he stood in Darwin Airport talking to Aran, Iyngaran started seeing social media posts from members of DASSAN, the Darwin Asylum Seeker Support and Advocacy Network. Did anyone know where the family were? Had anyone seen anything? The rumours all pointed to a motel complex near the airport and, since Iyngaran used to be a local, he knew exactly where to go—he'd attended medical conferences there.

'So I just wandered down there and then went into the actual premises. It's just like a whole bunch of villas and lots of townhouses, but it's totally open and anyone can walk in and out. And I'm just walking around. I didn't see the signage that this was an ABF area, but there's a whole fenced-off series of dongas [prefabricated cabins] towards the back that you can't just walk into. Which is sort of what initially gave me a bit of suspicion—by this time it's like three o'clock in the morning maybe—because I heard some adults talking to a little girl, and I vividly remember the girl asking about *Paw Patrol* [a children's TV show]. I thought it was a bit unusual. Like, what's going on? Why would there be people out at this time? And through the bushes I could see they were in uniforms. I wasn't familiar with what a Serco uniform looked like at the time, but then that got me suspicious about this particular area.'

Iyngaran's tenacity meant he didn't leave the spot for hours. In fact, he went further: 'I followed the fence line around and I found a gated entrance. And then there was an ABF sign there, and a white van parked just inside the gate. And there was one of those cheap dollar-shop bags, the stripey ones, sitting in the back window.

'I went back on Facebook and I saw that two people from DASSAN had actually been there, but they'd been waiting outside against the fence line. They'd posted photos of the family disembarking, and that same white van and that bag was visible in their photo. So I'm like, Okay, this has to be the place. This is where they are—and that must've been probably Kopika, because it sounded like an older child that was talking to the guards.

'I started wandering around the edge of the fence line and I got to the back of the donga that the family were in. I could see Kopika out on the verandah, and I was trying to be really quiet. But there was so much leaf litter, and four or five guards just on the verandah. I think they could hear me at times. They were out with big torches, like searching across the tree lines and things, obviously realising someone was out there. So I had to stay really still. I didn't know what I was going to achieve.

'Then I got close. The donga's only 2 metres from the fence line, and it's just an ordinary high fence. If I'd wanted to, I could've easily climbed it. I think one of my tweets was, like: "Come on, if we get enough people down here we could so easily just storm this place and break them out, it's just a bunch of Serco guards, like what are they gonna do?"

'But I could hear them talking through the back window, and I didn't want to give myself away. So basically I just kept tweeting, with different photos: "I can hear the family—come down guys."'

By this time it was very early in the morning.

'My dad brought me a sandwich. Thankfully I'd taken my battery pack, so I could keep recharging my phone, otherwise that would've been an issue as well. I don't know if he brought me another power bank or something, but they brought me some food and Dad was like, "What are you doing? You should come home." And my mum kept pestering me. But it didn't feel right to leave, something just kept me there.'

Iyngaran stayed, watching, all through the night. As the sun began to rise, people who'd heard about what was happening through social media and wanted to support the family started appearing. It soon turned into an impromptu vigil.

'About 40 people turned up, basically we were just keeping vigil outside. The journos came down as well, did some interviews. The Northern Territory's Unions people were even talking about blockading the motel to stop the family being moved. But then I think the news broke about the injunction being extended for five days or something . . . So this is Saturday morning, I think it'd been extended to the following Wednesday, and that's when people started dissipating. I think that came out at about eleven o'clock.'

That same morning, dozens of media colleagues started calling me. The footage of the girls screaming on the plane was going viral. Nades' quick-thinking camerawork was telling a story Australia had never been allowed to see before. Every television, radio and online news bulletin echoed with the screams of Kopika and Tharnicaa. Simone, Angela and the rest of the team were trying to manage a rapidly snowballing media event.

Nic Dorward at Change.org saw this as a crucial moment for the family and the campaign team: 'During the 2019 deportation attempt we pushed the petition as hard as we could, and we got it up to, I think, around the quarter of a million mark. These moments really, really matter in the life of a campaign.'

Journalists that didn't have the footage were calling me to track it down, and also ask more questions about what detention was like. These conversations with peers gave me an insight into how newsrooms of all stripes and inclinations were starting to view not just the last eighteen hours, but the last eighteen months, too.

I texted Carina several times that day to see if the department had communicated with her yet about the whereabouts and the plans for the family, now the plane had been grounded. Her responses chilled me: 'Nothing yet.'

In the meantime, a news crew in Darwin had tracked down where the family were heavily under guard. Video footage of tiny Kopika, waving cheerily at a uniformed Serco guard as she was escorted by even more guards, was promptly broadcast around Australia.

I didn't know Iyngaran was just metres away at the time the footage was filmed and was making more and more allies as he went. He later recalled: 'I think it was a press photographer who'd been around the back where you could get close to their window. He mentioned they had just started escorting the family out the front, onto the verandah. And we were like, "Oh my God, are they moving them? What's happened?"

'I ran back into the hotel, around the back way, and then I saw that a car had pulled up, just on the outside of the perimeter fence, and I got shooed away by the Serco guards. I knew then that they were about to move them. So I ran back out to the front to the nature strip and told the few guys, "I think they're gonna try and move them."

'I wasn't really familiar with all the entrances, but we thought they might be coming out of the entrance where that van was parked. But there's another road entrance on the other side, and thankfully my friend Linda had their car parked quite close. And then we saw the van.

'They obviously really wanted to get out of there quick smart. The van went round the back way, but they still had to come outside, out the main entrance of the motel, and we were stationed about 60, 70 metres down from that. So we jumped in Linda's car, and thankfully there was a bit of traffic coming through into the airport that kinda held up the van. That gave us time to catch up. We just started following it at speed. We didn't really know where it was going, but it was literally less than a kilometre back to the entrance onto the tarmac.'

As the van slowed at a security gate, Iyngaran jumped out and started shooting a video on his phone: 'They pulled up. It's a very slow-opening gate. That's when the footage starts, as I get out of the car. I didn't really know what to do, thinking, you know, they've got this injunction. We don't know why they're taking them back to the tarmac, we assume they were going to fly them somewhere. But we were like, "Are they flying them back to Melbourne? Or has something happened that the government thinks they can actually proceed with the deportation?"

We Will Fight for You

'So I just walked up to the van slowly. You know, the worst I've gotten is like a fine for running a red light once at 4 am in the morning, when I was driving some mates home from the pub and wasn't paying attention, and there were no cars around. So I've never really had any interactions with police and I wasn't really sure what to do, but I walked up to the van.'

When Iyngaran realised the family were in the van, he quickly moved closer. In the footage, Nades, looking out the window, raises a hand against the sun to see what the sudden movement is. He'd noticed Iyngaran following the van. In a slow-moving second, Nades' face breaks into a beaming smile, because he recognises it is someone who cares. He waves back as Iyngaran yells out to him.

Iyngaran says: 'I think Priya woke up Tharnicaa, or maybe she was asleep, Kopika was looking and Priya was telling her to wave. I went back to Nades, and he was trying to say something but I couldn't hear him through the glass. And I just said, "We will fight for you, Nades, we will fight for you." That was all.'

In the footage the gate finally opens, and the van speeds away.

It would be the last sighting of the family on the mainland of Australia for years to come.

Chapter 31

BACK TO CHRISTMAS ISLAND

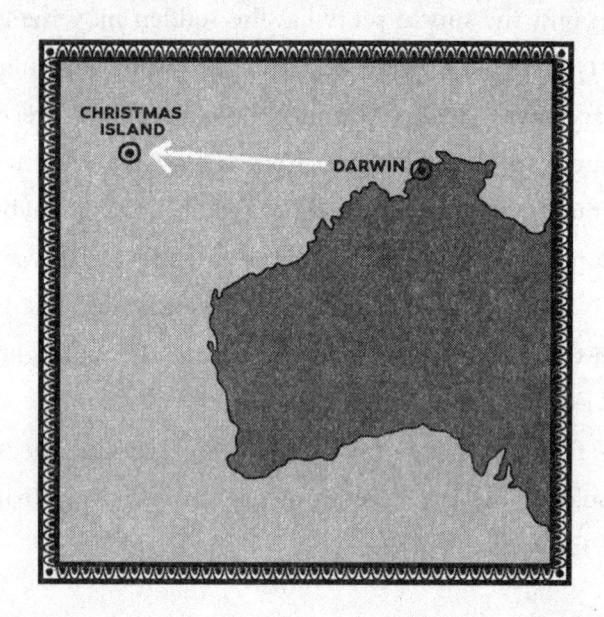

Christmas Island   **1 September 2019**

The immigration officer on the flight came over to us. 'You are being taken to Christmas Island,' he said.

I had heard those exact words almost six and a half years ago. But the feeling I had then was elation and relief. Now it was terror and suspicion.

I wondered why the Australian government was sending us

Back to Christmas Island

to Christmas Island. The detention centre there had closed five months ago. Maybe we were being punished; many Australians were supporting our community's Home to Bilo movement, and people were asking questions about our treatment. Maybe the government wanted us out of mainland Australia so the media couldn't report about us and the people would forget us. Maybe it was just easier to deport us back to Sri Lanka from Christmas Island without anyone knowing. Maybe it was all of those. Realising this made me very angry and upset.

It was around 2 am when we were taken into the Christmas Island detention centre. It was right next to the airport. It was pitch dark outside and lights were on in a couple of buildings inside the compound. It was a still night, very warm and humid. We were taken into an old demountable building and the guard opened the door to one of the cabins.

A stale smell hit us. Inside, there were two single-bed bunks. The bed frames were rusted, and the bed sheets were torn and stank of damp and mould. Tharni was asleep on Nades' shoulder. He was thinking twice about putting her on one of the dirty beds. Then he found a towel in the bathroom and spread it out on the mattress and got the girls to sleep. He told me not to worry—maybe they'd transfer us to a different cabin in the morning. If not, he said, he'd clean this place. So we sat on the floor, and tried to sleep.

In daylight, the cabin looked really run-down. There were large holes in the flyscreens and dead insects all over the floor. I wondered if it had been cleaned since the last detainees stayed here. We were in one of several demountable buildings on stilts. Ours had three cabins, a living room with a television, and a kitchenette.

HOME TO BILOELA

The children had no room to run around, but on one side of the building there was a small old slippery slide for them to play on. There was a recreation centre and an oval across the gravel road on one side and a large smouldering rubbish tip on the other side. The whole area was surrounded by bushland. Nades and I worried about how we were going to make this our home while they kept us here.

Having been on Christmas Island before, I knew that where we were was a different facility to the main detention centre, which had newer, more suitable buildings. Our detention centre was on Phosphate Hill, on the east side of the island. I was sure that they had put us here for one reason: they hoped we'd beg them to be sent to Sri Lanka. Why else would you put a hardworking family with two little children in a place like this?

I was surprised to see several Serco, immigration and ABF officers, some medical staff, cooks, interpreters and a psychologist all in the compound. There were no other detainees in the camp besides us. So, all these staff must've been brought here just for us. Nades and I wondered how much it was costing the government to keep this place open for us. If we had been left in Bilo, we would have been working and paying taxes. Instead, the government was spending all this money to try to break us down.

But they had picked the wrong family to make an example out of. If we'd lived in a big city in Australia, no one would've noticed us missing. But we were from Bilo; people who live in the country care about their community.

When I went inside the cabin to check on the children, a huge centipede, the size of a small snake, was crawling along the wall. I grabbed the children and ran out, leaving Nades to deal with it. It took me a few days to realise that wildlife was part of this detention centre. We had to get used to the centipedes, feral chickens, cockroaches the size of little birds, wild cats, wasps, large biting ants and crabs . . . oh, and the mosquitoes, lots and lots of mosquitoes.

Although the entire area was fitted with surveillance cameras, the Serco guards on duty watched us all day and night. Many wore body cameras. They'd walk into our cabin twice a day to do a headcount, whether we were asleep or in the toilet.

This annoyed me. I didn't know who was watching this footage. I was worried about images of me and the children—especially when we were sleeping or when I was giving the girls a wash—being watched by strangers. So I asked that the body cams be switched off when they entered our room. They refused. I ended up in a heated argument with them and their boss was called.

'This is for your safety,' the boss explained.

'But I don't feel safe. I don't want the guards filming me or the children.'

But he continued to justify keeping the body cameras on. I argued back that I wanted them off.

'No matter what, they won't be off!' he said firmly.

'We'll see about that!' I shouted after him as he left.

That afternoon, when I was given access to a landline to speak to my lawyer, I complained about this. Within two weeks, the body cameras had gone.

Many Sri Lankan refugees don't speak up for fear of jeopardising their visa application. They don't want to appear ungrateful or give the Australian government a reason to deport them. We were also brought up to be scared and respectful of authority. But not me. Even if I was deported, I knew that at least I had kept my dignity and fought till the end.

HOME TO BILOELA

On the third night after we arrived on Christmas Island, I had an accident in our cabin. As I was coming back to bed from the toilet, I felt the floor give way. Next thing you know my right leg had gone through the floorboards and I was stuck thigh deep. I didn't know what had happened. Hearing the commotion, Nades woke up and pulled me out.

Splinters had gone into my skin and they caused me a lot of pain and bleeding. I couldn't bend my knee either. The Serco guards took me to Christmas Island Hospital. The X-rays came back with no damage to the bones, so I was treated for the injury and was given painkillers and a wheelchair.

When I returned to the detention centre, they moved us to the adjacent cabin. I asked that we have a proper bed instead of the bunks as we wanted to sleep next to the children. We didn't feel comfortable leaving our little girls in a separate cabin on their own. The same day, Serco delivered an old queen bed that literally filled the room. You could hardly open the front door and, if you wanted to go to the toilet, you had to climb over the bed. All four of us slept on that queen bed for the next 23 months.

I often struggled to fall asleep till one or two in the morning, worrying about our lives and listening to Nades' snoring. His snoring was loud enough to keep the wildlife out. One night, about a week after we had moved into the new cabin, I was just nodding off when I suddenly felt like I had dropped. I tried to wake up Nades. He told me to go back to sleep and that it was a dream that everyone has. But I was right; in daylight we saw that this old floor, too, had given way, and the bed had indeed fallen through it.

When the Serco guards saw it during the morning headcount, they told us that they'd patch the floor up and we should be able to continue living there. I was furious. I asked if he'd guarantee in writing that we'd never fall again and take personal responsibility if we got hurt. So they moved us again; this time to the last cabin. But they reinforced the floors first.

I continued to fight with the Serco guards over many things: food, wi-fi, clothing and medication for me and the children. The food was very unappealing and barely nutritious. We were used to eating spicy flavours, so we found it hard to eat the same old boiled chicken and undercooked rice they gave us every day. So, after I complained, Serco let us cook our own meals in the kitchenette by dropping off chopped veggies and meat every morning. We still weren't allowed any knives.

The clothes they gave the children every six months literally fell apart after a couple of washes, so I argued with them for better quality clothes. When the IHMS doctor referred to my children as detainees, I told her firmly not to call them that; they had names and they were Australian-born children. But one thing I wasn't able to get was wi-fi or a SIM to call my family in India. In this fashion, the cabin became our home for almost two years, with a few wins and many losses, but we did our best to get through them all.

Even on Christmas Island, the immigration and ABF officers didn't let us live in peace. They came regularly in large groups with an interpreter and tried to persuade us to return to Sri Lanka. Nades and I told them a firm no every time.

Chapter 32

THEY DID IT

At 1 am Angela's phone rang. It was Priya. 'It just sounded so distant. Just the connection, and her words. "We're on Christmas Island." And I thought, They did it.'

Angela immediately initiated a group call with Simone and myself. In Melbourne I sat down heavily on my couch, in the dead of night, in the middle of winter, unable to believe the government had really dragged a family 5000 kilometres to a mothballed detention centre on a remote island, all to prove a point.

On that call I would tell Angela and Simone it was very unlikely that, as a freelance journalist, any newsroom would pay for me to go. I told Angela that, if she could afford to go, then she should; I was sure that Channel 10, a major TV network in Australia, would follow her.

Angela was very calm on the call, but the next day she felt significantly different: 'I'm really good at disassociating—that was how I'd

They Did It

survived the last five years. But the next morning I couldn't stop shaking. It was in that moment that I went: "This is just too big. I'm so out of my depth. We're now fully immersed in the government's torture regime." I felt they'd escalated it. We're no longer talking about Melbourne detention, in the city. Now they're actually really playing with us.'

Angela's husband, Alan, stayed up for hours, booking the earliest departing flights he could for his wife. She was on her way less than two days later.

The night before she left Biloela for Christmas Island, Angela was racing to get ready when she got an abusive phone call from a stranger: 'Some random got my number and was saying, "Why are you fighting for this terrorist family?" And I was in the bedroom sobbing, trying to pack, because I had to get to Gladstone Airport.'

Angela had to drive for 90 minutes from Biloela to Gladstone to start her huge journey to Christmas Island, while recording video updates for the Home to Bilo Facebook page. She flew from Gladstone to Brisbane, arriving in Perth after midnight. At Perth Airport the following morning, she met the Channel 10 news crew who were flying out with her.

After her second day of continuous travelling, and as soon as she landed on the island, the news crew wanted to get some footage before they lost light. But the problem was no one knew where Priya and Nades were being kept: 'We were driving down a dirt road. Christmas Island is the most beautiful place, it's gorgeous, but there were these huge robber crabs, and it felt like we were in this

Armageddon scene: a dirt track through the jungle, with all these crabs walking down the street, in the middle of the bush.'

Angela spotted what looked like a detention facility in the distance, and phoned Priya.

'I was asking her, "What can you see?" and Priya said, "I can't see anything. But I can hear kids. I can hear a pool." A local who was with us and had offered to help quickly worked out where they were. He realised the family were being held in some very old cabins just down the road from the recreation centre. That was what Priya could hear.

'So we hightailed it up there, and I phoned Priya and said, "We're here." I had to make sure I waited for the camera to be running, but I could see them. So I was running towards the fence, but they couldn't come to the fence 'cause they had guards with them. So they were just waving.'

Crucially, Angela had already made an application to visit before she left mainland Australia. But, ironically, on the lengthy online visit application she was unable to input Christmas Island detention centre as the location for the visit because the centre was officially shut.

'So I'm standing there with the guards, who are of course freaking out because there's a news crew there, and are saying, "You can't be here." And I said to the guards, "Just forget about them. I've come from Biloela. Can I please give my friend a hug? I've got my pass, I've filled in my forms, I've done all of this. Tell me what I need to do."'

One guard told Angela he would go and talk to someone. On returning, he said, 'Obviously the news crew can't go in.'

But Angela was allowed in on her own. As soon as she saw Priya, she was viscerally shocked. Priya bore the scars of what had happened over the last days. Her arm was bandaged, her shoulder injured from being dragged onto the plane in Melbourne, with other abrasions from being forced into a van.

'She just looked wrecked. We ended up sitting on the path, and there's all these chickens on Christmas Island, wandering around. So we just sat there on that footpath behind the fences for that first visit, and the chickens were just walking around us. It was crazy.'

The news crew, filming from behind the fence, saw Angela running towards her friends and embracing them. Their footage vividly captures the family trying to fold themselves into their friend from Biloela. While Priya collapses into her arms, Tharnicaa clutches her leg. Even Nades, in an unguarded moment and visibly upset, leans his head on Angela's shoulder.

They were all a very long way from Biloela.

Chapter 33

NOT QUITE OUT OF SIGHT

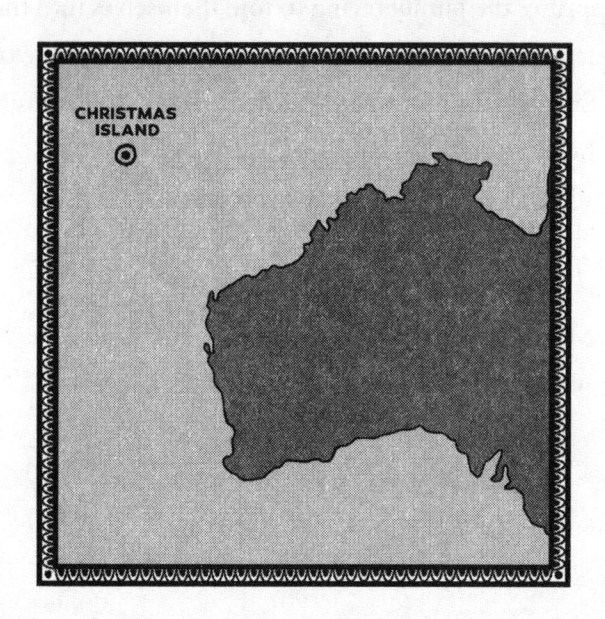

Christmas Island   **September–December 2019**

The highlight of our first month in detention was when Angela came to see us, all the way from Biloela. But they wouldn't allow her to come near our cabin so she had to stand under a tree in the compound and chat to us for ten minutes. We were all very emotional, especially the children, on seeing someone familiar and caring. She told us not to lose hope, and that the Bilo community would not let Australians forget us.

Angela visited us again a year later, this time with her husband Alan and our friend Vashini. But that wasn't without drama either. Typical Serco, they threatened to cancel their pre-approved visits with us after seeing them at the public recreation centre, where Kopi and Tharni had occasional swimming sessions. They had to leave without talking to us and I told the guards this was ridiculous, the rec centre was a public space and they were still trying to keep us in a prison.

In that first month, we also had a visit from the President of the Christmas Island Councillors, Gordon Thompson. He became a strong supporter.

Soon, a wonderful local woman called Robyn started coming to see us. Robyn had been helping refugees on the island here for about twenty years. She has a big genuine smile and sparkling eyes, and we felt happy every time we saw her. She'd visit with her two young daughters every Saturday for a couple of hours so our children could play together. I was happy that Kopi and Tharni were seeing what it was like to have aunties and cousins. My children didn't feel lonely because of her and her family.

Robyn's kindness was endless: she bought art supplies for the girls, Telstra SIM cards for me and Nades, and items we needed from outside the detention centre. She wasn't wealthy herself, but she went beyond her means to look after us during the time we were held in Christmas Island detention.

Eight months into detention, a young Indian family also started visiting us regularly. Their two children became playmates for my

HOME TO BILOELA

girls. The wife, Joslin, could speak a bit of Tamil; I felt very much at ease with her. She and her husband, Arun, were a great source of support for Nades and me. I don't think that I would've made it through those miserable days without the support of Robyn's and Joslin's families.

Chapter 34

THE FRONT DOOR TO AUSTRALIA

Christmas Island is a beautiful, tiny dot in the Indian Ocean, 1500 kilometres from the Australian mainland. The island is an Australian territory and therefore successive governments have for decades been able to establish multiple detention centres on the island, and define those centres on paper as being part of the Australian 'onshore' detention network. Absurdly, the island is simultaneously classified by Australia as an 'excised offshore place' for the purposes of anyone who arrives there by sea seeking asylum. This means refugees are excluded from making a valid visa application.

With a multicultural population of around 1200 people, Christmas Island is even smaller than Biloela. The main difference is that the tiny population is fluent in Australia's protracted and reflexive compulsion to disappear asylum seekers. With its location smack bang in the path of any boat sailing from Sri Lanka, the island is one of the front doors to Australia.

HOME TO BILOELA

One woman who has watched the evolution of how the island has been used for detention purposes by successive Australian governments for more than 23 years is Robyn, an educator and long-term Christmas Islander: 'When I first moved to the island in 1999, boats would arrive very, very quietly. The people would be taken off the boats, they would be put into the sports hall on the island, and local people, including myself, would go and bring them food, jumpers and blankets, whatever was needed. It was a very informal arrangement.

'Generally the boats that we saw then were coming from China and, because Australia had an agreement, they were sent back very quickly. That was heartbreaking, because we saw the people coming off the boats and they were looking very poor, in poor health. And I think it struck a chord, because we have a Chinese population on Christmas Island.'

Robyn noticed a change in the profile of those arriving in late 1999 and this time she became more involved in the work of processing arrivals: 'We started getting large boats, and these contained people from the Middle East. Once again, they looked like they'd had a tough life, they didn't look like wealthy people. And in those days—we call this time "Before *Tampa*"—there were only probably two or three federal police on the island; there were no ABF or customs officers. And so they would put the call out for anyone who wanted to go and process people coming in.

'I'd go to my job during the day and then in the afternoon go home, get changed and go to the sports hall, where I worked with an interpreter, who was usually a passenger from the boat.

'And so he and I would sit together, and there would be about seven little desks, little makeshift tables set up, and we would call the first person forward. I was given a list of questions that I had

The Front Door to Australia

to ask: "What is your name? What is the ID number they gave you when you landed? What is your occupation? Where are you travelling from?" My interpreter would translate for me, and I was very surprised to see how many people getting off the ship were poets. I think that was code for unemployed.

'Anyway, after we spoke to the people, we were then required to put on gloves and go through their hand luggage, any luggage that they were carrying with them, and look for photographs, phone numbers, anything that would be of interest to investigators looking into the people.

'I remember for one boat, it was an enormous job. There was an enormous amount of people on it, and I think we worked for seven nights interviewing people. And there was nobody in uniform at the interviews, there were just local people with a checklist. And the guy that was my interpreter, after about two weeks he was part of a group that were flown off the island and sent to the Woomera Detention Centre. A couple of years later I saw an interview with him on a show on the ABC, and he was working at Adelaide University as a microbiology lecturer. And I sent him a message through the program and he said, "Yes, yes, I remember Christmas Island."'

What Robyn was experiencing was the ability to interact with asylum seekers who arrived on the Australian territory, without the militaristic overlay that would soon become commonplace.

'We had, at the beginning, very personal connections with people coming off boats. We used to play volleyball—locals versus boat people. We used to have car-washing competitions, and it was very casual. People weren't scared of people arriving by boat in those days. We then had *Tampa*, and that just changed the entire landscape, the boat people landscape of Christmas Island.'

HOME TO BILOELA

What happened on the *Tampa* would not only change the social landscape of Christmas Island, it would also change the political and moral landscape of Australia.

In August 2001 a small 25-metre Indonesian fishing boat, overloaded with 433 asylum seekers, was in distress in international waters, just 140 kilometres off Christmas Island.

A large Norwegian container ship, the MV *Tampa,* was nearby and, under the direction of the Australian Maritime Safety Authority, the *Tampa*'s captain, Arne Rinnan, rescued everyone aboard the sinking boat. Without his swift intervention the hundreds of mostly Hazara refugees originating from Afghanistan would have drowned.

Understandably, Captain Rinnan then needed to look for a port that could dock such a large vessel. At this point, the Australian government of John Howard refused to give the *Tampa* permission to land, and an at-sea stand-off ensued.

For 48 hours the captain sent repeated requests to Australian authorities for assistance. Out of desperation, he decided to enter Australian waters. When the *Tampa* did so on 29 August, Australian authorities told Rinnan he was in 'flagrant breach' of the law. Australia then dispatched 45 heavily armed SAS troops to board the *Tampa*. Captain Rinnan was now being prevented from sailing to Christmas Island.

On Christmas Island, Robyn and the other locals had a front-row seat as these events unfolded: 'During *Tampa* we watched a military influx on the island. This is an island where it's illegal to have a firearm, but suddenly we see lots of very uniformed people running

The Front Door to Australia

up and down the streets with some serious hardware. They brought in heavy vehicles, I think. Helicopters were flying in, big planes were flying in, they closed Flying Fish Cove to general traffic, so that meant you couldn't go on your boat to go and catch your fish.

'People on the island were going, "Maybe these are bad people and we need to be scared of them. Why else would the government be doing this?" And I think from then on not only did the treatment of people that arrived by boat dramatically change, but also people's perception towards people arriving on boats changed, here and on the mainland of Australia as well.'

On 2 September Australia announced agreements had been reached with Nauru and New Zealand. The Royal Australian Navy would finally remove the asylum seekers from the Norwegian ship that had saved their lives. Of them, 131 would be taken to neighbouring New Zealand and 302 would go to Nauru and have their asylum claims processed.

Hundreds of the *Tampa* refugees would languish on Nauru for years to come before also eventually being resettled in New Zealand. Some in desperation would agree to returning to Afghanistan where, ten years after the *Tampa* affair, *Guardian* reporter Ben Doherty attempted to locate them. He found that at least twenty had been killed after they returned.

Chapter 35

HELLO, I'M YOUR FRIEND

After twenty years of close involvement with those seeking asylum, Robyn had watched the story of Priya, Nades and their young girls play out on the mainland. When the family disappeared in Darwin, she started paying very close attention to the comings and goings on the island: 'I saw on the news that they were missing. A group of like-minded citizens and myself were just ears to the ground, trying to find out what was happening. Straightaway there were workers put in to fix up some of the detention centre. Carpenters were being sent up there, air-conditioner people were sent up there, straightaway we knew that somebody was either in there or going in there. If a plane lands, it flies over my house, I hear it. Whenever there's a plane flying over, and it's a bit suss, you do some research. You find out, "Oh yes, that plane is from Darwin." And so with workmen, missing people, planes flying overhead, we were pretty sure that they were here.'

Hello, I'm Your Friend

Before any official confirmation that Priya and the family were on Christmas Island, Robyn's young daughters took it upon themselves to write to ABF and ask if a playdate could be arranged with Kopika and Tharnicaa. There was no response: 'We put that to Border Force [ABF] through another agency and that wasn't responded to. And then we heard for sure that they were definitely on the island, through people that had dealt with them at the centre. But the really hard thing about people in detention is that I have to write a request with their full names and their phone numbers and all their details to request a visit, and they have to do the same.' Robyn couldn't get that information until Priya had her name, and vice versa.

Robyn didn't know any of the family's core support crew in Biloela, so she had to rely on the smallness of the island to find the family. But she was in luck. Within days, she happened upon Priya and Nades being escorted by guards outside the detention centre: 'I was very lucky, I saw some people that were not local, people that looked very shrunken to me. So I ran as fast as I could to them and said, "Hello, I'm your friend, I'm here to help. Here's my number, here's my name."'

The Australian government had taken Priya and Nades nearly 5000 kilometres away from Biloela and placed them in detention on this remote island. But they had just met a practical and staunch local who would become a close friend and would do everything she could to support them.

When Robyn made her first request to visit Priya and the family, she made it clear she would be bringing her children so Kopika and Tharnicaa could meet them. Understandably, Robyn was more than a little curious to see where the visit would take place. Would she be allowed into the ancient worn-out cabins the family were being held in? Would the department insist on using the visit room at the large, nearly new (but still empty) detention centre on the other side of the island? How was the department going to manage locals keen to visit a family who had, purely through the government's own actions, become the highest profile prisoners in Australia?

When the answer came back, it contained a marked deficit of irony: 'I was told that the deal was I did not visit them in the detention centre. Because I requested that my daughters visit with me, I was told that the detention centre was no place for children.'

Robyn was told that the visit would be allowed to take place instead at the recreation centre, which was next door to the detention centre: 'We were allowed to visit for three hours on a Saturday in the creche. So there were kids' toys there, and room for the kids to run around and play. What would happen is I would arrive to the rec centre, my passport was checked, they eyeballed me and then we would go inside the creche, and the guard would remain outside the door. So whatever went on in that room was a really nice visit between my family and Priya's family. But we were confined to that room.'

After arriving on Christmas Island, Kopika and Tharnicaa were finally taken to school and kindergarten regularly but the daily trips during term time were still under guard.

Intermittently over the next two years, especially during the school holidays, when Kopika and Tharnicaa lacked the daily stimulation and companionship of their classmates, Robyn would ask if a visit might take place at a park or beach but was told no. Kopika and Tharnicaa would spend many hours locked in detention, able to clearly hear their school and kindy friends playing just across the road at the rec centre. All of this rankled Robyn.

Hello, I'm Your Friend

Even though Priya's family were the only people in the Christmas Island detention centre for nearly a year, they had the same problems, trying to access fresh and appropriate food, as they had experienced in Melbourne. After Tharnicaa's health issues and her surgery, doctors had noted that she was underweight, and Priya and Nades were painfully aware their two-year-old daughter needed to gain at least several kilos.

After interviewing Priya two months after they were sent to the island, I specifically asked the Home Affairs department if a paediatric dietitian was working with the family to assist in the weight gain of this child who had recently undergone surgery. I also reported that Priya was stymied in her attempts to make sure the girls had an appropriate lunch to take to kindy. An audibly frustrated Priya told me two startling details: she had asked for a second loaf of bread each week and been told it was 'too expensive', and she hadn't even been given containers to pack lunches for the girls.

In figures provided in response to Senate estimates questions, the Department of Home Affairs confirmed the cost of detaining the family on Christmas Island between 30 August 2019 and 31 October 2020 was $3.9 million.

After I filed my story, Priya let me know she had been given two lunch boxes for the girls.

———

Robyn knew there were usually at least 200 extra staff on the island when the main detention centre was open, but she was still surprised, after she had been talking to Priya, about the sheer number of people employed to detain a family of four: 'I remember chatting to Priya one day and we were talking about how many staff they had. Just on the day shift, we worked out that there would be something like ten people.'

Robyn knew, like many islanders, that those staff were given generous daily payments of up to $100, just for their own food. Robyn was struck by the inequity: Priya couldn't reliably get what she needed to feed her children.

'I remember Priya having a big argument with the caterers. *Caterers* sounds fancy—it wasn't sushi; it was certainly a long way from that. What happened was Kopika went to school and her classmates had grapes. And Kopi was desperate for grapes. But they were told, "Oh no, Priya, grapes are very expensive. You can't have grapes."

'Priya and Nades did their own cleaning, they did their own cooking, they did their own clothes washing. They were pretty much self-sufficient in this detention environment. But Priya has health issues and was very worried about the food that was provided to them. She wanted a healthier diet for herself and her family, but she had to work with what they were given.

'They were the only detainees on Christmas Island, with a huge number of staff. The staff were getting fed at work. So huge amounts of food were getting flown in, but Priya was having to fight for what she considered food that was healthy and necessary for her family.

'Something that I noticed, all the way through, is Priya was very strong at saying, "This is what my family needs. This is what I need and this is why." So she was not well liked by a lot of the detention staff that were there to supervise her. She wasn't treated with affection; her demands were seen as unreasonable. I felt that a lot of that was because she didn't sit quietly; she fought for her family and she didn't back down. So she was seen as quite difficult.'

Robyn worried what this would all mean for Priya.

———

In late 2020 I was interviewing Priya by phone for SBS when an opportunity to speak to and record Kopika presented itself. For over six months I had been weighing up how to handle that exact situation if it arose spontaneously. I had said to my colleague, Helen Davidson, 'If they keep those kids in any longer, they will be old enough for me to interview.' Regrettably, I was right.

After one very straightforward question to her about where she lived, Kopika's bright five-year-old voice bounced down the line at me: 'I like school and I don't like it here. I want to go to Biloela and I want to go shopping, and I want to go in my dad's car.'

Around the same time, Robyn's ten-year-old daughter had been troubled by how to answer Kopika's perfectly straightforward questions about why guards accompanied her family everywhere.

After a visit in the rec centre, Robyn and her children were walking Priya and the family back to detention. The two families were accompanied by the usual set of Serco guards but, after two years of living in detention, Kopika had questions. After the visit, Robyn's daughter explained to her mother what had happened: 'When we were walking back to the guardhouse, Kopi said to me, "Why are these people always with us? Why are these people following us?" And I didn't know what to say to her and so I said, "Oh, it's because they care about you."'

After that visit, Robyn's young daughter wrote a lengthy letter to Prime Minister Scott Morrison about the incident, and asked why her two little friends were still being detained. She didn't receive a reply.

Chapter 36
THREE GUARDS

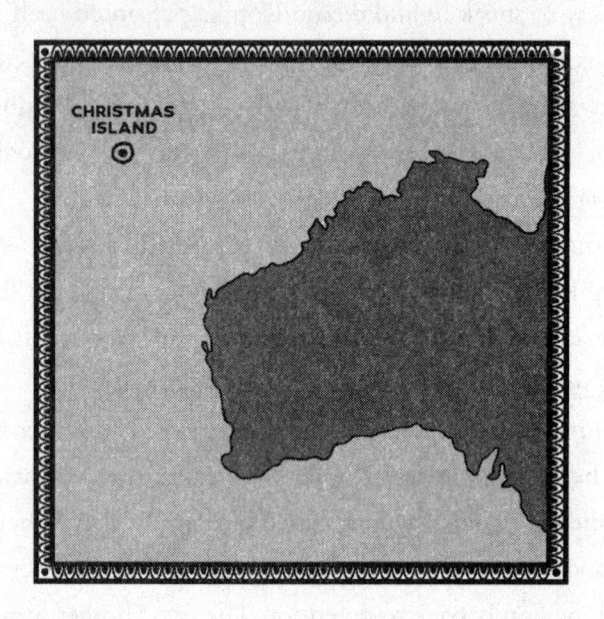

Christmas Island   **2020**

In 2020, because Kopi was turning five and Tharni three, Kopi was allowed to go to kindergarten and Tharni to a playgroup outside the detention centre. But three Serco guards would come with us on every trip and would stay watching us the whole time, like owls, and take notes on who we were talking to. They'd frisk us on our return, before letting us back into the detention centre.

One day Kopi complained that some of her friends were asking

Three Guards

why she had 'the police' come to school with her every day. She wanted to know why she wasn't allowed to have friends over or go to other's houses for playdates or birthday parties.

This broke our hearts. How could we answer these questions without telling our daughter that she was a child of refugees locked up in detention on a remote island? And that the government of the country she was born in was doing this to her? Nades patiently answered that we'd be back home in Bilo soon. There she would be able to go to a normal school and to birthday parties without the guards.

Then Covid-19 hit. That stopped them from frisking us every time they brought us back from outside. The guards also stayed 1.5 metres away from us. There was talk of making our detention centre a quarantine facility for Australians returning from overseas. This worried Nades and me; it was dangerous enough for us living here without the extra risk of catching Covid.

On 17 April 2020, we had some good news. Our lawyer, Carina, called us; we had won one of the grounds in Tharni's case at the Federal Court. The government had to pay for the legal costs because the minister should've allowed Tharni to apply for a visa. Nades and I had stayed up the night before, worrying. Carina was hopeful that this might mean the government might consider allowing Tharni to be released into community detention or receive a temporary visa. We'd been in detention for two years already.

Despite winning one part of the appeal, the government had not changed their position to grant a visa to Tharni, so we appealed to the High Court based on legal advice because the judge hadn't changed the minister's decision or permanently stopped Tharni's deportation. It seemed that this could drag on for many months.

HOME TO BILOELA

One day, in early May, I had to file a formal complaint against a Serco guard. I was alone in our cabin when he came and stood at the doorway and leered at me. I was used to them coming in without asking or knocking, but the way he looked at me made me feel very unsafe. He also seemed unsteady on his feet. I was frightened that he was about to sexually assault me. I managed to get past him and run out of the cabin.

After I made my formal complaint I never saw him again. But after that, I never felt safe for myself or the children. Nades and I kept a watchful eye over our girls all of the time and we never let them out of our sight.

Our days at Christmas Island detention were long, lonely and miserable. Being watched by Serco guards all the time, the stress of our uncertain future, the remote location—all these things made it hard to get through each day. And every day was the same; it was always hot and humid during the day, then it would rain heavily in the evenings and at night. After that, the humidity would rise very quickly. The sound of rain on the tin roof was so loud that we couldn't watch TV or sleep at night. We were usually able to get Western Australian TV channels, but often a slight wind or bad weather was enough to ruin it.

Other than speaking to my Bilo friends and my family in India, we had absolutely nothing to do. I'd cook something, but I could hardly be bothered to eat it myself. If I ate, then I would get indigestion. Some days Nades and I would just walk up and down the verandah of the cabins to kill time. We'd often do this in silence because we had run out of things to say to each other. It wasn't nice to be outside the cabins either; thick black smoke from the rubbish dump located next to the detention centre blew in every time they burned the piles of garbage there.

Three Guards

Kopi and Tharni developed welts all over their bodies from mosquito and ant bites. But I worried the IHMS doctor didn't take it seriously. The children were stuck inside also. After seeing some of those large centipedes on the only small slippery dip, I didn't want them playing on it. There was also a large wasp nest nearby.

One of the highlights of our stay there was whenever a team—consisting of an immigration officer, an interpreter and some Serco guards—regularly visited our cabin to pressure us to return to Sri Lanka voluntarily. Each time, Nades and I would say no and they'd leave. It was like a game; only it wasn't.

Nades stayed positive; he'd play with the girls during the week and tell them stories of our childhood in Sri Lanka and about our time in Biloela. He'd paint with them or play hide-and-seek. One time, he found fruit on a *murunga* tree and collected the seeds.

'Are you planning to live here permanently?' I asked him. 'Because I'm not.'

'I'm going to plant this back at our home in Bilo,' he said, smiling. 'We'll have a house with a decent garden one day and it's going to have mango, *murunga* and curry leaf trees, and I'm going to raise a few chickens also.'

That made me smile.

Chapter 37
I WANT TO GO HOME

After the family's first six months on Christmas Island, their lawyer started the longest trip she had ever made to visit a client. It took the Melbourne-based lawyer more than a full day to get to the island, flying across the entire continent of Australia followed by a good stretch of the Indian Ocean. Once there, she had to stay, because there are only two flights a week.

While Carina Ford wanted to see for herself her clients' living conditions, there was another equally pressing concern: 'Where you have a case that drags on, you've got to make sure your clients want to be a part of that case. It gave me an opportunity to make sure that they still wanted to, because at the end of the day it was their liberty that was being withheld. And I came away from that knowing they wanted to continue; I felt that very strongly from them. So it was definitely worth it, and meeting them in person was important as well.'

I Want to Go Home

The lawyer made it to Christmas Island just as the Covid pandemic was kicking off. Travel restrictions had not yet been enforced, but the Australian government had announced it would house evacuated Australian residents from Wuhan, China, in the enormous empty detention centre across the island from where the family were detained.

Ford managed to gain access to the area the family lived in, and her eyewitness accounts would be hugely useful to me months later when I wrote a feature about the family for SBS. The calm, plain-spoken lawyer described the cabins where the family were housed as being like a group of old tin caravans joined together.

The surprises didn't end there. Carina noticed that the playground was taped off and unusable. Her youngest clients had nowhere to play in the area where they spent the majority of their time.

'They had play equipment set up, but it had occupational health and safety signs that said you can't play on it because it was obviously considered unsafe. Even where the kids played, a lot of it was gravel. There were a lot of parts of it that just were not suitable for a family. I'm flabbergasted it costs that much in detention—that facility was so run-down. No one had lived in it in ages. It must have just been the cost of staff and housing them at Christmas Island that were the key costs. Later on, there might have been medical costs as well. I mean, why continue to rack up those costs?'

Angela, her husband Alan and Vashini arrived a month after Carina had been on the island. It was the second time there for both Angela and Vashini, but under completely different circumstances. Vashini had been detained on Christmas Island when she first arrived in Australia in 2012; this time, eight years later, she was going back as a free woman.

'The second time was different because I got to see Christmas Island . . . the beautiful island. Before, I had thought it was like a mining area, that there were no people living around it. I had no idea. But when I got there with Angela, I thought: Oh, this is Christmas Island. Such a beautiful place. And such beautiful people, like Robyn.'

To her surprise, Vashini realised that Priya and the family were being held in the same detention block she had been held in many years previously. Angela had been aware that returning to the island might be a complex emotional undertaking for the young Tamil mother.

Vashini recalls: 'Angela asked me, "How do you feel about coming back to kind of detention again?" But I said that it wasn't very stressful to me because coming from Sri Lanka was the stressful thing. Escaping from that was the stressful thing, but I had found a place that was safer.'

Vashini, Priya and Nades would all talk about their stints in Australian detention nearly a decade earlier as having been far less punitive. There were courses or activities to attend while they waited to pass their security checks and get their visas, which they all had. When I started interviewing refugees in detention in 2016, there were still occasional excursions—under guard—to church for those who were Christian.

By the time Priya and the family were taken back in 2018, conditions had changed considerably, even though this time they had their two small Australian-born children with them. On the island Vashini noticed five-year-old Kopika's dawning frustration as she realised her classmates lived very different lives to her. Kopika would say to her Aunty Vashini: 'I want to go home.'

Vashini would notice Tharnicaa repeating what her older sister was saying even though, by that stage, little Tharnicaa had lived more of her life locked in detention than outside of it. Vashini could see that both girls were comparing themselves to their new friends on the island and they could see that none of the other children were taken everywhere by Serco guards.

'They knew this was not their house. This is not their home, they know that all the kids from the school, when they finish school, they go back to a home and Kopika and Tharnicaa were not coming back to a home. They're coming with the guards in a van.'

Around this time Priya told me Kopika had been allowed to attend the birthday party for one of her schoolmates, but had been accompanied by no less than three Serco guards. I did not expect an answer, but I put questions to the department purely to mark the inauspicious moment. I asked:

'Did Serco staff accompany one of the children from detention to a children's birthday party? If so, how many?

'Could ABF please explain if there is a particular risk-management process carried out when deciding how many guards should attend a children's party? For example, is there a ratio of guards per five-year-old girl?

'Could ABF explain if the department considers small children detained on a remote island as a flight risk?'

My questions went unanswered.

Amid the deeply serious business of supporting Priya and the family, the core support group did have lighter moments. Such as when Angela, painfully aware of the lack of stimulation and contact Priya and Nades had, bought a tablet and thoughtfully downloaded books in Tamil for them so they at least could have some reading material while they were locked up on the island.

Angela, not a Tamil speaker, was looking at the book covers and choosing the novels to download based on that. It would be Vashini's job to tell Angela she happened to have downloaded an impressive amount of Tamil erotica.

Angela says: 'Vashini looked at it and she just cracked up laughing. I was like, they might enjoy that!'

Vashini had now been watching her friend Priya live with no privacy for close to two years and she was beyond impressed when Priya became indignant enough to say in interviews with myself and Helen Davidson from *The Guardian* exactly what that meant for a married couple. It didn't take a brain surgeon or a social scientist to know that a family of four being forced to share a bed would mean that freedom wasn't the only thing the government had removed from the family. They had also taken the intimacy that helps sustain an adult relationship.

Vashini virtually punched the air with jubilation and sisterly pride when her friend Priya stated the undeniable facts of that: 'Even though I was helping Priya, the relationship we had is like cultural sisters. In our culture you don't talk about things like that. It's a big no. So then when she mentioned that, I was like, okay. She's saying, "I'm up to it. I'm talking [about it], I will talk!" I was like, Oh my God, she's finally [said it], which is huge, I mean that's a huge part in a relationship, you have to have that intimacy or that privacy, whatever they call it.'

While the minister always had the option to use his discretion and grant the family their visas, which would have immediately restored their privacy and autonomy, as he had for thousands of other refugees, the department also had the option to restore dignity to the family. ABF could at any stage have chosen to let the family live in one of the houses on Christmas Island owned by the department. The children would have had their own beds. Priya and Nades would have had a curfew, but also a degree of privacy that acknowledged they were not criminals, they were an ordinary husband and wife.

After Vashini and Angela left the island, the department continued to keep the family in the one tiny cabin in which they were subjected to interrupted sleep from guards doing headcounts for another eighteen months.

Chapter 38

THAT'S ALWAYS GOING TO BE A PROBLEM

When Priya and the family were suddenly taken from detention in Melbourne and shifted to Christmas Island, it was only weeks after Tharnicaa had been under a general anaesthetic to have her baby teeth removed.

A diary note I had left myself reminded me that Tharnicaa was due for a post-operative check-up in Melbourne in early September. But by then she was thousands of kilometres away, on a remote island with rudimentary health services.

Most Christmas Islanders have to travel to Perth for health care at some stage in their lives, including anyone who gives birth. The crucial difference is that locals have the freedom of movement to negotiate and organise their own health care. No one in detention has that autonomy, and for Priya and Nades that frustration was compounded by trying to parent one toddler with serious health concerns, as well as manage Priya's own health issues.

That's Always Going to Be a Problem

Carina Ford, the family's lawyer, expressed disbelief to me that the department had seen fit to put Priya on the island given her history of diabetes and the degree of dietary management that required, let alone relying on guards to supply the required blood-testing equipment.

'They knew Priya had diabetes and yet it was fine to put her there. There was always potentially going to be a risk that they could get sick. Or have an injury—it rains a lot there and the floors used to get slippery. On Christmas Island you couldn't access proper medical attention 24/7 and often diagnosis is by phone, until someone can get there. The hospital is not a tertiary hospital and it's quite a long way away from anywhere. So if something goes wrong, that's always going to be a problem.'

In 2017 I interviewed a refugee woman who had just been released from MITA after fifteen months' detention. Like Priya, she had diabetes. During our conversation, this woman expressed her fear of the blood-testing equipment she had been given in MITA so I asked to see it. I know my way around a testing kit because of a family member with diabetes, so I was appalled to see she had been forced to use something that was meant for single-use only. No wonder she hated using the same increasingly blunt needle for who knows how long.

After I met Priya, I began routinely submitting questions to ABF about what provisions were made for her to safely test her own blood-sugar levels, in the hope she could avoid this woman's experience.

On Christmas Island, the locals are deeply familiar with the limitations of the available medical services. As a long-time local and Priya's new friend, Robyn knew there were many medical procedures that you had to get to the Australian mainland for: 'But Priya and her family, they had a different medical system called IHMS. So if they wanted some medical help, they would ring a switchboard over in eastern Australia and say, "My child is running a fever", and they'd go, "Okay". But sometimes the phone would ring out.

'I remember Priya and Nades showing me their phones and all the calls that got cancelled or that rang out. They would just keep trying to ring, ring, ring, ring, ring. Then if they got through to someone, they'd be told, "Okay, well, we need to contact the Christmas Island doctor or nurse." And that might take a couple of hours. So there was a big, big lag between them reporting something and actually having a medical practitioner with them.'

Another outcome of the family being moved to the island was that they effectively had no internet access. After they had their phones returned to them in MITA, they had been freely able to make video calls and send photos to the support team.

But once they were on the island, we lost the ability to show images of them and their detention. In the first few days they were on Christmas Island, I would text them and explain that other refugees had called me to say that they should try to make video calls from a couple of points on the fence line. Nades would promptly pace the fence, trying to call me on Facebook Messenger, but the calls would not connect.

None of this was a surprise to Robyn: 'Internet's very dodgy on the island. As soon as you leave home, you don't have internet anyway and you don't have mobile data. The family did not have wi-fi for the longest period of time. I think if you are going to deprive people of their liberty and house them against their will, you have a responsibility to allow them to be able to communicate. Especially with Priya and Nades' family being overseas, elderly and sick.'

That's Always Going to Be a Problem

In Melbourne, unable to lay eyes on the family, with no wi-fi and reliant on just phone calls, I began to have acute fears for their safety, particularly medically.

Tharnicaa's health issues had only been attended to in Melbourne following significant media coverage, which included graphic images of her swollen and infected mouth. I was aware there was not the same safety net available to the family on the island. Over the next year I would put innumerable questions to the department asking why the family had not been provided with their own internet router, but I already knew the answer.

This situation suited the government.

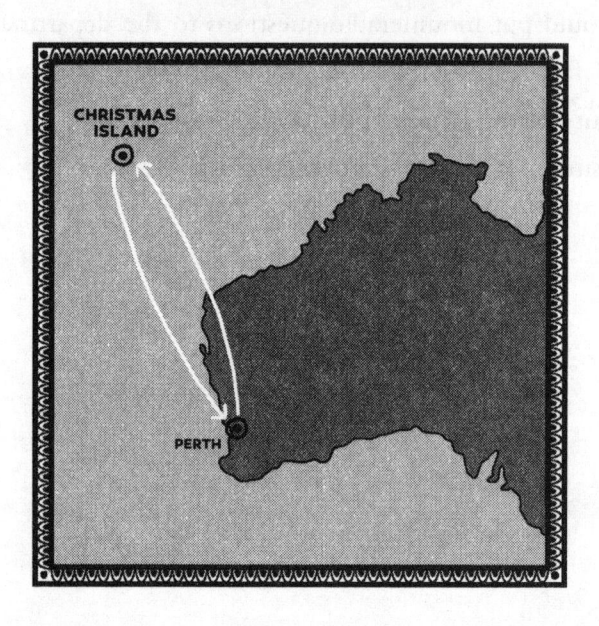

Chapter 39
MEDEVAC

Christmas Island 　　　　　　　　　　　　**July 2020**

In July 2020, my stomach problems got worse: indigestion, vomiting, severe stomach cramps and bloating, which made me look like a pregnant cow. As usual, IHMS kept giving me pain relief and tablets to stop my vomiting, but it wouldn't go away. I was taken to the Christmas Island Hospital, where I was kept for three days to do all the tests. Serco guards watched me the whole time and they wouldn't let anyone, other than Nades and the children, visit me. I phoned Aran and my Bilo friends and complained.

The doctors couldn't work out what was causing my problems. They said that I needed further tests, and transferred me to the Fiona Stanley Hospital in Perth by a medevac flight. I was there for twelve days in a separate room at the end of a corridor, with the curtains closed at all times. I underwent many tests: ultrasound, colonoscopy, endoscopy and an MRI for my shoulder injury. The tear on my shoulder ligament was 5 millimetres, so they didn't want to operate and gave me injections. ABF and Serco wouldn't let anyone visit me and controlled all my phone calls. I learned that, in support of me, the community in Perth projected a large cockatoo, a symbol of Biloela, on the hospital's outside wall. How different were the Australian people to their government!

The test results came back, showing that I had a digestive disorder as a result of my depression. They told me I would be returning to Christmas Island. Before discharging me from the hospital, I was in the middle of texting Nades when a Serco guard wrestled the phone out of my hands. I argued that I had the right to keep my phone. All I wanted to do was to update my husband. But she refused and said I'd get it back when we got to Christmas Island.

They took me to the airport in a van packed with seven of us, ignoring the Covid restrictions in place at that time. They flew me back to detention on the island on a charter flight. They could've put me on a passenger flight and saved government money, but no. Maybe they wanted the general public to think it was my fault that the government had to spend all this money. After arriving back on Christmas Island, I got my phone back and I put in a written complaint at the front office about all these things but, as usual, a letter came back defending their actions.

HOME TO BILOELA

On Christmas Island, the IHMS doctor tried to give me anti-depressants with my regular diabetes medication. But I refused. He tried to tell me that I had anxiety and depression, so I had to take it. If I had anxiety and depression, that was because I was being locked up indefinitely in detention; no medication was going to solve that.

I had seen what happened to other detainees who took anti-depressants. After an initial counselling session at a detention centre, they'd be prescribed small amounts of antidepressants and their dosage would be gradually increased. In the end, the detainees couldn't think properly anymore and would agree to being deported. I wasn't going to let that happen to me.

Chapter 40

WE ARE BETTER THAN THIS

Vigils for Priya and her family had started in the first week of their detention in 2018. By 2020 there had been rallies in every major city and many smaller towns across the country. Simone, Angela, Bronwyn and Nic from Change.org would be routinely asked by strangers what they needed to do to organise an event. This level of engagement went far beyond the reliable long-time supporters of refugee causes, who had closely watched Australia's woeful record on such matters.

In September 2019 Home Affairs Minister Peter Dutton said in a 2GB radio interview that Nades had travelled out of Australia after he arrived. But the core campaigners and family's lawyers pointed out that this was simply untrue. After being fact-checked by AAP, Dutton walked back this claim and said he was referring to the period *before* Nades had arrived in Australia.

In Melbourne Iain Murray had an idea based on other successful campaigns that had been forced to counter the spread of misinformation. He sent an email to Angela, Simone and Nic and proposed they set up a Facebook fact-check group to help counter both misinformation and disinformation. Iain's approach was simple: 'The tactic was to counter hate speech and trolling by encouraging people to leave new, positive comments under news articles instead of replying to the hateful comments.'

The core group agreed. Nic promptly set it up and Simone recruited a team of friends and supporters, including Biloela locals Brenda Lipsys and Jayne Centurion, who could safely and sanely negotiate the lava fields of online comments sections. Both women would take to this new endeavour with unbridled enthusiasm. Simone recalls that Jayne would even contact media outlets that got the facts wrong. Brenda was finding her feet, too, by countering falsehoods with positive and correct information.

In Sydney, Iyngaran, the doctor who had captured the last images of the family on the Australian mainland in Darwin, had started his own personal vigil. A week after what he witnessed in Darwin, he started going on a regular basis to the office of David Coleman, the then Immigration minister: 'I thought I'd go down there and start a little protest on my own. All I had was heaps of butcher's paper from when I'd moved. I wrote a few signs, you know, "Sri Lanka's not safe for Tamils" and things like "Biloela wants their family back". I went down to the office and just put the paper out with some rocks on the ground. I wasn't organised enough yet to even have tape.'

He soon would be. A group of like-minded Sydney locals sprung up around the doctor. Before long they had a name and a schedule. The group called themselves 'We Are Better Than This', and for the next year they would maintain a weekly protest outside the office of David Coleman. Iyngaran wasn't one to sit still, and the protests kept developing. 'One Friday I decided to go a bit more hardcore, so I printed out like a hundred A4 sheets with those same messages I had handwritten on butcher's paper. I went really early, at about 5.30 in the morning with a ladder, and covered his windows and the wall as far as I could reach with the ladder.

'It made a dramatic photo, but there was very little foot traffic. Then, once the staff got there, they called the local police, who came and told me, "You've got to start taking all this down." So I just started really slowly taking the pieces of paper down. I think the police left once they'd seen me taking at least one or two down—and I was like, "Nah, I'm not taking any more down."'

Over the next months the protestors would repeatedly try to talk to the minister, who enjoyed a reputation as a far more reasonable person than many of his hardline counterparts. But the group were never allowed in, despite repeated requests for a meeting. A reasonable number of the group were constituents in the area and Iyngaran was puzzled that they weren't shown respect on that basis alone.

The group and Iyngaran would never even see the minister, only occasionally catching glimpses of his car. But there was one notable change after six months of the vigil. In December 2019 the Minister for Immigration David Coleman would take indefinite leave for personal reasons.

In Melbourne Nic was seeing a tangible groundswell from certain quarters that weren't usually sympathetic to refugee causes.

'When you have *The Australian* reporting favourably on the side of the family, you feel like you're getting somewhere. As lovely as the other media are—as fantastic and wonderful—those stories aren't going to add 100,000 signatures to your petition.

'The grassroots impact of this campaign was phenomenal. Your phone's ringing off the hook; day and night emails flowing in, so many emails. And the wild thing in this campaign was you had so many "Holy hell!" moments. Like when Alan Jones came out in support of the family. Now this is someone who is not exactly a champion of progressive values, but he speaks directly to a particular demographic in this country and his support really signalled that this was going way beyond the usual spaces.'

Jones, an ex-Wallabies rugby coach and a notably conservative radio and television personality, invited Angela Fredericks onto his radio show in 2019 to speak about Priya and the family. Jones said on air that he had personally written to the prime minister to argue that the family were exactly the kind of people rural Australia needed, while also pointing out that the government's assertion they had got all children out of detention was patently untrue.

The core 'Home to Bilo' campaign team was spread across Australia, but the furthest away was Simone, who was living in Malaysia from August 2018 until June 2021. Not only was the full-time law student and mother of two responsible for breaking down legal language and concepts for the core campaign team, she was often deployed to manage and answer incoming queries from people who wanted to offer support: 'That was more about trying to tell them the tone that we wanted to set for the vigils. We definitely didn't want the signs that say, you know, stuff like "Dutton kills babies". We weren't after that tone.'

On 24 April 2020, there was a rare legal victory for the family: a Federal Court action taken by the government was partially dismissed. As Simone Cameron explains: 'There were two grounds in this appeal. We won one, and the department won the other. We won the ground that argued Tharnicaa was denied procedural fairness when the department had conducted an assessment of her. And we lost the ground where we had argued that a protection visa application that Carina had lodged for Tharnicaa was a valid application. This argument had centred on whether the bar had been lifted for *all* children of asylum seekers who had arrived by boat.' Both sides appealed each decision.

While on one level this was a victory—the court ordered the government to pay the family's legal costs—it also brought into stark relief what Simone and the campaign were up against: 'This was a sobering moment, as it was when we realised the limits of administrative law remedies. The courts were not able to make any assessment or determination about who is a refugee or not. The courts were only able to look at decisions made by the minister and department, and assess the *process* by which those decisions were made. So the Federal Court and Full Federal Court did find that Tharnicaa had been denied procedural fairness in an assessment made by the department. But while the courts quashed the decision of the minister, he was free to make the same decision again, as long as it was done *fairly* the second time round. And with what we knew about how the Immigration minister has been vested with so many "God Powers", it was actually frightening to think about how successive parliaments had made it very difficult for the courts to review decisions made by the minister.'

HOME TO BILOELA

By Christmas 2020, there was a palpable sense that ordinary Australians thought the family had been locked up for too long. Australia was a year into a pandemic that showed no signs of abating, massive multi-state fires the previous summer had found the federal government unprepared despite multiple warnings from experts, and businesses were desperate for an influx of foreign workers to staff jobs exactly like those at the meatworks in Biloela where Nades had been employed. The government's fixation on locking up two tiny girls and their parents in a distant detention centre was becoming a hard sell.

The campaign team had made a decision in November 2020 to channel the goodwill into something tangible for the family. The call went out that Priya, Nades and the girls would love to receive a Christmas card from any supporters who could send one. The response was immediate.

On Christmas Island Robyn saw thousands and thousands of cards and gifts and messages arrive: 'It was just mind-blowingly, phenomenally amazing. They had this little room with a bunk bed in it. The entire bunk, from bottom to top bunk was full of piles of envelopes and Christmas cards and greeting cards, and bags of toys and bags of reading books and bags of jigsaws and hand-knitted teddies and hand-embroidered textiles. They were from grandmas, they were from little kids. People from all over Australia sent them well wishes. It was overwhelming the support it gave Priya and Nades; they showed me photographs of it.'

In Melbourne Nic was noticing that the broadness of the support base continued to grow: 'At any refugee rally around the country, you can bet on seeing lefty folks, unionists, grandmothers, people from the core GetUp! community, women of a certain age, and blokes that think that Julian Burnside is a real top bloke. Not saying he's not, but that he's definitely their guy. But we started to go broader than that. It started to be the sort of thing that butchers and hairdressers were talking about.'

Back up in Biloela, Bron was seeing the same: 'There were times like at some of the rallies you'd be thinking, Oh gosh, you know, no one's gonna come. But then there'd be more people there and you'd be like, Oh, this is so wonderful.

'Sometimes the types of people who would turn up, that would be the thing that would make me go, "Oh yeah, oh, we can do this, we can do this." Because I would've pegged them as being totally anti-refugee or they'd not spoken up before now. So you do get a bit buoyed by that.'

Chapter 41

A RISING FEVER

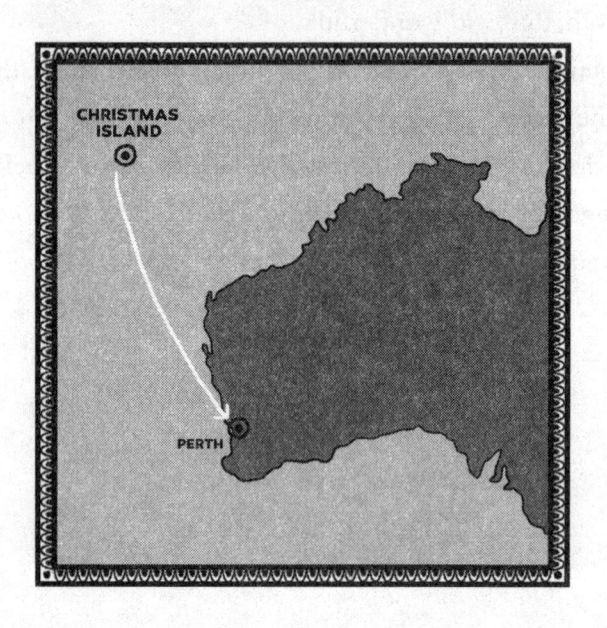

Christmas Island   **February–June 2021**

On 16 February 2021, ten months after the government's appeal to the Federal Court on Tharni's case, the decision was to be made at 5.30 am Christmas Island time. By 5 am, Nades had showered and had his breakfast and was telling us to do the same. He'd been doing this since the dawn raid—being prepared for whatever the day brought.

I was feeling very unsettled. Outside, I noticed that the Serco guards were unusually busy for that time of the morning. There

A Rising Fever

were about fifteen new ABF officers I'd not seen before. They were talking to each other in low voices and rushing about hither and thither. Also, and out of the ordinary, a passenger plane had come in last night. Normally passenger flights only arrived on Christmas Island on Tuesdays and Fridays, not on Monday nights. Smaller ABF and cargo flights arrived on other days.

I said to Nades, 'Something is cooking because I heard the passenger plane arrive last night and now the guards are running around like headless chickens.'

'Stay positive,' said Nades. 'If they deport us, then let's die together. Don't keep fighting. You've tried enough.'

I tried hard to stay positive, but I couldn't control the anxiety that crept into me. Then my phone rang. My hands shook as I answered the call; it was Aran Mylvaganam.

The first thing he said was, 'You won't be deported for now.' That helped me breathe again. Then he explained that both we and the government had lost our appeal.

Within minutes, a senior Serco officer came over to us and asked what the verdict was. I knew this was a game, so I replied that we didn't know yet. She left and came back an hour later and asked the same question. I told her to go and check her email.

The same afternoon, the passenger plane left, carrying those ABF officers. It was now clear to us that the government had sent in a plane with officers in readiness to deport us as soon there was a negative verdict. This realisation really upset us.

We'd tried staying positive throughout this process, but it was beginning to get us down. Why did they hate us so much? What had we done to deserve this? There were so many other refugees in Australia in a similar visa situation to us, but they didn't receive this kind of treatment from the government. It was hard to accept.

Our lawyer, Carina, called later and told us that we wouldn't be deported for a few months, while the case went to the High Court. Although we were safe from deportation for now, we didn't know if we'd continue to live here in detention, or whether they would send us to live in the Christmas Island community with reporting conditions, or let us go home to Biloela.

But nothing changed.

———

In April 2021, Labor Senator Kristina Keneally visited us. Serco didn't let that one go smoothly either. We were at a church service one Sunday with the guards when we saw her for the first time. I had put in my request to go to the local church three weeks earlier and had no idea she was going to be there also. She came over and introduced herself and had a quick chat. The Serco guards interrupted our chat and told us that we weren't allowed to speak to her, and they were going to cancel her actual appointment for a formal meeting with me, booked for the following day. Senator Keneally left the church after that. I later heard a rumour that those Serco guards were suspended from work for two weeks for letting us speak to her.

The next day we were a little early for our scheduled meeting with her and were sitting in the waiting room when we heard she was outside. But the guards wouldn't let her in straightaway and watched the clock to the minute before they would let her in to see us. We thought that she was a genuine and caring lady. She

A Rising Fever

brought the children gifts and talked to them kindly and spent the hour playing with them on the floor. They adored her. She asked us lots of questions and told us that many senior Labor and Liberal members of parliament wanted us released, but Peter Dutton and Scott Morrison didn't. They had nearly stopped her from visiting us.

Kopi and Tharni gave her a shell necklace that they had made with Robyn. She kept her promise to them and wore it to parliament on her return and spoke up for us. I was grateful that she made sure that Australians didn't forget about us.

One morning, as I went to wake up the girls for preschool, I noticed that Tharni felt warm. She was also unusually lethargic. So I got Nades to look after Kopi and took Tharni to the IHMS with the help of guards. She definitely had an increased temperature, so they gave her pain relief syrup and took a urine sample for testing.

But over the following week, her condition got worse. She was now complaining of a sore mouth, and had ear and stomach pains. Serco guards helped me to take her to IHMS again, but the medical staff gave her only more pain relief medication. She was refusing to eat.

On Friday, 4 June, Tharni vomited twice. We had to call the IHMS head office in Sydney because it was after hours and there were no local staff. After waiting for about one hour for someone to answer the phone, one of the Serco guards came over and gave Tharni pain relief. But the next morning her mouth was swollen. I asked the guards for more pain medication but they refused, saying that they needed a new authorisation. So we were back on the hotline, and it was Saturday afternoon by the time they gave us more pain relief medication for Tharni.

By midnight, her temperature had risen to 39.9 degrees and she had vomited twice. On Sunday morning, she complained about pain in her head and then she vomited. She also had diarrhoea. So we were back on the hotline, and they sent us a doctor. He gave her some pain relief medication and medicine to stop vomiting. He thought that she had the flu and gave us some information on flu symptoms.

But Tharni didn't improve. Her temperature stayed up and she looked weak and lifeless. Seeing our daughter like this, Nades had had enough. He put her over his shoulder and went up to the guards. He said: 'If you don't take us to the hospital right this minute, I'll walk there myself! Try stopping me!'

The guards tried to make excuses, but he stood his ground. The doctor came back and organised for Tharni to be sent to the local hospital.

On 6 June Tharni was admitted to the Christmas Island Hospital. On Monday 7 June the doctors at the hospital told us that Tharni's temperature was too high for them to manage on Christmas Island and that they'd arranged for her to be flown to Perth Children's Hospital.

Only one parent could go with her. I immediately said that I would go. Nades tried to tell me that it was better for him to go, because Tharni was used to being with him all the time and I mightn't stay calm under pressure. But I couldn't bear to be separated from my sick baby. So that afternoon, Tharni and I got on a medevac plane to Perth. As I looked out the window and watched the island disappear from sight, I didn't realise that this would be our last trip out of Christmas Island.

A Rising Fever

Perth   June 2021

I had to hold Tharni on my lap for the whole of the four-and-a-half-hour trip because the only bed on the plane was taken up by another patient. Tharni was becoming confused and distressed at this stage; her pallor changed, too. It was hard to watch. I was very upset, but I told myself to stay strong. The doctor on the flight asked me to keep her lucid by talking to her.

As soon as we landed, we were whisked away to Perth Children's Hospital by a waiting ambulance. Tharni was burning up as we arrived. I kept placing wet paper towels on her forehead to keep her temperature down. The staff at PCH immediately attended to her and did all the tests.

Finally, two weeks after her first high temperature, Tharni was diagnosed with pneumonia and blood poisoning. The doctor told me that she was very lucky that her kidneys weren't damaged. It was the height of the Covid-19 pandemic in Australia, so all the staff who attended to her were wearing full PPE. Neither of us were allowed to leave the room. Nades, Simone, Angela, Bronwyn and Vashini would call me multiple times a day, asking for updates on Tharni's health.

In that first week it felt like we were still in a detention centre. Serco guards were posted right outside the door of Tharni's room and took the name of anyone coming in and out.

With Tharni and I locked up inside the hospital, it was hard to feel hopeful all that way from my husband; we both missed him terribly. Nades was very worried about Tharni. He was physically on Christmas Island, but his mind was here with us the whole time. There were times in those first few days when I felt overwhelmed being alone with Tharni while she was so sick and I cried and cried.

HOME TO BILOELA

It was all too much. Nades had been right: Tharni was missing him and Kopi so much. She kept asking for them and wouldn't stop crying. I struggled to keep her and myself calm. I was also very lonely, not being able to interact with friends or family.

On top of all this, I was getting wound up seeing the Serco guards standing by the door, peering through the glass every few minutes to check on us. No matter who came to check on Tharni—be it the doctor, the nurse, the interpreter or the child psychologist—they'd question them and log their visits in their notebooks, even if the same person came in multiple times. There were Serco guards at the entrance to the ward and down at the entrance to the hospital. I was still angry at Serco for not looking after Tharni when she had the temperature back on Christmas Island.

During that first week in the hospital, Tharni turned four; it was her first birthday outside a detention centre. Nades and Kopi came on a video call filmed by Robyn and Joslin. They were holding a birthday cake they had made for Tharni in the detention centre's kitchen. Nades burst into tears seeing Tharni. Although my heart was breaking into pieces, I tried my best to assure him that Tharni was being taken care of by the best medical team and he didn't need to worry. It was a very emotional video call.

Later, Angela, Simone, Bronwyn, Vashini and Aran called to send Tharni their birthday wishes; they reported that many Australians were sending their best wishes through social media. All the mainstream media were reporting on Tharni's situation and a group of Western Australians were holding a vigil outside our

A Rising Fever

hospital in the cold and pouring rain. They were holding placards and singing 'Twinkle, Twinkle, Little Star' for Tharni, and passing cars were tooting their horns in support.

Even the WA premier Mr McGowan had told the press that we should be allowed to stay, and many ordinary Australians were speaking in support of us. All this news made me feel very emotional. I was still lonely and sad inside the walls of a room in PCH, but knowing there were people outside thinking and talking about us filled my heart with gratitude.

Tharni was still crying every day that she wanted her Appa. I started to feel that she thought I was a bad parent and that this isolation and all the pain from needles were my fault. I was also desperate for adult company. I wanted to argue and fight for the truth, like I always have, but the years of being locked up were taking a toll on me.

But by the second week, things changed. The medical staff were treating us kindly but they seemed to become even more supportive. They told me to press the buzzer whenever I needed anything. They brought in coffees and muffins for me. They moved the Serco guards further down the corridor, so they'd no longer be peering into our room all the time.

I felt a little less lonely when the medical staff made these efforts. Maybe they spoke to the protestors outside or looked us up on the internet and began to understand how we had been treated.

As Tharni began to get better, one of the nurses told me that I could take her out so she could have a play within the hospital. But Serco wouldn't allow me to do that. So the nurse told them firmly that she was the carer and she had the right to take her. With that, she picked Tharni up and walked out. I followed her. After that, the nurses would come and take Tharni out to have a play; they told the guards not to come near, as Tharni was getting stressed.

The wonderful medical staff at the hospital wrote to the WA Health Director General. They asked for Nades and Kopi to be reunited with us; for us to be kept in community detention in Perth or Queensland, and not to be sent back to Christmas Island.

I couldn't believe that over the past four years, starting from Biloela, so many Australians were speaking out against the government and even putting their jobs on the line to support us. My heart fills with gratitude whenever I think of them. The only way my family can repay their kindness is for us to contribute back to Australia.

Chapter 42

THEY'VE GONE, ALL GONE

Shortly after Priya and Tharnicaa landed on the mainland, *The Saturday Paper* contacted me and asked whether I could do an interview with them.

As well as interviewing Priya for a print feature, I would record audio for the paper's podcast. I was hoping that, after years of speaking to me, Priya would feel safe enough to explain what had happened in English. While I believed her English was good enough, I also understood the stress on her was unprecedented.

As soon as I dialled Priya and saw Tharnicaa on my screen, it hit me all over again how serious this was, how close to disaster this had come, with one tiny girl repeatedly paying the price for political brinkmanship.

Priya had climbed into the hospital bed to hold her daughter, who leaned back against her mother. Priya's eyes kept darting to the door, where she knew multiple guards were posted, checking the IDs and taking the names of any hospital staff who entered the room. She was tense but ready to talk.

Several times staff would come in, and Priya's greeting to them would immediately signal to me that I should be quiet. No one needed to know she was doing an interview with me.

Clearly there was no privacy available. So, whether we liked it or not, the youngest child detained by the Australian government would also be part of this interview.

Resting against Priya, Tharni's tiny arm was bandaged, and I could see the gaps in her mouth from the missing baby teeth. For years I had been watching this little girl carefully smile with closed lips. I wasn't even sure what to say to her anymore. I started simply. 'I hear you were very brave.'

It was only a few days until Tharnicaa's birthday. On the video call she started to tell me about a cake Robyn was organising for her back on Christmas Island. But halfway through the description, she suddenly and tearfully said, 'I want my dad.'

―――

The Saturday Paper published my story on the front page four days later, on Tharnicaa's birthday. Even though it was her first birthday outside a detention centre, she was still surrounded by Serco guards. On the Monday morning the podcast was released, and Australia could hear her voice. It was the first time Tharnicaa had ever been interviewed.

Less than two hours later, the Australian government announced that the family would be reunited and, after more than three years in harsh closed detention facilities, they would be allowed to live in a community detention unit in Perth.

They've Gone, All Gone

Confusion broke out and my phone started ringing. Various newsrooms I worked for had completely understandable questions.

Were the family being given visas?

No.

Were they going to be allowed back to Biloela?

That was another no. And they couldn't even leave Perth.

The government had finally cracked, but barely. The family were definitely not safe from deportation and they were still thousands of kilometres from home.

That same morning, on Christmas Island, Robyn was woken before dawn by her phone: 'Nades video-called me and I was fast asleep so Nades got a face full of old lady, fast asleep. I was quite scared, because I had said to them to call me if anything was happening to them.'

Nades explained that he and Kopika had been told they would be taken to Perth and reunited with Priya and Tharnicaa. The family were going to be allowed to live in community detention.

Nades also told Robyn he had insisted that Kopika had to be allowed to say goodbye to her friends this time.

'He fought hard. He put his foot down and said that Kopika needed to go to the school and say goodbye to her classmates, because everywhere else they'd been disappeared. So Nades took Kopika into the school and she was able to say goodbye to her teachers and to say goodbye to her classmates and say goodbye to friends.'

Meanwhile Robyn was quietly and usefully informed by another local what time the plane taking Kopika and Nades would leave:

'I raced up to the airport with my daughters, so we could say goodbye. The Shire President was up there to say goodbye. The Catholic church people were there. Some classmates of hers, too, the parents had grabbed them out of school and taken them up there. A lot of the parents of Kopi's classmates were very, very supportive of the family. Then they were just getting on a plane and going. And it all happened so very quickly, although we'd been waiting for them to leave for two years. Every week we visited them, we would go, "Well, hopefully we don't get to visit you next week."'

In Melbourne I was still trying to make sense of what community detention would mean for the family. But more immediately I wanted to know if the Serco guards had been removed from the hospital. I knew they had no right to be there if the family were now effectively under community detention conditions.

I rang Priya. Exactly a week after the air evacuation and three years of interviews, I had one last question for her that week: 'Priya, are the guards gone from outside your room?'

Her face lit up. 'Yes, yes. They've gone, all gone.'

Chapter 43
REUNION

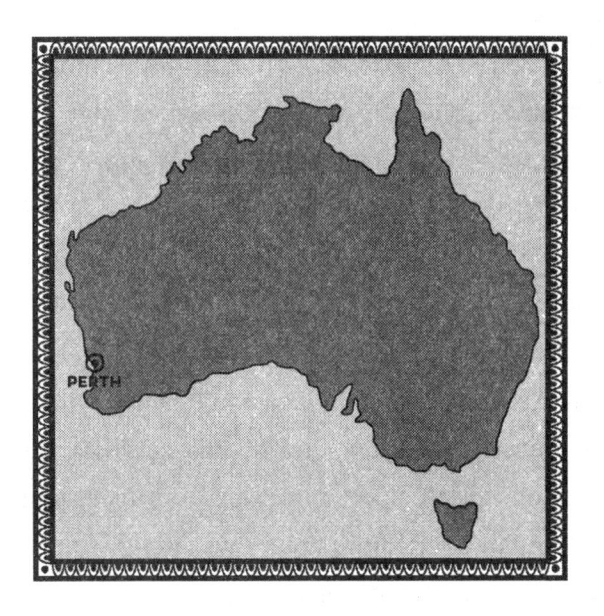

Perth   **15 June 2021**

On 15 June, the Australian government listened to the medical community, our lawyers and supporters and allowed Nades and Kopi to come to Perth. It was a very emotional reunion when Nades and Kopi burst into our room. Kopi ran up to Tharni and jumped on her in her bed against my protests. Nades couldn't stop smiling as he held Tharni in his arms and showered her with kisses. We held on to each other, and I couldn't stop crying. Little Tharni clung to

Nades and said, 'I missed you, Appa. I don't want to ever leave you or *acca* ever again.'

Angela and Alan flew in from Biloela, and Vashini and her husband Riswan flew in from Brisbane with their newborn, Aaliya, to be with us that day. There are no words to describe what this meant to me. I had been so lonely over the past two weeks; to know that my children had people who cared so much about them was a really wonderful feeling.

Nades told me that around 50 Christmas Islanders, including many staff and families from the girls' school, had come to the airport to send them off with a fanfare. Some of them had taken time off work to do so. This wonderful Christmas Island community, along with the rest of Australia, had supported us over the past 22 months, both emotionally and physically. Without them, I'm certain that we would've been broken.

We stayed at Perth's Ronald McDonald House while Tharni was still being treated. Meanwhile, the child psychologists and teachers at the hospital school spoke with Kopi and documented her life in Christmas Island detention. Four days after our reunion, Tharni was discharged from the hospital.

We were called into the office of the charity MercyCare, not far from the hospital. There we had a call from an immigration officer and Carina. It was good news: we were being released into community detention in Perth on a three-month visa. It's hard to put into words how Nades and I felt when we heard those words; it was a mix of enormous relief, happiness and gratitude.

As Tharni needed to visit the hospital for regular check-ups, the staff from MercyCare assigned us a caseworker and we settled into community detention. The furnished three-bedroom house was a ten-minute drive from the international airport. Although we had 23 conditions to obey, overall our situation was much more relaxed than during our previous detention. We were not being locked up; we had no security guards watching us all the time; we were allowed to move around Perth as long as we were home by 6 pm.

Our caseworker visited us every week and checked on us; at times an immigration officer came with him. Because we were now eligible for a Centrelink payment, they deducted rent before giving us the remainder; it was hardly enough. We were keen to buy our children the clothes, toys and foods they had missed out on. Nades was trying to find a job, but who'd give a job to someone on a three-month visa?

Chapter 44

NOW EVERYONE KNOWS ABOUT THIS FAMILY

With Nades and Kopika having been reunited with Priya and Tharnicaa in Perth and the announcement that the family would now be able to live in a community detention unit there, the core campaign group expected the frenzy of the last seven days would start to dial down. But the media interest didn't abate.

The increased appetite for coverage of the family received a boost from an unlikely quarter—Home Affairs Minister Karen Andrews. The minister appeared on a Brisbane 4BC radio interview and suggested the four-year-old was not as sick as had been reported and that media reports were inaccurate.

Reaction from media was swift and when the minister was asked exactly what details had been reported incorrectly, she was suddenly reluctant to elaborate further.

Up in Biloela, Bronwyn Dendle was more than happy to elaborate: 'Oh, I got fired up. I said in one of the interviews I did: "Well, we're getting our information from real doctors. Karen's getting her information from spin doctors, LNP spin doctors. And that's a different type of doctor."'

The day Karen Andrews decided to comment on the reporting of Tharnicaa's health, Angela and Vashini were travelling the entire breadth of Australia to get to the family. Bron had hoped to make the trip with them to see Priya, but she couldn't step away from the responsibilities for her own five children. However, what Bronwyn could do by June 2021 was to go on the record for the family, because she had left her job at Queensland Health.

Her ability to now speak out publicly was useful to the whole campaign amid the ongoing frenzy, as there was yet another moving part in the core team. Simone and her family had moved back to Australia from Malaysia but were in hotel quarantine—the very week of Tharnicaa's evacuation. Simone's family had spent the last three years watching the incalculable hours she poured into the campaign, but at least they had been able to shut a door on her when they needed to. In hotel quarantine, the family of four had two small rooms, so now the only room where Simone could do meetings with a closed door was the toilet.

'I used to crawl out of bed and sit on the toilet with the little sliding door and do the daily Home to Bilo 7 am meeting from there, and also do media interviews from there. I remember a radio producer saying, "Oh, it sounds very echoey where you are right now." And I replied, "That's because I'm in a toilet in hotel quarantine." And she went, "Oh, how's that going?" And I said, "Hmmm . . . about as well as you'd expect."'

Also in Melbourne, campaign teammate Iain Murray had come to a major decision. He was going to leave his day job and work, unpaid, on the Home to Bilo campaign full-time for the next six months: 'After that incredibly stressful time with Tharnicaa's air evacuation, everything just blew up. I knew I couldn't continue to work full-time and do voluntary work on the side. So I decided to leave and volunteer on Home to Bilo. It was a critical time for the family and I think it was the right decision to make.'

In Perth, Priya was waiting for her friends Angela and Vashini, who had arrived less than two days after Nades and Kopika. As usual, Angela had to hit the ground running. Arriving at the hospital just 30 minutes before a scheduled press conference, she had to speed through a special moment, her very first guard-less interaction with the family.

'Nades actually came down to get us from the elevator because we were lost, so that was quite a moment, just seeing him walk up to us on his own.'

Angela only had ten minutes to see the family before fronting the media pack in the downstairs foyer but noted that, while Tharnicaa was sitting up, she was noticeably quiet and flat.

In the days that followed, besides her campaign duties, Angela needed to use her social worker skills to help organise the transition to community detention for Priya and the family. When Tharnicaa was finally well enough to be discharged from hospital, several weeks after the air evacuation, Angela was shocked that the family were essentially dumped out of detention without much meaningful assistance.

She ended up renting a car and driving Priya and the family to their new home in Perth, a nondescript single-level community detention unit with a small courtyard. Out of all the strange and arduous trips Angela had undertaken to see the family, that short car ride was one that stood out: 'I remember that car trip because with the girls, there's no traffic lights on Christmas Island. So there were all these new things for them and they're saying to me, what does the red light mean? But with all these new experiences there was the other side of it, so we were all in the car, but the girls got car sick 'cause they'd never gone any distance on a road. So then we had Tharnicaa throwing up, then Kopika throwing up. Then we get to the unit and I'm taking the footage, because I still have to do that part of the job.'

The reality of what had happened over the past few weeks hit Priya hard as she stood in the garage of the community detention unit. While there were no guards and the girls were excited that they could finally have their own bedroom and walk to school, it was bittersweet because the family were still not home in Biloela. Angela watched her usually strong friend collapse: 'I remember, it was in the garage. Priya broke down, and she was just in Nades' arms. Because she was so disappointed that they were still not home. It was just that mix of knowing we've finally got our own unit and some privacy, but we're in Perth and we still don't have any security. And knowing this isn't permanent. Nades was there saying, "Everything's going to be okay," and holding her.'

Later that afternoon Vashini and Riswan arrived at the unit, which meant Angela could switch back to social worker mode: 'I had to leave and go and get Tharnicaa's medication. So I'm off finding pharmacies and I took Nades, but I was tearing up. It was just this moment of: "What have we done to this man?" Because they had no money, I paid for it. Tharnicaa hadn't even been given a Medicare number. So I paid for the shopping, and it was just so disempowering for him. He'd done his shopping and he's there at the check-out, and then the white person has to come and pay. It was just so heartbreaking.'

The next day Riswan stepped in and took Nades to a Sri Lankan grocer, so the family could finally get the food and ingredients they had been missing for the last three years.

A degree of normality was restored to the family finally, the girls now attending a local school and kindy without Serco guards and Nades was allowed to work. But Priya was often left alone for many hours while the rest of her family got on with life.

If the middle of 2021 hadn't been overwhelming enough for Priya and the family, there was more to come.

On 23 June the family's lawyer, Carina Ford, was told three of the family would be granted bridging visas. All except for Tharnicaa, who would continue to be detained in Perth.

Vashini was shocked: 'When they transferred to Perth, I thought, This is all over now, this is gonna end. I thought, Okay, they're gonna come home. But then, by giving only three of them a visa and putting Tharnicaa in detention, Priya was very, very broken. It really made me sad. Sometimes I felt depressed.'

As well as supporting Priya, Vashini had been dealing with fallout from the difficult breakdown of her first marriage. The responsibility of supporting Priya with daily calls, as well the pressure of translating complex legal matters and vital information back into Tamil for Priya and Nades, became all-encompassing for the young wife and mother.

In Melbourne Carina was nonplussed that her youngest client had to remain in detention, even though the rest of her family were issued with bridging visas: 'It meant that effectively they had to remain in Perth. It was clearly a strategic decision. And at the time I thought, How cruel is this? You are issuing bridging visas to three people because you really have to, and you could have done that at any point in time throughout this whole matter. And instead what you've done is to say, "Well, I've granted these, but we are going to keep you there because of the youngest child. We're not going to lift the bar and we're going to keep them in community detention."

'So it was pretty heartbreaking. And also, at that point in time, I just thought, Gosh, how much more hardship and cruelty do you need to put a family through? What is the point of this?'

Up in Biloela, Bron was frustrated. She hadn't seen Priya and the family in over three years and now they were being forced to stay nearly 5000 kilometres away in Perth. There was a discussion between Carina and the core support team about making a request for Tharnicaa to temporarily leave detention and travel to Biloela for a holiday with the whole family.

But complicating matters was the fact that Western Australia had kept its borders shut for much of the Covid pandemic. It was decided that the request would not be made because it was so unlikely the government would allow four-year-old Tharnicaa out of detention.

Bron was worried about how Priya was coping in the third detention facility the government had forced the family into in as many years. With Nades now at work and the girls attending school and kinder, Bron knew Priya's days were often lonely, and that she felt a long way from her home in Biloela.

'Sometimes I felt like dropping my bundle a bit. For a long time, most of my friends had been politically conservative, so it wasn't until more recently I'd got to know a few progressive left-wing people. I actually lived around right-wing people, even in family circles.

'That's a bit isolating sometimes in a town like this, because things were happening that I was emotional about or that I was passionate about or that I was worried about. And it got to the point where at barbecues or social gatherings, people would avoid the topic or if I'd start to say something, they would just shut it down. It was hard not to take it personally, like really hard. So I regularly swung between thinking, That's okay, that's just where they're at, and Oh, well, fuck 'em—they're not coming to the next barbecue.'

After four months in Perth, September saw a flurry of activity. On 20 September 2021, an episode of *Australian Story* aired on the national broadcaster, the ABC. With extensive interviews with Biloela locals and the core campaign team, as well as with Priya and Nades, the episode summarised the family's lives since the trauma of the 2018 raid.

Long-form, extensively researched television stories have a way of making politicians sit up. Three days later another newly appointed Immigration minister, Alex Hawke, extended Priya, Nades and Kopika's bridging visas.

But for a second time, Tharnicaa was ignored. And with no visa, the four-year-old had to remain in community detention in Perth.

It was clear the government hoped to bury the hot-button issue of the family's fate far beyond the 2022 election, a day of reckoning for which the date had not yet been set.

Chapter 45

I WANT TO GO BACK TO OUR BILO HOUSE

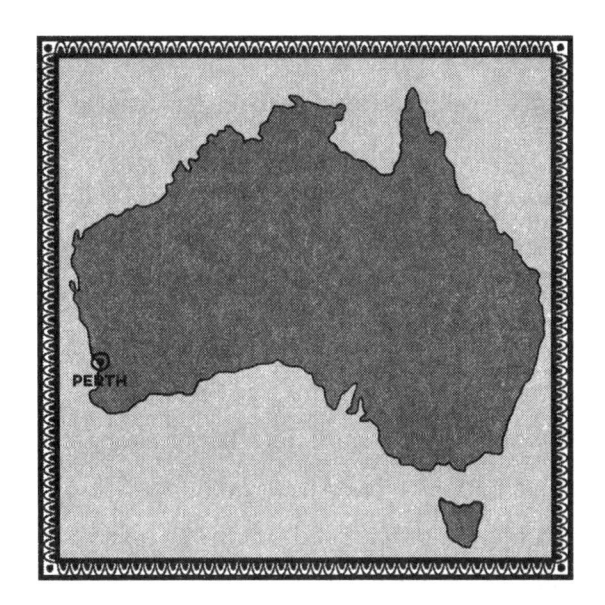

Perth   **late June 2021**

The news of us being in Perth must have spread like wildfire among the community; in the first week, many people contacted us. An Indian dance teacher called Shobana Gopu Iyer rang us one day and asked about the wellbeing of Kopi and Tharni, then she offered free dance lessons at her classical dance studio. Renuka, a friend from my time in 2013 at Christmas Island detention, was now living in Perth and got in touch. Several other Tamil locals began to offer us support. Members of the public would stop to talk to us at the shopping centre or on the street; they'd welcome us to their city and apologise for the treatment we were getting from their government. The people of Perth were truly wonderful to us.

Kristina Keneally paid us another visit; she brought many gifts for the kids and spent hours playing with them. This time I was able to offer her some of my homemade sweets. The emotional support I received from all these people carried me through the one year we spent living in Perth.

You'd think I would've been relaxed and happy. But so much was going on under the surface of the normal life we were trying to live. Our visas were only temporary, and Tharni was still without a visa or Medicare card. Court cases regarding our residency were ongoing. Living so close to the airport was a constant reminder of the threat of deportation. Any day the government could cancel our visas and put us on a plane back to Sri Lanka.

My body would tremble uncontrollably every time someone knocked on our door or if I saw a car pull up near our house. Even seeing a policeman in public made my heart beat faster and made the blood drain out of my head.

Kopi would often ask us if this was our new home. 'Appa, are we going to live here forever?' she'd ask. 'I want to go back to our Bilo house.'

Nades would always answer, 'We'll be back in Bilo soon, Kopi. You just wait and see.' I would say nothing but my heart would be breaking.

On top of all this, I received the news from my younger sister in India that both my parents were sick. I spoke to them through

FaceTime. Amma had been diagnosed with bone marrow cancer, and was getting chemo and radiation. She couldn't afford private care and so she was making regular trips to the cancer hospital miles away in Chennai. Appa had had a stroke. Neither of them was any longer able to eat well so, every time I was about to eat a meal, I'd think of them. I found it hard to swallow.

I felt very guilty that, as the eldest daughter, I wasn't able to do my duty and look after them, and my *thangachi* was doing everything. When I told Nades this, he decided to send part of his wages every month to cover their medical bills. I felt a little better after that.

Perth   23 September 2021

Three months after we had arrived in Perth, we were asked to come to the MercyCare office again. We were always asked to go there when there was any news about our visas. At times we would have to wait for an hour or two before someone from the minister's office rang in with an interpreter and our lawyer joined the call.

This time, the government gave Kopi, Nades and me twelve-month bridging visas. But they didn't give one to Tharni and they wanted her to stay in community detention. This meant that we all had to remain in detention and we were not able to return to Biloela. We couldn't understand the point of this. Why did they even bother to give the three of us these visas? But we had no choice, other than to obey their rules.

Nades took on a second job, as a cook at a Sri Lankan restaurant a few suburbs away. I became a school mum, taking Kopi and Tharni to school, just a five-minute walk from home, and to their other activities. Kopi was now in Year 1 and Tharni in preschool.

HOME TO BILOELA

During the day I'd speak to my Bilo community or Carina, who kept me updated with what was going on with our visas. Some days a local friend or two would pay me a visit. Then I'd do household chores and cook dinner. We remained like this in Perth for a year.

I continued to FaceTime with my family in India. By early 2022, Amma was still undergoing treatment. Appa was now in hospital on a ventilator; he was having trouble recognising his own children. I was feeling down that I wasn't there for them.

Then, on 21 May 2022, Australia had its federal election. As temporary visa holders, neither Nades nor I could vote. But the election results would change our lives completely.

Chapter 46

ELECTION

On 10 April 2022, after weeks of procrastination, Prime Minister Scott Morrison announced the next Australian general election. It would be just five short weeks away, on 21 May.

The day Morrison announced the election date, I realised I could get to Perth and spend election night with Priya and the family, as Western Australia had just opened the borders to Melbournians. I hadn't seen them in person since days before the August 2019 deportation attempt from Melbourne.

At the 2019 general election, polling had indicated a trouncing lay in store for Morrison, and Labor had promised that the family would be sent home to Bilo. The election result that year—victory for Scott Morrison and his Liberal National government—had taken the entire country by surprise. Possibly even Morrison himself, who said upon winning that he 'believed in miracles'.

After the 2019 experience I, like many others, was sceptical about the positive polling for Labor. If Morrison was re-elected, I had no doubt the family would be subjected to yet another deportation effort.

Despite numerous Liberal and National MPs and senators asking their own government for the family's release, neither Dutton nor Morrison had shown any interest in sending them home to Biloela. By May 2022 it was clear that the family's lives depended on a change in government.

One of the benefits of being a freelance journalist is independence, which naturally is also one of the downsides. I decided to take support to Perth, in the form of my son Francis and his partner Mia. They could help me shoot footage and record audio, even though I didn't have a commission locked in. After years of doing this work by myself, I knew it'd be extremely difficult to finish this story alone, especially if things went wrong.

All I knew for sure was that election night would be completely unpredictable, but it was essential to be there. With Nades having to work, we didn't even know if he would be home with Priya by the time the result was announced.

On the morning of the election, breaking news alerts ricocheted around the country. The Australian government had announced that a boat full of asylum seekers from Sri Lanka had been intercepted close to Christmas Island.

It was a completely unprecedented announcement for a government that had refused for years to comment on what they called 'on-water matters'. But that wasn't the end of it. Australian citizens,

Election

many of whom were heading out to vote, started receiving texts from the NSW Liberal Party. The text read: 'BREAKING—Aust Border Force has intercepted an illegal boat trying to reach Aus. Keep our borders secure by voting Liberal today.'

A detailed chronology released later showed that just before midday on election day, Karen Andrews, the then Home Affairs minister, asked the commander of the Operation Sovereign Borders taskforce to issue a statement. The commander was told to finalise a statement within fifteen minutes: 'The Prime Minister wants a statement.'

Andrews then requested the statement be emailed to a list of journalists identified by the minister's office, but the department secretary directed staff not to comply with this request. His staff would inform the minister's staff that the statement would be loaded only onto the ABF news and media site, but no more amplification would be conducted by the department.

The statement regarding the boat from Sri Lanka was loaded onto the ABF website at 1 pm but did not appear immediately. Three minutes later Scott Morrison began a press conference at a primary school. When the statement did not appear online, staff from Andrews' office sent a flurry of texts to ABF staff, including, 'Is it live?? PM is speaking' and 'A lot of people are furious'.

At 1.06 pm, Morrison was asked about the reports of an asylum seeker boat. He told the assembled media, 'I've been here to stop this boat. But in order for me to be there to stop those that may come from here, you need to vote Liberal and Nationals today.' Morrison did not take any follow-up questions. The statement was live on the ABF media site by 1.09 pm, two minutes *after* Morrison had answered the question.

On Christmas Island, Priya's friend Robyn watched the breaking news about the texts being sent out in disbelief: 'I felt physically sick. A little part of me was not surprised. I felt that all sorts of public relation tricks were needed for the government. I really wasn't surprised when I heard it. But then I got really scared and thought, Okay, is this going to affect voters at the polling booth? Thankfully it didn't. I think maybe the whole of Australia had become a little bit more cynical.'

Robyn noted other islanders also shared a discernible degree of cynicism about both the timing and specificity of the boat announcement: 'Among my colleagues and friends on the island, we knew that occasionally boats were being intercepted with secrecy, so the big announcement was pure political showboating.'

———

That evening, as I drove to the family's community detention unit, the huge Perth horizon put on a display of heft at dusk, with massive mauve clouds marching towards the sea. Inside our rental car, the colours lit up every surface. I was preparing myself for the worst outcome, but I needed to make a plan with my two assistants, who weren't as familiar with the particular stress of reporting on someone's life in close-up.

Priya had been sick with stress all day and a few years earlier Nades had quietly told me that she sometimes had heart palpitations. The contingency plan in case she collapsed and needed medical attention, especially if Nades wasn't home, would be that Francis and Mia would stay with the girls while I called an ambulance.

The unit that Priya and the family had been forced to live in since June 2021 sat in a nondescript Perth suburb. Larger family homes

Election

were being built on the flat streets surrounding their brick unit. In a small internal courtyard there was a washing line and several plants Nades was growing in plastic storage containers.

The immense pressure on Priya was palpable as soon as we pulled into the garage. I had asked Francis to start rolling audio as soon as we stepped out of the car and the first noise captured was Priya letting out a long sigh, followed quickly by me saying, 'Oh, I know, I know.'

After four years I really didn't have any more questions for one of the most persecuted women in Australia. She had said everything, and tonight I just had to watch and witness what the country she had arrived in nine years earlier would do to her next.

Nades was already out at his kitchen job when we arrived. He had been unable to get the night off because a co-worker had gone off sick. Priya planned to cook us a meal, but it would become clear she couldn't keep any food down herself. Her phone was regularly pinging with messages of support. So was mine, with updates from colleagues in various newsrooms. One merciful benefit of being in Perth was the three-hour time difference from Australia's east; if the election was resolved tonight, then we would hopefully know by mid-evening.

At the very least, Francis and Mia could distract Kopika and Tharnicaa while we waited. I discovered Priya had thought exactly the same thing. She asked if Francis and Mia would sit with the girls in their room.

On the small television in the sparsely furnished unit, Priya had the ABC's election coverage on. Three years previously I had been in MITA for an evening visit and watched the same political journalists navigate a totally unexpected election outcome. Serco guards had projected the election coverage onto a wall of the visit room. As the night wore on, but before the election outcome was clear, various refugees had asked me what I thought was happening. The unspoken question was: Did they stand any chance of release? On that occasion, I was conscious of being watched; my reactions were being scrutinised for any scrap of hope.

Three years later, there were no guards but Tharnicaa was still detained. For the first hour, the little girls amused themselves by giving the two young adults extensive makeovers. My son emerged sporting a bold blue eye, enthusiastically applied by the youngest child detained in Australia. Kopika ran after him with a final touch, a flower crown of hers. 'Here you go, old man,' she said, adjusting it. My 24-year-old son looked across the room at me and raised a blue eyebrow.

Results were beginning to trickle in.

'Is it good?' Priya asked.

It felt too early to be overconfident. I hedged my bets: 'Some of this is good . . .'

Kopika and Tharnicaa strolled in to check on us after having applied make-up and nail polish to every accessible part of Mia and Francis. The girls showed an awareness of what was happening on the television screen; but, when they came in for any longer than a few seconds, Priya and I would take turns to dial the volume down. 'Red is good,' Kopika said to no one in particular.

Driving over that night I had wondered if any of the pre-produced news packages that election night coverage depends on to give hosts a break would include footage of the family. By turning down the sound, I was hoping to avoid any remote chance of the girls seeing footage of themselves, particularly the clip of them screaming on a plane three years ago as their mother was dragged past.

Election

The day before the election, Kopika had asked about the last time they had seen me. Priya said, 'Oh, Aunty was in Melbourne', and I took out my phone and showed both girls photos of their much younger selves sitting on my knee in the detention visit room. I had wondered if the girls might say something that demonstrated their understanding of what had been done to them over the past four years, so I nodded at Mia to start filming. In the footage both girls lean in to see themselves on my phone screen.

'That's when my sister didn't smile,' said seven-year-old Kopika. She was right.

After Priya made us dinner, the girls hauled Francis and Mia back into their room for a photoshoot to capture the makeovers.

I was keeping an eye on my phone because Nic was in Biloela with Angela, Simone, Vashini and Bronwyn. They had all spent the day campaigning with Home to Bilo signs and T-shirts and were now gathered at Angela's parents' house with a huge number of the local supporters. Nic had asked me to help Priya with a victory call if the election was going Labor's way.

The seats for Labor and the teal independents were really starting to stack up. Nic had been in extensive conversation with teal candidates who were unanimous in their support for the family. Their cross-bench support was crucial to ensure Labor didn't retroactively get cold feet.

By this stage Priya and I were quietly sharing the couch, watching the coverage.

The teal candidates were doing astonishingly well, as the Liberals dropped further and further behind. Soon it became clear that the

HOME TO BILOELA

Liberal treasurer, Josh Frydenberg, had lost his seat in Melbourne to a teal candidate. In conservative Queensland, the Greens were enjoying a surge and looked like going from no seats to three.

For twenty minutes this meant Priya and I were exchanging more and more emphatic versions of the same sentences to each other: 'Good?' 'Yes, actually yes. This is looking good.'

I was keeping my voice very even, but I was nearly mute because I didn't think Priya could take any more.

At around 7.40 pm, Perth time, my phone rang. Up in Biloela Nic had run the numbers: 'Can you help Priya join a Zoom call? We're going to call it. They're coming home.'

I asked him for a few minutes so we could get ourselves together. But he had already hung up.

I told Priya that a call was going to come through and it was good news, so she and the girls should get ready.

I didn't need to say anything more. She was up and changing herself and the girls into their red dresses immediately. I could hear the girls hammering their mother with questions and giggling through the bathroom door.

Mia and Francis appeared beside me, scanning my face for clues, both too nervous to ask what was about to happen. I told them Nic was sure it was safe to call it. It was around 10.30 pm on the east coast, so we had to get ready to film.

We set Priya's laptop up on a coffee table beside the couch, ready for the call, my audio recorder sitting beside it. There was still no sign of Nades. I wondered if he knew anything yet. Had anyone told him?

Election

Francis and I did some quick calculations. The Home to Bilo team needed to record the Zoom call because this was a historic moment. But both girls were beginning to tire. How could we keep them in shot with their mother?

We decided I would sit at one end of the couch and act as a human wedge with one of them sitting on my knee. That meant both girls would be visible to the supporters and recorded for posterity, but I could lean back and effectively disappear.

My phone pinged and I realised Nic had sent the Zoom link to me instead of Priya. I flicked it through to her via Facebook Messenger. In doing so, I could briefly see where the last four years of our messages and calls had taken place. Many messages simply asked: 'Can I call you?' This had come to mean several things: Are you alone? Are guards with you? Do you have wi-fi?

There was no other story I had ever covered for this length of time, and we were nearly at the end.

Priya and the girls came in, all three of them wearing red. In the footage both girls sit on the couch watching the laptop screen as the call tries to connect. I can be heard saying to them and myself 'nearly, nearly' while pointing at the screen. Tharnicaa sits on my lap and leans into me. She's tired. It's 7.58 pm, past her bedtime.

As soon as the call connects, we can see a very blurry image of Bronwyn, Angela, Simone and Vashini all jammed together in Biloela. Almost immediately Kopika starts kicking the leg of the coffee table and the laptop shudders. I hook a leg around the table to weigh the whole thing down so the shot stays solid as Angela starts to tell Priya and the girls they are coming home to Biloela.

HOME TO BILOELA

I can see Simone is starting to cry. Priya leans back and covers her face with her hands. After a breath she starts telling her friends how hard the day has been and how hard she has been praying.

Kopika leans up and says to me quietly, 'Why is Mum crying?' I explain in a whisper that she's happy, because they will all get to go home to Biloela. Tharnicaa reaches over and wipes the tears off her mother's face using her hand. Kopika stands up and gets Priya a tissue. Angela says, 'Girls, give Mum a big hug.'

Both girls reach over and hug Priya, and Tharnicaa settles onto her mother's knee. I lean out of shot to turn off Priya's ringing mobile phone, my leg still hooked around the table to stop it shaking from Kopika's nervous kicks.

Up in Biloela the laptop is spun around so Priya can see everyone's faces. I spot Nic hunched over his laptop talking on his phone. He looks up and waves. During a pause in the conversation, I explain to the campaign team that Kopika has asked why Priya was crying. It gives them a chance to reinforce to the girls that what is happening is good.

After the call finishes, I ask Priya if she's had any message from Nades, but she hasn't. She gets the girls ready for bed and ten minutes later, as I walk past on my way to the bathroom, I see them both in the same bed, curled up and fast asleep.

Priya makes us a tea and we watch the rest of the results come in. When her phone rings with a video call, she turns the screen to me and introduces me to the caller. It's Robyn, calling from Christmas Island: she's thrilled.

Barely an hour later, I hear a noise in the garage and realise it's probably Nades. But I'm sitting in the wrong spot to get a good angle, so I throw my phone to Francis and point at the door: 'Go, go!'

Election

He starts filming and captures Nades walking in. He looks taller and younger. He's beaming at us. Priya crosses the small room in just a few steps, embracing her husband as she bursts into relieved tears.

We can hear Nades telling Priya not to cry, speaking half in Tamil and half in English: 'Don't cry, happy.' His voice is muffled as he holds her.

Nades looks across at us and says, 'This is okay, four years . . .' He kisses his wife on the top of her head.

In the background there is another sound: a voice I recognise.

I glance across the lounge of the community detention unit the family now know they can all leave. The small TV we watched all night is still playing election coverage. Priya and the girls have placed six cockatoo toys they've been gifted, the namesake of Biloela, on top of it. The birds form an askew, furry yellow and white chorus looking down at the man on the screen.

The voice I recognise is Scott Morrison's. He is making his concession speech.

Chapter 47

BACK IN BILOELA

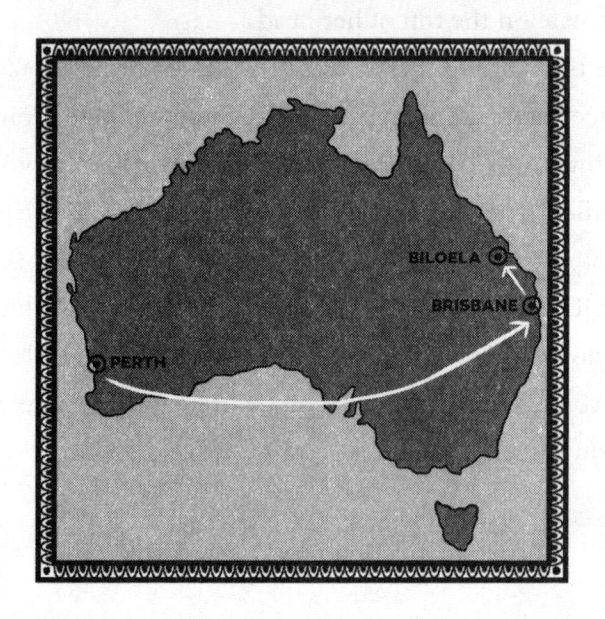

Perth   **May 2022**

Australia had a change of government. The Liberal prime minister Scott Morrison was gone, and the new prime minister was the Labor Party's Anthony Albanese. All our supporters were happy. They said that he was a compassionate man who had always spoken in support of us.

There was a good chance we could go and live in Bilo permanently soon. But the children, Nades and I were sad that Kristina

Back in Biloela

Keneally didn't win her seat. Kopi kept asking if there was anything we could do to make 'that lovely Kristina auntie' win.

On Friday 27 May, we were asked to go to the MercyCare office again. Unlike previous times, we were excited. After a long wait, Jim Chalmers, the new treasurer, came on the phone with our interpreter and our lawyer, Carina. He told us that we were all being given bridging visas and we were free to go and live in Biloela or anywhere in Australia.

The Labor Party had kept its promise. I couldn't believe that they'd done it within a week of them winning the election. It was a great feeling to think we were one of their priorities; it was really something. Nades and I were very happy and explained to our children that we could now go back home to Biloela. I laughed when I saw Kopi clap her hands and jump around, and little Tharni copying her. I hadn't experienced happiness like that for four years. We rang and told our community in Bilo the good news.

By the time we got home, well wishes were coming in like a flood. A friend and her family brought us flowers and hugs of congratulations. We couldn't stop smiling that day.

Next morning, I was feeling exhausted. But I told myself that it was because of all the emotions the day before. By the time I went to bed that night, I was feeling quite unwell, with body aches and shivers. That night, I kept dreaming about Appa.

I woke up the next day feeling very unsettled. I had spoken to my *thangachi* only the day before, telling her our news. She had told me that Appa was home and was feeling great for an 87-year-old man who'd had a stroke. That worried me; he was feeling good before he was about to go bad, like it happens to many people.

HOME TO BILOELA

I did a home test for Covid and it was positive. Just as I was about to call my friend to tell her that, she sent me an SMS saying that she had tested positive and that she was sorry if she had passed it on to us yesterday. Then *thangachi* rang in the evening to say that Appa was doing better and had asked after me. I told her to give my love to him and that, if I could, I'd be there by his side.

But within a few minutes of us hanging up, the phone rang. It was my *thangachi* again. That very moment I knew that my Appa had died. I didn't want to answer the call. My heart raced and my hands trembled. *Thangachi* was screaming and crying on the phone and could hardly utter the words that Appa had gone. Nades came home from work immediately to be by my side. I sobbed and sobbed thinking of my dear Appa.

When I was little, I had been Appa's favourite; when he returned home from Colombo, he'd bring me rambutans and pineapple. He'd sit by me at lunch and dinner and chat to me. I in turn would defend him whenever Amma got annoyed at him for buying late-harvest vegetables or not shopping for the right items. I felt really sad that Nades never met him in person.

My children didn't get to know their wonderful *thaatha* and were now robbed of time with him. Perhaps we'll have that opportunity in our next life. But I knew that I had made Appa happy by having a family of my own. It was almost as if he'd held on to life till he heard the news of us returning to Bilo. His funeral was held the very next day and we couldn't be there to be part of that. We felt stateless, all of us without a passport.

My Covid infection left me with a bad stomach and a hacking cough. Nades and I had been given two shots of the vaccine back at the hospital, but I still had a severe reaction to the virus. Luckily,

Back in Biloela

Nades and the children didn't catch it. Meantime, my Bilo community had booked our flights to Bilo for 8 June.

Nades did all the cooking and all the packing. Not knowing what to discard and what to keep, he gave most of it to charity to be sent to an orphanage in Sri Lanka. We ended up with six boxes of our belongings. Only after arriving in Bilo did I realise that three of those boxes were full of cards from well-wishers. Nades wanted to keep them all for Kopi and Tharni, as reminders of how the Australian community had supported us. He had left the expensive wet grinder behind that I used for making the *idlis* and *dosas* that Tharni loves so much.

My quarantine period ended on the 7th, so I was still able to make the flight. I had been waiting for four years for this special day of being able to return to Biloela, but I now found it hard to be truly happy. My body was still recovering from Covid and my heart was still heavy from the loss of my Appa.

The day of our flight marked the tenth day after my Appa's death. It was still within the thirteen days of the Hindu mourning period. During this time, we are not supposed to leave the house, cook any meals or engage in new experiences. Here I was, doing all of these. I had no choice. That morning, in honour of Appa, all four of us put oil on our hair and bathed. Then I prayed to Appa, asking for his forgiveness and his guidance.

We boarded a flight to Brisbane on the 8th, accompanied by many of our supporters. Everyone was smiling; the mood was jovial. The girls were so excited about returning to Bilo. Kopi was telling Tharni about Bilo and about all her friends. My heart swelled with happiness for them. I hoped that we'd never be forced into a plane again.

HOME TO BILOELA

We stayed at Simone's house in Brisbane for two nights. Because Simone and her family had visited us in MITA, my children felt at home with them. After enjoying their wonderful hospitality, we flew to Biloela on the 10th. Our small plane was full of supporters, except for two other people. Many, including Aran Mylvaganam, were driving from Brisbane and were already on their way.

We could hardly believe our eyes when we landed in Biloela. There were hundreds of people calling our names, waving banners and applauding our arrival, as if we were VIPs. There were local and international media. I was so overwhelmed seeing so many people care about my family. All the emotions from the past four years burst out of me. I couldn't stop sobbing.

As we do in our culture, I wanted to fall at the feet of those I wanted to thank, to show my respect, but there were too many people. So, instead, I fell to the ground and kissed the precious Biloela soil. I had longed for this day for the past four years. Words can't describe the gratitude I felt. This was real; at last, we were home in Bilo. In that moment, I felt that I had reached the ultimate reason for my life on earth.

Chapter 48

WE DID IT

On the morning of 8 June 2022, Priya and her family left Perth and started their two-day journey to get back to Biloela. But they didn't leave the city alone. Yet again Angela and Vashini had flown all the way across Australia so they could be on hand to help get the family home.

The trip contained many firsts, not least that it would be the first time since 2018 that Priya and her family walked into an Australian airport as free people. It would also be the first time Tharnicaa or Kopika had ever been on a plane that wasn't an air ambulance or organised by the Department of Home Affairs.

Pulling up at the airport, Angela was shocked by the size of the media contingent. Camera flashes lit up the dark Perth morning and it wasn't over once they got inside. Amid the chaos of getting bags out of the van and organising the check-in process for six people, Angela noticed one persistent photographer getting too close to

Tharnicaa: 'I've met some amazing, beautiful media people who are so respectful and then you've got the ones who are in the kids' faces with the cameras flashing. So, while it looked like I was being very loving when I picked Tharnicaa up, I was literally doing it 'cause this photographer was in her face and I just purposely picked her up and turned away.'

At Brisbane Airport, Simone and her daughter Isabelle were waiting for them. Bronwyn Dendle had dispatched her brother Scotty as a back-up driver for Simone. As the group from Perth made their way to the arrivals area, they could see Simone and her squad waiting on the other side of the barriers, holding up signs welcoming the family.

But at the last security barrier, enthusiastic airport security staff suddenly stepped in and escorted Priya, Nades, the girls and Angela and Vashini into a private hallway. Perhaps news of the media scrum in Perth had filtered through, but no one knew for sure why they were getting this special treatment. Simone was left wondering where everyone had gone.

Angela had to point out to the overzealous guards that they had a welcoming committee waiting, so eventually the security staff let Simone through. She found herself ushered into a very industrial-looking back corridor, which one of the airport staff said was where singer Taylor Swift had been hidden safely away from paparazzi. This was where Simone would finally see Priya and the family for the first time since 2019. The last time they were all together had been in a Melbourne detention centre visit room.

We Did It

For the next two nights in Brisbane, Simone's three-bedroom, one-bathroom house burst a little at the seams. As well as her own family of four, there were Nades, Priya and the girls, plus Angela.

The party of nine was augmented the next night by the arrival of another three people. Aran Mylvaganam and Barathan Vidhyapathy, from the Tamil Refugee Council, had flown up from Melbourne. They would camp a few hours in the lounge room before leaving at dawn to make the drive to Biloela ahead of Priya and Nades's final flight home.

Thursday night also saw Iain Murray from the core Home to Bilo campaign team arrive. Iain had never actually met the family, even though he had spent more than four years helping them. It was Kopika and Tharnicaa who greeted him when he first arrived.

The intense ordinariness of the scene hit him as he walked up the steps of Simone's house: 'The first members of the family I met were the girls as they ran down the hall. They took it in their stride that here was another person arrived. Something that astonished me all the way through those four years was what extraordinary parents Priya and Nades must be to keep those kids safe, to protect them as much as they could from this disgraceful system. That night, I just kept looking at Priya and Nades, and thinking, Thank goodness. You are finally free to sit around and eat pizza and talk politics, while the kids tear around the house.'

In Brisbane that night Angela was struck by how very close to the finishing line they all were: 'Priya had a glass of wine at Simone's to celebrate and I was just standing with Priya and Nades on Simone's balcony, looking out at where we were. And I said to them, "You're in Queensland. We did it. You're back in Queensland."'

HOME TO BILOELA

On the morning of 10 June at the crack of dawn two carloads left Brisbane to make the seven-hour drive through to Biloela ahead of Priya and the family's arrival later that day.

Priya, the family and the now sizeable Home to Bilo crew were scheduled to fly in the early afternoon to Thangool, the airport closest to Biloela. But, before she could leave Brisbane, Simone had to quickly go into the Refugee and Immigration Legal Service where she was working as a paralegal. When she woke up, Simone expected her many house guests to be asleep; instead, she found Nades ironing a work shirt for her, watched over by Kopika.

Simone quickly took a photo of the beaming Nades. The man whom she had taught English to was clearly revelling in doing something for his friend. Later, Angela informed her via a text that Nades was still keeping himself busy, vacuuming the house.

―――

By early afternoon, the entire group had made it to Brisbane Airport, to get on a plane and finally take the last leg of their journey home—a one hour and fifteen-minute trip to tiny Thangool.

When the small twenty-seater plane took off from Brisbane, everyone on board cheered. The supporters packing the plane cheered again as it landed.

As they taxied towards the little group of buildings, Angela looked out the window and could see that it was going to be a memorable homecoming. The dusty little airport was swarming with locals and media. There were multiple TV cameras set up to live-stream the family's arrival.

'Looking out and seeing this mass of people, that was just surreal.

We Did It

I was sitting across from Priya on that flight and I was like, "Yeah, you're home. We've actually done it."'

Among the people waiting in the crowd was Bronwyn Dendle, who hadn't seen Priya and the family in person in the four years since the dawn raid. The homecoming came at a difficult time for Bron, as she was running for parliament in a by-election as the ALP candidate for the state seat of Callide. She knew it was unwinnable, but she was right in the middle of her campaign and giving it everything she had.

That morning Angela had asked Bronwyn if she could make a quick speech at the airport and Bron agreed. But she only had a few moments in a car packed with her family to try to compose something.

———

When the plane finally touched down, many news networks were streaming the event across Australia from the edge of the tiny Queensland airfield. After more than 1500 days apart, Bron was finally about to see Priya again. But after years of telling the story of the family snatched from Biloela, there would be no discreet reunion for the two of them.

'They got off the plane and everyone cheered. We waved, they went inside and then they were in there for a bit. They had to stay in the airport until the media got set up and ready. In hindsight, I should have just gone in, they would've let me in. But someone from the media had said, "We'd love to capture the moment when you first see them." You're torn between what you really want as a human versus the optics. And we'd been training ourselves for four years to work on optics.

HOME TO BILOELA

'So we were ready and waiting, and they were finally opening up the doors. And I heard someone at the back sing out, "And action." And I don't know whether it was a media person or someone else. And when they said that, I'm like, well, fuck this.

'It was just, it was a bit surreal. 'Cause I ended up going to hug Priya first, but someone beat me to it. So I hugged Nades first and then went to Priya and felt so . . . it sounds weird to say it . . . like an out-of-body experience. The campaign had finally ended and there was a feeling of "Oh my God, we've got them home". But I didn't feel the reality of them being home until a little later.'

About a month later, Bron dropped by Priya's house. The girls had started at school in Biloela with Bron's youngest. The two women started discussing what their kids liked to eat in their school lunch boxes: 'It was just a random conversation between two mothers at the kitchen table, about putting bananas in the kids' school lunches, and I felt myself getting choked up. I got in the car afterward and was bawling with tears and I thought, Ah yeah, this is the shit I needed us to get back to after everything. Just a conversation about our kids. And that was it, that was when it felt like they were home.'

Chapter 49

AFTERWARDS

The ripples of the family's homecoming impacted the family and their supporters in many different ways. For the core campaign team, the space that had been consumed by the desperate push to save the family was now filled with the substantial administration of helping a family of four back into something like normal life. There were also the continuing media requests for the family, who weren't just the most well-known residents of Biloela, they had become the most famous refugees in Australia.

A long month and a half later, Angela was with Priya the day in early August 2022 when the family were finally told they had permanent visas. Priya admitted that she had been feeling numb until she knew for sure.

As Angela recalls: 'She said that day, "Oh, I can actually live again." But the thing that has been horrible is we had these big moments, but then we had to go straight into media appearances so we didn't have time to sit with the moment.

'That day we were straight into doing radio and TV together, and media would say, "Oh, you'll be celebrating!" And we would say, "Yes, we are off to the pub," and all that stuff. But in reality it was the two of us having a cuppa.'

That day, after doing countless media appearances together in Priya's lounge, Angela noticed Kopika had disappeared. 'I thought I'd just check on her and found her tucked up in bed. And she told me she was scared. So there I am, trying to explain to her that what has happened today is a good thing.'

Down in Brisbane, two of the core campaign team became aware of the sudden space left by the absence of the campaign.

Vashini would later look at the campaign and comprehend the time and effort she put in, but would frame it up as simply the right thing to do as a Tamil woman: 'I'm really grateful that I was part of this campaign. As a Tamil person, one of your responsibilities you should have is for your own people. So when people are actually talking about your problem, your country, that's your problem. And that I got to play my part, too; that was my opportunity.

'You know, when you come from a country where you are not allowed to speak, you're not allowed to have freedom, but you want to scream to the world about Tamil persecution and our pain, the pain we carry, that's hard. The pain we are carrying about how our people were killed, thousands of people being killed and the disgusting things they did to women, our sisters, all this we are carrying inside, and so that gives you courage to speak up. Maybe that's how I did it, because I didn't have the proper English to speak, but what happened to Priya gave me the courage to speak up, because I think that's the feeling I had inside me, and it was pushing me to speak.'

Afterwards

She realised there wasn't a tidy way to end the last four years: 'After the campaign was done, everybody was busy with life. And we never had the conversation with everybody about how are we? How is everyone going? Because we never had this healing thing. After the campaign, everybody went off and I didn't talk to anybody after that. I was just talking to Priya, of course, but I can't talk about this stuff to her.'

———

Now the family were home, Simone had been left with similar thoughts. Over the time that the family had been locked up, Simone had lived in three cities and two countries. She had studied and then graduated with a Bachelor of Laws. Her constant companion through that time had been the Home to Bilo campaign, which now felt like something of a ghost limb: 'Because the group formed so organically, without a formalised structure, we didn't have any good sustainable strategies and we were so reactive to every single drama. And in a way, when you're doing something as a part-time thing and you've got your own work and your own family, in the quiet periods, no one was interested in making time for some long-term sustainable planning because it was like, "Oh actually, I have to go and talk to my kids again." Sorry, they forgot who I was for the past week because I just didn't talk to them!

'So we just sort of had to hop from one drama to another. And then, at the end, I can remember thinking I don't know what to do, feeling like a balloon that had all the air taken out of me.'

Simone graduated in April 2022, one month before the federal election that saw the family freed. She was admitted as a legal practitioner in September, just weeks after the family were given their permanent visas.

Bron was also beginning the process of re-entry into family life.

'I have carried a lot of guilt around not being able to go to things, or being busy all the time, in meetings or on the phone. And the kids would be trying to talk to me about something and I'd be, "No, I'm doing interviews, everyone needs to be quiet." And I've been so conscious of that the whole time and felt that guilt.

'After the deportation footage was on *The Project* on TV, my son happened to see that. Harry was only seven at the time and he was really upset about what's gonna happen to the family and what they are doing to them. So I'm like, "It's all right, mate. We're doing what we can, you know, we're gonna get them, we're talking to the boss of the country and all the other bosses." And he says, "Well, I wanna talk to the boss of the country."

'It was seven o'clock at night. So we rang Scott Morrison's electoral office and I knew they wouldn't answer. I didn't actually think Harry would say anything, to be honest, but he did and I wish I had recorded it. Because he called and got onto voicemail. He was on speaker phone and I said, "Oh, they're not there, you can leave a message." And so he said, "My name's Harry from Biloela and I just want you to let my friend Kopika come home."

'That was his message to Scott Morrison on the voicemail and I was broken-hearted, thinking I've scarred him for life because he saw that plane footage. But I look at that and think there we are: a seven-year-old making a phone call to the prime minister's office.

Afterwards

'But there were other nights, when I'd be putting him to bed and randomly he would ask me, "Mum, what would happen if they do have to go to Sri Lanka?" And I'm saying, "We won't let that happen."'

'"But what if they do?"'

'You know, he couldn't sleep. So I would say, "Well, mate, we've got some extra money saved up. We're just gonna put bodyguards around them, so they'll be safe."'

'He said, "Around all of them? You'll have four bodyguards?"'

'"Yep. We'll have four bodyguards, and they'll be protected all the time."'

'It really did impact him, which is why, now they are back at school all together, he's like a big brother, monitoring Kopi and Tharni and saying, "No one's mean to my little sisters."'

'So, while I do kind of carry that guilt about the chaos on my kids, I also feel like they couldn't have learned this at school. No book could've taught it to them. And we did get the win. So that's a positive for them to see. That if you stand up, and even if you have to stand up for a long time, and even if you're the only person standing up in the room—do it anyway. But you know, maybe that's just me trying to make myself feel less guilty.'

Bronwyn Dendle didn't win the election she only had two and a half weeks to campaign for, but she did win the fight to get Priya and her family home.

———

After the election and years of work, lawyer Carina Ford had to manage her own expectations about when the family would be granted the permanent visa status promised to them upon their release from community detention in Perth. Carina had travelled to Biloela for the family's return and was surprised that they still weren't at the end of the process.

'When I went to Biloela we only had them on bridging visas and, to be honest, we were a bit let down by that. Because we got a call, it was an interim minister and they said they had granted bridging visas and our faces just nearly ... Not that we weren't grateful, but it was just like, "Oh my gosh, it's still going."'

After three and a half years of representing the family and a change of government, Carina was finally able to inform Priya and the family in early August 2022 that they had permanent visas.

'I hope that, for the rest of my career, I am not having to represent children in detention. And I also hope that I don't see families put in such a remote place, just to make a political point. Hopefully both sides of government have learned from that. You can make a point, you can have a policy, but you don't have to actually bring humans into it, humans whom you're going to effectively make their life hell. Because, at the end of the day, all the people who arrive by boat need to be treated fairly, equitably and with dignity, and not be made an example of. In particular, children should never be made an example of.'

As of January 2023, Carina and her firm are still acting for Kopika and Tharnicaa in matters regarding their citizenship.

———

Out on the chook farm, Brenda Lipsys, the retired teacher and local farmer who had become an online stalwart and frequent caller to

Afterwards

politicians' offices, hadn't seen the family since the chaotic scenes when they landed at the airport. One quiet afternoon a car she didn't know appeared on the dirt driveway that overlooks her farm. Brenda was busy sorting a few chooks for another key supporter and friend of the family, Margot.

'Margot had just been visiting Priya and Nades, and they must have decided, "We'll go out and visit Brenda, too." When the car pulls up, I'm thinking, Who's this? But then I see it's them. It's Priya and Nades and the girls. And it was, "Oh! Hello, hello." Then hugs. Hugs.'

Brenda was struck by how much better Nades looked, now he was back in Biloela. She had noticed it even before his feet had hit home ground: 'From when he stepped onto the stairs to walk off that plane at the airport, I loved that moment, it was brilliant. The door opened on the plane and from the top of the steps, he just stood there and waved. There was joy in his eyes.'

The last time the family had been out to get eggs or a chicken off Brenda, Tharnicaa could barely stand up. Now both girls ran around Brenda's farm trying to find hen eggs and chicks. Slowly, something closer to the normal life Priya and Nades wanted for both of their daughters was unfolding.

―――

In October 2022 Nev Ferrier is still the mayor of Biloela. He enjoys the small town's new-found fame as a place that stood up and kept standing up for Priya and the family. But he defers all glory to the local women who led the campaign. Asked what it was like to watch that small group take on such powerful political forces, he unexpectedly starts crying.

'It turns me into a sook, to tell you the truth, that's what it does. I am so proud of them, they were incredible. The ones here in Biloela doing the talking, Bron and Ange, what they did was incredible, an incredible job, the respectful way they went about it. Just with decency, not abuse. And men can't do that, honestly. They fire off too much sometimes.'

Nev admits a couple of locals registered their opinion with him that he was doing the wrong thing in supporting the family and the local women: 'A few said to me, in a friendly warning kind of way, "I think you're on the wrong track." And I said, "I might be, but I'm going to go with the heart. I'm not doing anything else."'

Nev also quietly told those warning him that he didn't care if he didn't get in at the next election: 'I've been in bloody council since 2004. I need a break, I'm bloody near 70. It was pretty easy to listen to them, though, only a few spoke out. You've got to listen to everybody, but I think it was the kids being born here that had everybody onside. People couldn't believe that we'd do that in Australia, that we'd kick our own kids out.'

It has taken the mayor a while to absorb that the name of his quiet town is now known nationally: 'I didn't realise what was going on in the rest of Australia, because we were just having our own little fight here without thinking what was happening down south. Then we'd see the newspapers, headlines, all that.

'My son married a girl last month. She's Victorian, and so all her family came up for the wedding in Cairns and they asked me where I'm from. I explained it's a tiny place between Biloela and Rockhampton, and they said, "Oh Biloela, we know Biloela, that's where the family are."

'And these are country Victorians, not from Melbourne or anything. I just met a couple come through town in a caravan. They're

Afterwards

basing themselves here for a month-long holiday, just because they had seen us on the news.'

Nev remembers back to 2018, when he heard about the family being taken in the raid, despite his having discreetly contacted the local member of parliament the year earlier: 'It was very shocking when they came in and grabbed them in the morning. I've got four grandsons and then my little granddaughter came along; she's the apple of my eye. And every time I see those two little girls, I go, "Oh, Christ." Obviously they're just like my little girl. You just tear up. Especially what happened to the little one. I just kept saying all the time that the mental stress, it must've knocked them around.'

Asked if Peter Dutton and Scott Morrison had underestimated small-town Australia, Nev agrees: 'Yeah, for sure. It was the kids, and the whole of Australia would have thought that.'

In October 2022 I flew to Biloela to do the interviews for this book. It was the first time I had ever seen Priya and the family outside of the detention environment. While Nades and Priya made us tea, Kopika and Tharnicaa took me outside to show me the backyard. They were both very keen that I push them around on the Hills hoist washing line, like hundreds of thousands of other Australian children before them.

As we went to go inside, there was a noise above us. A white bird with yellow blazes on its wings flew down low over our heads. Both of the girls looked up and at the same time said, 'A cockatoo!'

As it flew off, Priya put her head out the door and told us the tea was ready.

Postscript
PRIYA

The first four days in Bilo were a blur. A visit to the Catholic church, to thank Mother Mary. The wonderful celebration and honour we received at Flourish, Bilo's annual multicultural festival. The Indigenous smoking ceremony. The celebratory dinner at a local restaurant. And Tharni's fifth birthday party, at the park for all the community to attend. It was her first birthday out of detention, so it was very special to see her celebrating like any other child would.

I was so honoured to see how Biloela had embraced us as one of their own. They made us feel very, very special. They had tirelessly fought for us for four years and now given us a welcome that was fit for royalty. I felt very lucky and blessed.

We are now settled in a nice three-bedroom red-brick house in Bilo. The backyard has mango trees and plumbago shrubs with a Hills hoist in the middle. A generous mystery owner gave it to us rent-free for six months. Many people donated the furniture in the house including Brett McInally from the Beds R Us store. Angela's

Priya

mum, Anne, stacked our fridge and pantry with groceries. Neighbours and people on the streets would stop and wish us well.

Nades got his job back at the meatworks and the children have started at school again. I am full of happiness when I see them getting ready for school or playing in the backyard. These are things many people take for granted, but not us. The school principal really cares about my children and checks in on them regularly. She often asks me if they're happy or if they're stressed. There's no word in Tamil for stress; we're just expected to get on with things. Australians care about feelings.

My Bilo community continues to be part of our lives. Vashini calls me in the morning every day; Bronwyn, Matt and their children are often in and out of our house as we are at theirs. Bronwyn arranged counselling for us also. Angela and Simone are still managing all our media requests. Many local Bilo people continue to be supportive. When we are out and about, some senior citizens of this town will come and talk to us, and pick up Kopi and Tharni. Both children have had a few of them go to the school for Grandparents Day.

Although Nades and I were born in Sri Lanka, we consider Biloela as home, and that's where we want to bring up our children. What I love about Biloela is that it's a country town, where people are family-orientated. They are conservative and caring, so I feel it'll give a good foundation of values to my children. Kopi and Tharni believe that Bronwyn, Angela, Simone, Vashini, Joslin and Robyn are their aunties, and that their families are part of our family. Margot, Marie and Anne are their other grandmas.

Thursday, 4 August 2022, was a chilly winter's day in Bilo. When the phone rang, it was Carina, telling us to expect a visit from immigration officers the next day with some good news. We wondered if they'd extend the visas, or give us all permanent residency. Nades and I explained to the children about the visit and told them not to worry.

That afternoon, Angela came to offer us moral support. But, as soon as the two officers arrived, Kopi ran to her room and got into bed. She refused to come out. Angela had to stay with her. Kopi later told us she was scared that the men had come to take us away again.

'But we all told you that those people weren't here to take you away,' said Angela.

'Appa and Amma told us that before, but it still happened,' Kopi replied.

Nades and I looked at each other; we only lied to the children to protect them. I worried that they might not trust us anymore. Angela realised this straightaway and told them that only good things will happen from now on, and they can trust us.

The officers had spoken to the Immigration minister, Andrew Giles, on the phone and now passed on the message through an interpreter that we had been granted permanent residency.

Just like that, our ten-year ordeal came to a quiet end—no papers to sign, no certificates awarded and no drama. I didn't know what to feel! Nades was emotional and so was Angela. We all hugged each other, trying to take it all in.

Later Nades complained that I didn't look as happy as I should've. Of course, I was really happy and grateful. I had to explain to him that my life wasn't perfect at this moment. I was still recovering from the physical and emotional pain of the past four years; my beloved father had died only recently; my mother was in hospital with cancer and my *thambi* was still unmarried in his forties. I had

Priya

lived the past ten years on the highs and lows of a huge wave. I may have landed safely on the ground now, but I was unable to feel undiluted joy.

The pain of having missed out on so much life is hard to shake off. We can't make up for the four years of childhood my children missed. They have undergone so much trauma: being homeless and dragged all around Australia; being forcibly separated from each other at times; suffering ill health during their formative years. As a couple, Nades and I had missed out on intimacy; we weren't able to enjoy each other's company or make love for almost three years in MITA and Christmas Island. Just because we are refugees, we are not without feelings and needs.

I feel that I have aged so much in the past four years. My health has suffered; my teeth have rotted; I have issues with digestion; my mental health is not good; my shoulder is still painful and needs ongoing treatment. I also struggle to sleep; when I close my eyes, I think I'm back in detention.

I can't bear to look at our pictures or videos online. I know I look sad and miserable in most of them. Most women post their pictures on the internet with full make-up, wearing their best clothes and all their jewellery, but look at me.

We have also missed significant events like our siblings' weddings, the birth of their children and my father's funeral. I feel so very sad when I light the lamp every morning in front of the photo of my father that my sister sent me and I think of him. But that's life; you can't let the past get in the way of living now.

I know people say that I'm tough and resilient. I wasn't always like this, but when the guards hurt my wrist and shoulder and threatened to handcuff me like a criminal, I had no choice but to become tough. I have done nothing wrong in seeking asylum, because I'm a genuine refugee, as it says in the UN definition. Nades and I came here by boat because that was the only option left for us. I can't understand why we were treated worse than criminals or why even senior ministers spread lies about our background.

I know that there are thousands of refugees stuck in Australia without a permanent visa, and I want them all to settle and have a happy life. I've now made it my mission to fight for them. But I wish people wouldn't compare other refugee families to mine. Everyone's story is unique.

One of the reporters asked me once: 'The Australian taxpayers spent $60 million on your family. What would you say to your children if they ask you about it in the future?'

I told him that I will clearly tell my children that we were not the recipients of the $60 million, but it was Serco, transport around Australia on vans and charter flights, court cases, the running of the detention facility, which at times held only us. The Australian people's hard-earned money was wasted on just trying to keep us locked up in the time we could've paid taxes ourselves. All we got was torture and misery. The Australian taxpayers didn't want it either and they showed that by their votes. That's why we are now back in Bilo.

Many people ask me why Nades doesn't say much, and why our English is still poor. Those who are close to us know that Nades is not a man who wastes his words; he's quiet by nature. After all the trauma and stress, he has some issues with his memory; he can't even remember the exact day he arrived in Australia. As for not speaking English, in the ten years we've been in Australia, we've spent almost half of it locked up in detention. When we were out,

Priya

we did attend classes, but we were also busy earning a living and looking after babies. How many people who go and live in another country, especially at our age, learn to speak fluently in the local language straightaway? Now that we are settled, my goal is to improve my English and to learn to drive.

The community of Bilo travelled this four-year journey with us. They fought for justice for our family; they have protested tirelessly, seeking answers from the government for their actions. Their love and support were our only strength through the hardest times of our lives. They continued to fight for us when I felt like giving up. I can now live a peaceful and content life because of them. Their work was recognised at the 2022 Human Rights awards in Sydney.

I'm inspired by the power people have in Australia. Together with my Bilo community, I'm now advocating for those refugees who continue to live in limbo. I want to be a normal mum and make up for all the lost time.

Nades wants to start a business running a Sri Lankan food truck. Let me tell you that he's a great cook.

I'd like Kopi and Tharni to be accepted as Australians, and not be labelled as the children of Sri Lankan refugees. What they want to do as adults is up to them, but I want them to give back to the community that gave them a future.

By the way, Nades has planted the *murunga* tree sapling, raised from the seeds found on Christmas Island, into a pot in our backyard.

'We'll move this to the ground when we get our own house one day,' he says.

That's Nades for you!

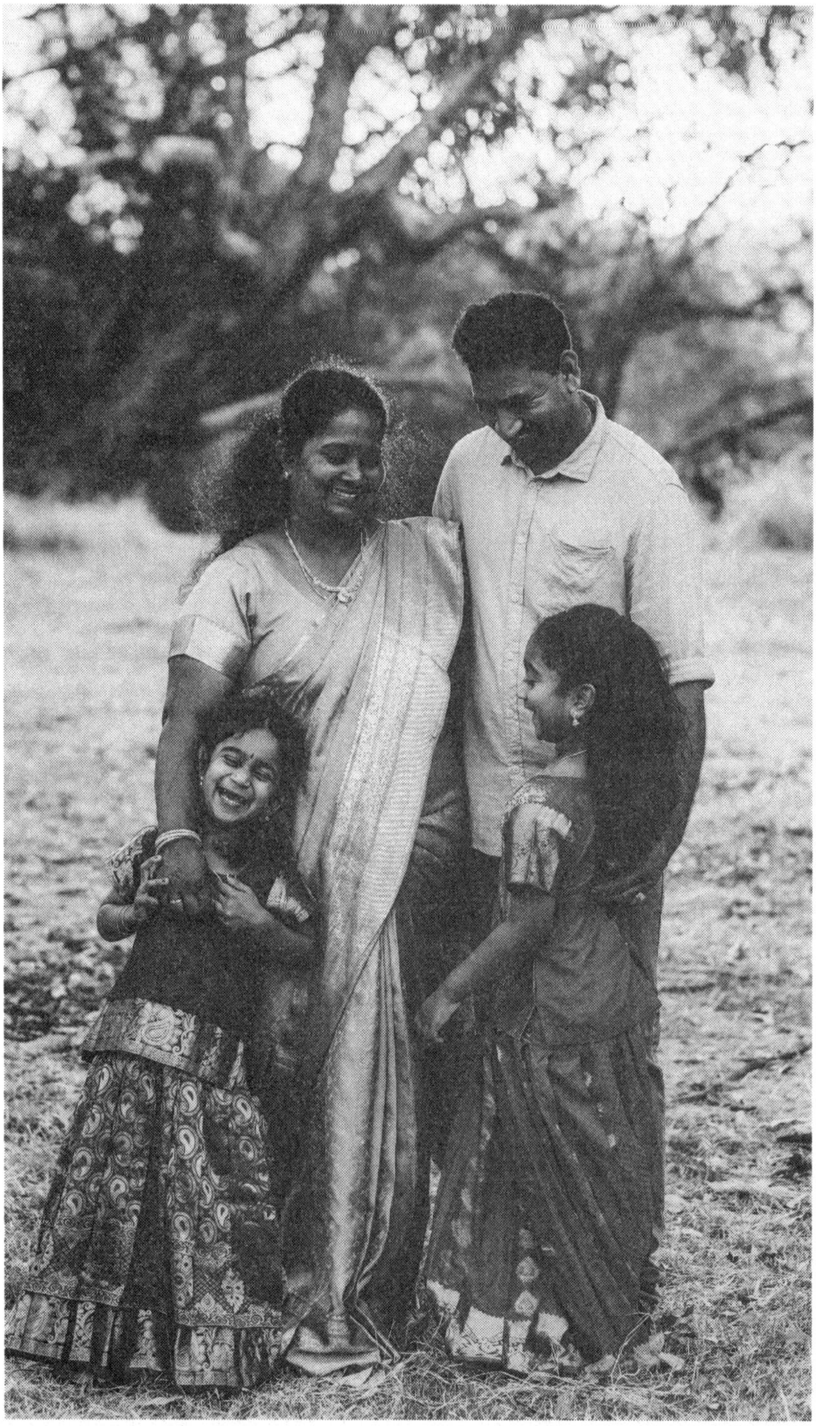

Acknowledgements

PRIYA

First and foremost, we want to thank my friends; Saivashini Jayakumar, Bronwyn Dendle, Angela Fredericks, Simone Cameron, Iain Murray and Nic Dorward. I wouldn't be here telling our story if it wasn't for you and your families. My heartfelt thanks for your commitment, love and support. You gave us hope when we were in the darkest of places. We shall continue to work together to make a change.

Margot Plant, Marie Austin, Jenny Ralaca, Marion Meisner, Lorraine Webster, Jayne Centurion, Anne Smith, Alan Fredericks and all the Home to Bilo support crew and the extended community of Bilo.

Aran Mylvaganam, Senthuran Mahendran, Umesh Perinpanayagam, Ben Hillier, Brad Coath and all at TRC, Father Pan Jordan, Sally Rugg and all at Change.org, Dulce Manoz and all at Mums for Refugees, Grandmothers for Refugees, RAR, Kristina Keneally, Kon, Jana, Marcella and Carolyn and all at ASRC, Dr Iyngaran, and all those who took the time and effort to visit us in detention centres, you know we can't name you all here but you're all in our hearts. We sincerely thank you.

A very special thanks to Robyn, Joslin and Arun on Christmas

Island. Without you and your beautiful children, my family wouldn't have survived that jungle prison. Michael in Perth. Your generosity is endless.

My wonderful friends and supporters all over mainland Australia, especially the community of Perth and on Christmas Island, to those friends who want to remain anonymous, and the Australian medical community—for your kind words and prayers, phone calls and letters to your ministers, your petitions and vigils, thank you.

Prime Minister Anthony Albanese and the Labor government for keeping their election promise and helping us return to Bilo, we are grateful. For the support of politicians on all sides, including Liberal Party ministers who spoke in support of us against their party, spiritual leaders, and everyone who fought for our freedom, to all the people who advocated for us; a special thanks to Michael Caton, Craig Foster, Joe Leach, Leah Vandenburg, Miranda Tapsell, Justine Clarke, the Campbell family, Charlie from Hi-5. Thank you to the journalists and activists who didn't let Australia forget us.

Niromi de Soyza for giving up your evenings and holidays to listen to us patiently and write our story vividly and beautifully in English. Thank you also for all your support and encouragement throughout. Rebekah Holt for your care over the past five years and telling the complex background story for this book. Richard Walsh and Elizabeth Weiss for your support and giving me the opportunity to share my family's story with Australia and the world. Our heartfelt thanks.

Our parents, siblings and extended family in India and Sri Lanka for travelling this emotional journey with us and all your wonderful support, we thank you. We can't wait to introduce our children and see our new extended family.

Acknowledgements

Most importantly, my husband Nades: I'm really lucky to have found you; you are the best husband and father there is. We are in this together forever. Kopi and Tharni, you are the reason we fought for freedom and the Australian community fought alongside us. It is because of your wonderful spirit that we are now back in Bilo.

REBEKAH

Many thanks to my Australian editors for showing repeated faith in freelancers: Bhakthi Puvanenthiran, Meg Watson, Maddison Connaughton, Erik Jensen, Elle Marsh and Kate Sullivan.

My widely distributed colleagues for their esprit de corps: Helen Davidson, Ben Doherty, Behrouz Boochani, Rachael Hocking, Abby Dinham, Eden Gillespie, Sean Marsicovotere, Mel Jones, Gus Gillies, Dan Lake, Mitch McCann, Conor Whitten, Tova O'Brien, Jim Moir, Ceinwen Curtis, Jenna Lynch and Ingrid Hipkiss.

The itinerant showbiz *whānau*: Nathan Wild, Susie Yousef, Sammy J. McMillan, Heath McIvor, Shaun Micallef, Michael McMahon and Tony Ayres.

Thanks for essential clinical guidance and comradeship, Anne O'Connor.

Francis and Jonathan Brough, for many years of photographic, sound, video, IT, meal delivery and family support, usually all of the above, and right on deadline.

Research assistants and caffeine suppliers: Georgia Wohlgemuth and Lizzy Carmine.

For legal advice I could swear by Michael Bradley, Daisy von Schoenberg and the team at Marque Lawyers.

Lawyers Carina Ford, Nina Merlino, Leah Perkins and Alison Battisson for their endless patience in explaining the unexplainable.

HOME TO BILOELA

With thanks to Lauren Martin of the Kaldor Centre UNSW for always answering last-minute emails that government departments won't.

The long-distance welfare monitoring telephone tag team of Sarah Hall, Leza Corban and Jacqui Dillon.

The Home to Bilo campaign team, Bronwyn Dendle, Nev Ferrier, Brenda Lipsys, Robyn, Dr Iyngaran, Nic Dorward and everyone who so generously told me their story for this book.

To the refugees who must remain anonymous but were reliable sources for many years despite substantial discouragement, my gratitude always.

To Priya, Nades, Kopika and Tharnicaa, thank you for having trusted me with your family's story.

Lastly, the best bicoastal PA, sound recordist, transcriber, photographer, navigator, tick remover and Paul Simon enthusiast, Mia McCarthy.

About the authors

Rebekah Holt is a journalist and writer. Born in Aotearoa/NZ, she trained in broadcasting before establishing a career as a media and communications adviser to political parties, finance institutions and the NZ police. After moving to Australia she became the only journalist to gain regular access to the country's onshore detention centres, giving her work a rare level of insight into the day-to-day reality of those imprisoned. Her reporting has appeared in *Crikey*, *The Age*, *The Guardian* and *The Saturday Paper*, and on SBS and Radio NZ.

Niromi de Soyza grew up in Sri Lanka, speaking fluent Tamil and Sinhala. As a teenager, she was one of the first female fighters with the Tamil Tigers in the Sri Lankan civil war. After being granted political asylum in Australia, she gained several university degrees, and is now an educator and motivational public speaker, living on Sydney's North Shore. Her community involvement includes roles as ambassador for the Australian Red Cross Blood Service, the Bone Marrow Institute, Multicultural NSW and refugee advocacy. Her memoir, *Tamil Tigress*, was published in 2011.